Praise for *The Extended Enterprise*

"As the expression goes, 'a mind once stretched never returns to its original shape.' Whether you are a student in academia or a veteran supply chain practitioner, you will benefit immensely by stretching your mind with this well-written tome. Ed and Robert have an extremely thorough understanding of their subject and have done a masterful job of crafting a very thought-provoking book. It belongs in your collection of supply chain management reference material."

—Mike Gray,
Senior Manager,
Global Supply Chain Strategy,
Dell Inc.

"Required reading if you're looking to lead the process of developing new value propositions, bring ideas from your strategic supply partners into your value streams, and execute plans that deliver results."

—R. David Nelson,
Vice President,
Global Supply Management,
Delphi Corporation

"Supply chain management has sorely needed a comprehensive text to outline its development and strategic opportunity. *The Extended Enterprise* may well be this book. The book provides a historical perspective of supply chain management and explains why collaborative SCM is an imperative for 21st century companies. Moving from a strategic vision of SCM's role in corporate strategy, *The Extended Enterprise* provides practical suggestions to companies seeking to manage their supply chains more effectively. Individual managers learn the benefits and challenges to managing resources and processes beyond the boundaries of their separate companies. This book should be mandatory reading, not only for procurement and materials management professionals, but for CFOs, CEOs, and Board Directors as well."

—P. Jeffrey Trimmer, Chairman,
National Initiative for Supply
Chain Initiative (NISCI),
Former Director,
Procurement & Supply Strategy,
Chrysler Division,
DaimlerChrysler Corp.

"The authors have done an excellent job of combining their knowledge of general alliances to a specific area of a company. The use of examples throughout the book clearly shows the benefits of an Extended Enterprise. Without question, the ability to apply this concept effectively is critical to companies today, and will be how they will succeed in the future. The chapter on trust conveys its importance in any successful alliance, as well as how one goes about achieving this difficult relationship trait. This well-written, easy-to-comprehend book explains a subject that is difficult to successfully implement. The authors help make the task easier through real-life examples and practical alliance applications."

—*L.D. Metcalfe*,
Global Director,
Strategic Global Alliances
and Planning,
Whirlpool Corp.

"*The Extended Enterprise* provides a fascinating historical look at the evolution of supply chain management from its lowly origins as no more than 'purchasing' and 'materials management' to today's concept of using supplier relationships to dramatically increase the capabilities of an organization. The authors underline the competitive requirements behind this evolution and stress that the goals of the Extended Enterprise are not only to reduce unit costs and working capital but also to grow sales and market share through leveraging the capabilities of the organization by developing a new series of relationships with key supplier partners. The book closes on two of the key ingredients to making the Extended Enterprise work: the people and the metrics. The keys to success are identified as the managerial competencies of the organization to create and maintain the right relationships with supplier partners, new non-traditional metrics to promote correct behavior with all parties, and the proper attitude of management to allow the Extended Enterprise to flourish. The book is a clear useful guide to understanding both the why and the how of the Extended Enterprise."

—*Kent Brittan*,
Vice President of Corporate
Purchasing,
United Technologies

THE EXTENDED ENTERPRISE: GAINING COMPETITIVE ADVANTAGE THROUGH COLLABORATIVE SUPPLY CHAINS

EDWARD W. DAVIS

Oliver Wight Professor of Business Administration
Darden Graduate School of Business Administration
University of Virginia
Charlottesville, VA 22901

ROBERT E. SPEKMAN

Tayloe Murphy Professor of Business Administration
Darden Graduate School of Business Administration
University of Virginia
Charlottesville, VA 22901

FT Prentice Hall
FINANCIAL TIMES

An Imprint of PEARSON EDUCATION
Upper Saddle River, NJ • New York • San Francisco • Toronto • Sydney
Tokyo • Singapore • Hong Kong • Cape Town • Madrid
Paris • Milan • Munich • Amsterdam
www.ft-ph.com

Library of Congress Cataloging-in-Publication Data

Davis, Edward W. (Edward Wilson), 1935-
    The extended enterprise: supply chain alliances, strategic partnerships, and why your
company can no longer afford to go it alone / Edward W. Davis and Robert E. Spekman.
    P. cm.
    Includes bibliographical references and index.
    ISBN 0-13-008274-0
    1.   Strategic alliances (Business) 2. Business networks. 3. Business
logistics--Management. 4. Competition. 1. Spekman, Robert E. 11. Title.

HD69.S8D392 2004
658'.044--dc21

                                    2003053153

Editor-in-Chief: Timothy C. Moore
Editorial/Production Supervision: Donna Cullen-Dolce
Development Editor: Russ Hall
Manufacturing Manager: Alexis R. Heydt-Long
Manufacturing Buyer: Maura Zaldivar
Cover Design Director: Jerry Votta
Cover Design: Anthony Gemmellaro
Interior Design: Gail Cocker-Bogusz
Composition: Daly Graphics

© 2004 Prentice Hall PTR
Publishing as Financial Times Prentice-Hall
Upper Saddle River, NJ 07458

Financial Times Prentice Hall offers discounts on this book when ordered in quantities for bulk
purchases or special sales. For more information, please contact U.S. Corporate and Government
Sales: 1-800-382-3419, or corpsales@pearsontechgroup.com. For sales outside the United States,
please contact International sales: 1-317-581-3793, international@pearsontechgroup.com.

Printed in the United States of America
1st Printing

ISBN 0-13-008274-0

Pearson Education LTD.
Pearson Education Australia PTY, Limited
Pearson Education Singapore, Pte. Ltd.
Pearson Education North Asia Ltd.
Pearson Education Canada, Ltd.
Pearson Educación de Mexico, S.A. de C.V.
Pearson Education—Japan
Pearson Education Malaysia, Pte. Ltd.

FINANCIAL TIMES PRENTICE HALL BOOKS

For more information, please go to www.ft-ph.com

Business and Technology

Sarv Devaraj and Rajiv Kohli
The IT Payoff: Measuring the Business Value of Information Technology Investments

Nicholas D. Evans
Business Innovation and Disruptive Technology: Harnessing the Power of Breakthrough Technology…for Competitive Advantage

Nicholas D. Evans
Consumer Gadgets: 50 Ways to Have Fun and Simplify Your Life with Today's Technology…and Tomorrow's

Faisal Hoque
The Alignment Effect: How to Get Real Business Value Out of Technology

Economics

David Dranove
What's Your Life Worth? Health Care Rationing…Who Lives? Who Dies? Who Decides?

John C. Edmunds
Brave New Wealthy World: Winning the Struggle for World Prosperity

Jonathan Wight
Saving Adam Smith: A Tale of Wealth, Transformation, and Virtue

Entrepreneurship

Oren Fuerst and Uri Geiger
From Concept to Wall Street: A Complete Guide to Entrepreneurship and Venture Capital

David Gladstone and Laura Gladstone
Venture Capital Handbook: An Entrepreneur's Guide to Raising Venture Capital, Revised and Updated

Thomas K. McKnight
Will It Fly? How to Know if Your New Business Idea Has Wings… Before You Take the Leap

Erica Orloff and Kathy Levinson, Ph.D.
The 60-Second Commute: A Guide to Your 24/7 Home Office Life

Jeff Saperstein and Daniel Rouach
Creating Regional Wealth in the Innovation Economy: Models, Perspectives, and Best Practices

Stephen Spinelli, Jr., Robert M. Rosenberg, and Sue Birley
Franchising: Pathway to Wealth Creation

CONTENTS

Chapter 5   OUTSOURCING IN THE EXTENDED ENTERPRISE   109

Chapter 6   INFORMATION SYSTEMS AND TECHNOLOGY ISSUES IN THE EXTENDED ENTERPRISE   131

**Chapter 8   DEVELOPING THE
   EXTENDED ENTERPRISE**

The extended enterprise has been discussed for a number of years, beginning, we believe, with Tom Stallkamp, former purchasing head at Chrysler. He transformed supplier relationships at Chrysler by building bridges to its suppliers, and he changed the adversarial model that had ruled the U.S. auto industry for decades.

The term *extended enterprise* connotes the collaborative relationships among supply chain members. Buyers and sellers work toward a shared vision—gaining a competitive advantage and achieving greater end use customer satisfaction, relative to other supply chains. Chrysler and its suppliers competed against Ford, GM, and the non–U.S.-based OEMs and their supply chains. It is interesting to note that since the Daimler merger, the collaborative model at Chrysler has slowly been supplanted by a different approach to procurement that, we believe, has done very little to foster the tenets of the extended enterprise as put forth under Stallkamp.

Some of the alleged gains from a more collaborative supply chain are easy to document, whereas others require a leap of faith. For instance, it is easy to point to purchase price reduction, lower inventory costs, or quality improvement. We can show, albeit with slightly more work to gather data, how the total cost of ownership has been reduced or how cycle times have improved. We have a more difficult time demonstrating how customer satisfaction, market share, or customer retention can be attributed to closer ties with our supply base. Statements of how OEMs have learned from their suppliers and improved their processes, and how these gains have led to better supply chain-wide performance are likely to be met with some skepticism.

Yet the extended enterprise is really about creating a defensible long-term competitive position through strong supply chain integration, collaborative behaviors, and the deployment of enabling information technology. Herein lies the challenge we face in writing this book. We advocate close ties among supply chain partners and argue the importance of the extended enterprise as the preferred business model for the new millennium. If we look at the current state of affairs, most companies fall short of our normative paradigm. Our observation is that most firms are not even close to developing the requisite mindset; they lack the skills and competencies needed and cannot implement the processes that lie at the heart of the extended enterprise.

We are open to criticism that we have created an ideal world and that we are naïve. Our objective is to share our vision of how supply chains should be. We acknowledge that most firms struggle to transform their supply chain relationships. We are aware that there are obstacles that must be overcome. At the same time, there are a small number of exemplar companies that are much farther along this path. These companies do demonstrate extended enterprise behaviors and are reaping the benefits of cross-company integration or an ability to institute design product and process changes with suppliers instantaneously and on a global basis. We will document these best-of-breed examples and use them to support our vision. These examples demonstrate that the time for extended enterprise thinking is now. To wait is to jeopardize the future competitive position of your company.

We advocate that extended enterprise thinking forces the company to consider supply chain-wide effects for actions taken and strategies developed. Concurrently, such thinking also encourages the development of evaluative criteria that examine cost savings and revenue growth. Metrics for evaluating supply chain-wide performance cannot emphasize one to the exclusion of the other, although we admit that the cost-focused measures are more prevalent. Despite the acknowledged nascent state of metrics that examine extended enterprise performance, we believe that valid and reliable measures are being developed and that any attempt to measure these benefits is a step in the right direction. If not measured, the hard work will never be done. For the extended enterprise to be successful, it has to be viewed as an investment. It is an investment in the lifeblood of the firm and is necessary if the firm seeks to attain a sustainable competitive advantage.

In part, supply chain integration begins with goal alignment. The challenge is to align goals on two levels: corporate and supply chain-wide. For many companies, procurement has come a long way from its lowly origins to now being considered a strategic partner in the planning process. Many of us can recall the time when purchasing did not enjoy such status. Armed with an understanding of the corporate mission and strategic plan, extended enterprise managers (purchasing) can initiate and/or facilitate the requisite cross-functional linkages and cross-discipline dialogues that support corporate-wide supply chain initiatives. The true challenge, however, is to accomplish this alignment across all components of the supply chain to ensure the same level of coordination and collaboration that can exist within one firm. The challenge of serving as a catalyst to bring together the skills and capabilities of independent companies working together to accomplish mutually achievable goals is a non-trivial problem.

For too many years, relationships among buyers and suppliers have typically been tenuous at best and often less than harmonious. Distrust, self-serving/opportunistic behavior, and a concern for only my objectives have left both buyer and seller quite cautious and, in a number of instances, wary of letting down their guard. Yet the handwriting is clearly on the wall: Cooperate or fail.

There are benefits to be gained from the formation of alliances and other supply chain relationships that unleash the power of partners working jointly to bring value to the marketplace. We are even more committed to the idea that a sustainable competitive advantage will come to those buyers and sellers who master the principles of the extended enterprise. Charles Fine, in his book *Clockspeed*, suggests that success will come to those firms that have a core competence in designing supply chain networks where virtual integration links partners that share a common vision and are committed to a set of common goals.

This book builds the case for the extended enterprise. Chapter 1 first introduces the extended enterprise and states the case for its merits. Here, the idea of the extended enterprise is defined, and factors that drive such thinking are discussed. Chapter 2 traces the development of the extended enterprise from the 1970s, when corporate purchasing morphed into materials management, then into strategic sourcing, and then to supply chain management. Each of these transitions is discussed and compared with the principles of the extended enterprise. Chapter 3 discusses the rise in technology and the importance of enterprise-level software that facilitate the linkages across the supply chain. Technology is the enabler that brings firms together by bridging the boundaries and facilitating the flows of product and information to each member of the supply chain. State-of-the-art technology alone cannot ensure the development of extended enterprise thinking or behavior. People are responsible for the content of information shared, its richness, and its degree of sensitivity.

In Chapter 4, the extended enterprise is presented in its entirety. Our view of the extended enterprise grows from our work in alliances and other collaborative relationships. Here, the criteria for success are developed, and principles by which members must abide are delineated. Management must be committed to the concept, and partners must be comfortable with the transparency of information that is shared. This new paradigm for how supply chain members interact requires new rules of engagement.

Chapter 5 discusses outsourcing as a potential example of the extended enterprise. We develop the notion of outsourcing from the more traditional forms to business process outsourcing. To some extent, business process outsourcing is a metaphor for the extended enterprise. To fall within the context of the extended enterprise, outsourcing must be approached from a core competence perspective. Merely shifting costs from fixed to variable is no longer a viable rationale. Outsourcing is less about reduced costs and more about leveraging capabilities. When selecting an outsourcing partner, firms now raise questions that center on how partners can work together to combine and leverage complementary skills and to improve end use customer satisfaction.

Chapter 6 builds on Chapter 3 and talks about the use of information technology to manage information flows and workflows across organizational boundaries more effectively. We describe the differences between technology and information technology. Here, technology is presented as a strategic tool to support and empower the tenets of the extended enterprise.

Chapter 7 truly differentiates this book from more traditional books about supply chain management. In Chapter 7, we develop the concept of trust. Trust is essential to the extended enterprise because without it, there can be no lasting collaboration. This chapter describes how trust is built, what its dimensions are, and what the impact of trust on supply chain relationships is. Trust lies at the core of the extended enterprise.

As stated previously, the extended enterprise requires a new approach to working with suppliers and customers. As such, skills and capabilities of managers must adapt to reflect this new world order. Chapter 8 argues that the type of procurement manager who was successful in the traditional role of buyer is not likely to have the skills or competencies to survive within an extended enterprise environment. In this chapter, the explanation for a new mindset and behaviors is given, and requisite skills are developed. Criteria for selecting extended enterprise managers are presented.

Chapter 9 focuses on performance measurement and presents metrics for the extended enterprise. Here, we extend traditional performance metrics to include both behavioral and enterprise-wide measures that reflect the difference level of analysis required, as well as measures that capture the less quantitative and softer metrics that depict the relationship qualities required by the extended enterprise. This discussion is couched within the Balanced Scorecard perspective. Chapter 10 brings the book to a close and highlights the key points made throughout the book.

This book is a departure from other books written about supply chain management on several levels.

- We simultaneously build the case for adopting new technology and the case for adapting traditional behaviors and attitudes. Devoting chapters to building trust and developing roles and behaviors that enable extended enterprise thinking to transcend the traditional supply chain is not typically done in supply chain management texts.
- Devoting a chapter to metrics and measures that capture the principles of the extended enterprise extends traditional wisdom.
- The emphasis given to the kinds of changes in attitudes/behaviors needed to develop extended enterprise thinking brings to the fore the importance of relationships.
- Our focus on the organizational processes and structures required to support the extended enterprise brings attention to issues that often are neglected in a traditional supply chain text, although structural and process-related obstacles can derail the best collaborative intentions.

The path to the extended enterprise and supply chain integration is not an easy one to follow. Yet the gains are well worth the effort. This book is our attempt to build the case for the hard work that must be done. Extended enterprise thinking requires a different way of thinking, a different culture, and set of values that for many managers is too far removed from their life experiences. Over the last 20 years, adaptations and accommodations have been made. However, we still have a long distance to travel. Perhaps it is best to think of the extended enterprise and its principles and precepts more as a journey than as a destination. We will argue in this chapter for the importance of extended enterprise thinking as we begin our journey. During the course of the book, we will continue our travels.

As we begin our journey, we are struck by the challenges faced by Lewis and Clark, who began their journey in

Charlottesville, Virginia, 200 years ago. We are the first to admit that the magnitude of our challenges pales in comparison. As faculty at the University of Virginia, however, we are aware of the fact that Thomas Jefferson was a long-time promoter of the expedition. His curiosity was unencumbered; his mind thirsted for facts. He was driven by practical knowledge—the chance to contribute to science and improve mankind. Among the directions he gave to Lewis was, "Your observations are to be taken with great pains and accuracy to be entered distinctly and intelligibly for others as well as for yourself, to comprehend all the elements necessary."

It is in the spirit of Mr. Jefferson's thirst for information and knowledge that we lead the reader from the past to future competitive realities and the role of the extended enterprise.

This project began several years ago as we were discussing the work each of us was doing. Although our functional areas are different—Robert is in Marketing, Ed in Operations—we saw a great deal of overlap in our teaching and research interests. Like all Darden faculty, our titles are Professor of Business Administration, not Professor of Marketing or Operations; as such, we are not confined to narrow functional homes but are expected to work on significant business problems that, almost by definition, cross-functional areas. Our work together began by jointly supervising student field projects; we hosted two conferences on supply chain management, we collaborated on several case projects, then we started this book.

We are grateful for the financial support provided for this work by the Darden Foundation and the Batten Institute of the Darden School. Our first thanks to Darden colleagues go to Bob Bruner, Executive Director of the Batten Institute, and Sankaran Venkataraman, Research Director of the Batten Institute. We also thank former Dean Ted Snyder, now Dean at the University of Chicago's School of Business; Darden's current Dean, Robert Harris; and Associate Dean Jim Freeland for their support. Many faculty colleagues have provided insight and support, but we especially thank Brandt Allen, John Colley, Paul Farris, Bob Landel, Tim Laseter, and Joe Spear (at James Madison University).

In addition, we owe a debt of gratitude to all the practitioners with whom we have worked and from whom we have learned. Special thanks go to our friends at United Technologies, particularly Kent Brittan, Vice President of Corporate Purchasing, and Ken Marcia, Director of Supplier Development. L.D. Metcalfe, Global Director of Strategic Global Alliances and Planning at Whirlpool Corporation, was a constant source of information and encouragement. We have also benefited greatly from our interactions with Jeffrey Trimmer, Batten Fellow at Darden and a former DaimlerChrysler executive. His comments, insights, and conversations were invaluable to us.

We would also like to thank Steve Williams, President of DecisionPath, Inc., who contributed most of Chapter 6 and provided encouragement throughout this project.

Our thanks also go to present and recent past doctoral students who have contributed to our intellectual growth over the years. Special thanks are due D. Eric Boyd and Jay Lambe, who have worked with Robert over the years. Both of us also wish to thank Niklas Myhr, whose dissertation helped solidify some of our thoughts regarding supply chain management. We also are grateful to John Kamauff, Jr. for his efforts and insights in previous case projects and academic articles. Our work is better as a result of his collaboration. John provided invaluable input to Chapter 9—thank you, John.

Our Administrative Assistants, Karen Harper and Debbie Quarles, worked under tight deadlines, managed our anxieties, and did so with constant professionalism and smiles. Marie Payne, graphic artist, learned new software for this project and contributed her considerable talent and imagination.

Finally, our major debt of gratitude goes to our families. Their support, love, and patience were invaluable during the writing of this book. It is to them that this book is dedicated.

Edward W. Davis and Robert E. Spekman

INTRODUCTION

This chapter introduces the concept of the extended enterprise and argues for the benefits of collaborative behavior among supply chain partners. Given the economic turbulence in recent years, it is not surprising that firms are trying to make their supply chains more cost-effective, transparent, and responsive. The rewards of doing so can be great. Successful companies show that leaner inventories, lower working capital, higher profits and productivity, and better customer service are among the benefits.[1] Companies such as Wal-Mart, FedEx, Procter & Gamble, Dell, and IBM have demonstrated that superior supply chain management (SCM) can lead to industry dominance.

Supply chain management systems and Internet-based solutions have become the focus of many reengineering projects aimed at solving supply chain problems. For instance, HP's Internet-based exchange has saved over $100 million in just 18 months. AMR Research reported that expenditures for supply chain technology grew to $5.6 billion in 2001 and are expected to grow another 12 percent in 2002. These technology applications all promise to deliver greater control over portions of the supply chain. These gains are not guaranteed and can mistakenly redirect management's attention away from the importance of integrated processes and people issues.

Technology might enhance better information flows among supply chain members but the quality of information shared is far more important. The level of trust among the supply chain drives the quality of information. AMR also reports that most firms are nowhere near exhibiting the level of trust needed to achieve the range of supply chain benefits. When suppliers and their OEM customers were asked what level of price discount would cause them to switch suppliers, their responses were 7 and 10 percent, respectively. The data suggest very strongly that loyalty and collaboration are worth very little in practice.

Even more disturbing is a study published in *Purchasing*[2] regarding buyers' responses to a CEO's mandate to improve profits in the sluggish 2002 economy. Buyers have beefed up their cost control programs with an average expected cost drop of 5.8 percent. Among the tactics employed are greater reliance on long-term contracts to lock in prices; leveraging size through consolidation of purchases; harder negotiations; use of reverse auctions and search for lower cost labor opportunities; and buying on the spot market. Some buyers are trying to reduce costs through value engineering and product redesign. Although a number of these approaches make sense and have merit, the more popular approaches are focused on the short term and ignore any attempt to think strategically about collaboration and the benefits that accrue from the extended enterprise.

THE NEW COMPETITION:
THE EXTENDED ENTERPRISE

Although the ideals of the extended enterprise are relatively new, there have been small numbers of firms that have begun to employ its principles. Competitive pressures, an instinct for survival, and a realization that their traditional business model was likely to fail typically have driven these firms. For example, in 1970, a consortium of four of Europe's aerospace companies joined fortunes to create Airbus, a response to the European's shrinking share of the commercial airline business. France's Aerospatiale, Britain's Aerospace, Spain's CASA, and Germany's Daimler Aerospace each would build sections of planes that would be assembled, marketed, and certified in Toulouse through a separate management company owned by the four partners. Achieving this level of cooperation from firms (and countries) that have competed (and fought) against each other has not been a trivial obstacle to overcome. These partners acknowledged that alone they had neither the skills nor the resources to compete effectively against Boeing, Douglas, or Lockheed. With the introduction of the A320 in 1988, Airbus demonstrated that the consortium and its suppliers could produce a superior plane and make a profit. Despite the debate as to the impact governmental support plays in its sales, Airbus stands today as an example of a network of collaborative partners who compete very successfully on the world scene. In fact, press statements released in January 2003 suggest that Airbus sales this year might exceed Boeing's sales for the first time.

This consortium has seamlessly linked its four prime partners and is currently in the process of incorporating its first-tier suppliers into its information exchange process through the use of bar codes on parts. These codes reduce logistics processing and cycle time relative to service-related problems. Successful horizontal consortia are built on a model of trust where all members must win if the group is to win.

An area in which problems arise is associated with letting go of the reins and letting the group make decisions on behalf of the members.[3] Firms are less willing to relinquish control; however, we are beginning to hear a common rallying cry: *We must cooperate to compete*. The extended enterprise symbolizes a revolutionary approach to competitive behavior and how firms view their exchange relationships. We are witnessing a transformation in the nature of relationships within a value chain (or a supply chain), and this transformation will forever change the manner in which firms compete and cooperate. To begin the journey of understanding how the extended enterprise changes the face of SCM and creates additional value for customers, we first need to appreciate the impact of the new competition.

CHANGING THE FACE OF COMPETITION

The capabilities derived from integrated SCM are delivering benefits across a range of businesses as diverse as construction and software development. These gains are far more powerful than inventory reduction and more efficient than logistics, encompassing new product development, improved cycle time, improvements in customer responsiveness, and overall improved productivity. For instance, Lucent has reduced its warehouses from 200 to 33 as a direct result of better technology that allows monitoring of order status throughout its supply chain. As it relies more on outsourcing, it has reduced inventory and carrying costs. Increased visibility is a result of a seamless information technology system that links suppliers and notifies Lucent of any delays or problems in fulfilling a customer order.

Supply chain-wide thinking is a fairly recent phenomenon, and procurement managers have not always viewed their world through this lens. Adversarial relationships between buyers and suppliers have long been the rule, and price reduction has been the key metric by which success has been measured. Traditional supply chain thinking was based on the premise that lower prices add value. Although price is important, value is created in ways that render price considerations secondary and emphasize innovation and information as critical elements in the value equation. Today, buyers realize that supplier involvement in new product design and processes provides benefits to the buyer that span areas such as engineering, testing, tooling, and other capabilities.

Changes in both the nature of competition and how competition is defined have demonstrated that the previous adversarial model is inappropriate and, in many instances, is harmful. It makes perfect sense that a firm cannot optimize its operations without consideration for its customers, its customers' customers, its suppliers, and its suppliers' suppliers. The notion of the extended enterprise takes SCM to the next level and focuses on those factors and characteristics that link supply chain members by far more than workflow and logistics. The extended enterprise captures the idea that firms are also linked as learning organizations. Knowledge becomes the currency of exchange, and the goal is to create value for customers so that each supply chain member benefits. Withholding needed information from other supply chain members or creating technological barriers to prohibit supply chain-wide learning shows a lack of appreciation for how winners/losers emerge.

Whirlpool looks for qualities in suppliers that go well beyond competitive costs and quality. It attributes its overall productivity improvements and innovative product introductions to a supply base that helps reduce design costs and assists in migrating innovation globally. Part of its mandate is to leverage existing relationships with suppliers to deliver competitive advantage globally. Whirlpool created a world-class supply base by working with suppliers to develop new supply technologies and by trusting that both were working toward similar goals. Margins in the appliance business are quite slim, and there is little room for noncollaborative partners who do not share insights and capabilities and are not willing to transfer knowledge across the boundaries of the two companies.

However, firms are slow to adapt; a recent study by AMR shows only 6 percent of companies are actually connected throughout their supply chains. Nonetheless, these extended enterprises symbolize flexible, creative, learning organizations whose managers seek new business approaches and are quick to respond to marketplace changes. Texas Instruments (TI) is in the process of installing supply chain event management

(SCEM) software to track exceptions over time and identify and correct bottlenecks. The goal is to provide visibility from suppliers to customers on a global basis. TI estimates that just being able to confirm deliveries electronically will pay for the system.*

As supply chain members begin to think of themselves as adaptive networks that can respond to changes, they are on their way to extended enterprise thinking. These new organizational forms require a transformation in both internal and external processes and procedures. More efficient internal processes alone no longer measure operational excellence; it now entails more effective and relevant responses to customers' needs and requirements that often cross organizational boundaries. You would think that cross-functional cooperation is easily understood and implemented. However, many managers cannot rise above a reward system that provides incentives to individual department thinking based on behaviors that reinforce little consideration for the leverage that accrues when business units (or departments) act in concert, sacrificing individual gains for the benefit of the enterprise. Metrics that emphasize individual unit profit and loss rarely encourage such joint actions where win-win thinking rules the day.

Externally, extended enterprises are managed to optimize efficiency in workflow and to maximize the flows of information/knowledge among partners. To appreciate aspects of supply chain learning better, a survey[4] of global firms showed that companies that value learning across the supply chain often see information as a shared asset and exhibit very collaborative behaviors. These findings are summarized in Table 1.1. The results suggest that when learning is valued and shared across supply chain members, purchasing efficiency is enhanced, and supply chain partners are better poised to gain a sustainable competitive advantage. Not only are supply chain-wide costs reduced, but these supply chains are more responsive to customers'

---

* We caution that systems such as SCEM are relatively new, and their full benefits are untested at this juncture. Although the software might not deliver as promised, it is the change in mindset that is important because it signals a movement in the right direction.

TABLE 1.1 Positive Effects of Supply Chain Learning

Greater support for supply chain learning is associated with....	Better performance regarding: ■ On-time delivery ■ Adaptation to change ■ Responsiveness to partner needs
	Contributions by supply chain partners to: ■ Customer satisfaction and value creation ■ Differentiation of offerings in the marketplace ■ Increased account penetration ■ Reduction in inventory levels ■ Reduction in cycle time and new product development

needs and requirements. By leveraging skills and capabilities across the supply chain, revenue-creating opportunities exist.

A Survey of CEOs and the Extended Enterprise In 2002, *The Economist*[5] surveyed CEOs to understand the effects the extended enterprise is having on senior managers in global companies. Interestingly, over 65 percent of the respondents report that they have become and will become more dependent on external relations to achieve their business objectives. In areas related to supplier relationships, the three most critical factors for selecting partners were high levels of expertise, reputation, and an excellent knowledge of their companies. At the same time, over 65 percent feared that such relationships would lead to a lack of control and heightened vulnerability. An equal number of executives said they lacked adequate metrics to assess whether these partnerships were successful. This survey highlights two key points:

1. CEOs acknowledge the critical importance of the extended enterprise.
2. Few firms are adequately prepared to accept the loss of control or have sufficient metrics to measure performance.

An Illustration of Extended Enterprise Thinking The previous discussion paints a broad landscape of extended enterprise thinking but lacks the clarity of a more focused portrait. To understand better the nature of the new competition and the rise of the extended enterprise, we offer an illustration from the oil business, with focus on underwater drilling. FMC Energy Systems (FMC) (a U.S.-based multinational manufacturing company) manufactures precision equipment for the oil industry that is used at wellheads in thousands of feet of water to direct the flow of oil and gas from underground reserves to the surface. These "Christmas trees," along with other highly engineered products and services, provide mission-critical applications and solutions to oil companies that drill globally for oil. You can only imagine the severe conditions found working at the surface and the floor of the North Sea in depths exceeding 6,000 feet of water. Working with many of the major oil companies in locations as dispersed as the coast of Brazil, the North Sea, West Africa, and the Gulf of Mexico, FMC adds value to its customers well beyond lowered total costs of operation. It also works in partnership with its customers (and other suppliers) to provide customized solutions to technical problems in safely ensuring the flow of the oil and gas from these depths to the surface. Although cost, faster system delivery, and other traditional purchasing measures remain important, both FMC and the oil companies have come to realize that their destinies are inextricably linked. Common goals foster a belief that success for one results in success for both.

As part of its value-added capabilities, FMC touts its product innovation and state-of-the-art technology that provide its partners an advantage when competing for global market share. These technological gains can be achieved only if there is a high level of cooperation internally among different functional units, all of which have their sights set on achieving customer satisfaction. In addition, buyers and sellers work more collaboratively, share plans and strategies, and work toward a mutually shared set of goals and objectives.

This scene is a far cry from behaviors of a decade ago, where the oil companies and their suppliers attempted to gain advantage at the expense of each other. It should be noted that in some instances, spot market transactions still exist in the oil industry, and buyers still attempt to leverage their size and power. Yet for strategic purchases, such an approach makes little sense. These more critical relationships are based on trust and mutual respect. Purchase price still matters but it is counter-balanced by a number of other factors that are driven by a different mindset. In fact, as part of the proposal process, oil companies have included a survey that is intended to shed light on the collaborative behavior of the potential suppliers. A potential supplier might score high on its technical merits or on the elegance of its design/solution but score low on its partnerlike behavior and attitudes. This profile might be sufficient for the buyer to drop the supplier from further consideration.

The decision to work with a supplier is based on both quantifiable and qualitative data. In addition, technical skills, price-related factors, *and* the extent to which the supplier is seen as a potential partner are viewed as key criteria.

Factors Driving Extended Enterprise Thinking   In the oil industry, firms are dependent on a number of other companies to provide a total solution to the technological challenge of drilling for oil in deeper waters all over the globe. Both Shell and Exxon Mobil are listed among *Fortune's* top 10 global firms, with Exxon Mobil being number one at revenues in 2000 of $210 billion. Yet if you were to add the revenue of all the firms that partner with these companies to explore, drill, and extract oil from the ground, the total revenue for these extended enterprises would be close to $1 trillion.[6] These global alliances act in concert as single entities, and when their assets are combined, the total exceeds the GNP of many nations. For example, Brown & Root Energy Services has signed a 10-year alliance with Chevron in the Gulf of Mexico to provide project management and other topside and subsea services, along with Aker Maritime (floating platforms), Saipem, Inc. (pipe laying and heavy lift), and Han-Padron Associates (design and development of deep-water systems). This risk- and reward-sharing alliance allows Chevron to rely on the expertise of its partners as it develops its deep-water leases.

Implicit in the new competition and extended enterprise thinking are several key factors:

- Environmental changes that affect technology development, access to markets, or the ability to predict
  changing consumer demand are increasing at a faster
  rate, and competitive responses must be swift and deci-
  sive. World-class suppliers often provide insight into
  these issues and contribute to reducing uncertainty for
  companies.
- The recognition of fragmented markets and the existence of microsegments have forced firms to respond
  faster and with greater precision to changing preferences
  as needed. Agility[7] is required to anticipate these
  demands and to create bundles of products and services
  to meet the needs of these different segments. It is
  unlikely that one firm has the skills or capability to do
  this alone. Dell, for example, has demonstrated time and
  time again its flexibility and speed in adapting to new
  technology without the inventory problems or
  unplanned obsolescence that plagues many of its
  competitors.
- Technology, new product innovation, and the product
  life cycle are all subject to greater time pressures, such
  that it is often difficult to achieve a long-term advantage.
  Product life cycles are shortening; long-term patent pro-
  tection in some instances is illusory. Supply chain partners allow firms to leverage speed and to shortcut the
  innovations process. In the pharmaceutical business,
  each day that a new drug is delayed in its introduction
  can cost upward of $5 million in revenue. Supply chain
  partners can improve speed to market.
- The globalization of markets, free trade, and new
  economic development serve to accelerate all of the
  conditions listed above. Although there are increased
  opportunities, there are also new challenges, not the
  least of which is how to manage these loose federa-
  tions/networks and/or supply chain relationships that
  extend beyond the boundaries and reach of the single
  enterprise.

One implication is that a new leadership style is needed—
a style that embraces change, encourages flexibility, and

simultaneously takes on a firm-wide and extended enterprise perspective. There are few supply chains that have fully implemented metrics to reward system-wide thinking and capture systemwide performance. For instance, one key issue is how to determine profitability at the firm and the supply chain levels. A truly win-win supply chain examines profitability at all levels and ensures that profits are distributed equitably, based on a model in which supply chain partners share risks and rewards.

Such changes must begin with a corporate vision that transcends the single firm to encompass the partners that comprise this extended enterprise. Managers must learn to utilize assets and coordinate activities they do not directly control or own and cannot directly see. In addition, they must now consider their suppliers' views on resource needs/constraints, threats/opportunities, and weaknesses/strengths when considering setting goals and objectives.

To meet the volatile demands of the semiconductor market, MKS Instruments (a maker of gas-flow controllers and throttle valves) maintains capacity at 85 percent so that it has the flexibility to react to the needs of Intel and other key customers.[8] It has also worked with its suppliers to ensure that the entire system can react in time to the changing demand requirements of its customers. In its commitment to customer service, MKS willingly holds some stock on consignment at customer locations. Although 19 days of finished inventory might not be considered "lean," MKS sells its products for less than $10,000; they are part of final products priced in excess of $1 million. MKS understands where it sits in the customers' value equation and feels that such actions are a sign of commitment.

DIFFERENT VIEWS AND PERSPECTIVES

For the CEO and the senior management team, the level of analysis is the full constellation of cooperating companies that work together toward a commonly shared set of goals and objectives. For instance, when Shell attempted ultra deep water (8,000 feet) exploration in the Gulf of Mexico, its prime partners were other exploration companies from Amoco, Mobil, and Texaco who helped share the risk of this deep-water opportunity. In addition to the principals who shoulder the financial risks, there are numerous other partners who manage the platforms, oversee the daily operations, and do the work of drilling.

Combine the needs of these risk-sharing partners with the efforts of those firms that provide drilling platform management, deep-water equipment and services, seismic expertise, and the entire range of operational activities; it is fairly easy to envision the complexities inherent in coordinating and integrating the members of the extended enterprise. Competitive assessments are now made up and down the supply chain, and the constellation of cooperating companies is as strong as its weakest partner.

Boeing and Lockheed Martin competed to build the Joint Striker Fighter, the next-generation multi-role fighter. Both assembled teams of supplier partners who are core to the success of the effort. The partner firms that comprise the Boeing team (one extended enterprise) competed against the Lockheed team for a prize in excess of $200 billion in orders to be delivered over the next 20 years. On October 27, 2001, the Pentagon announced that the Lockheed team had won the competition. To understand the competitive realities, the playing field does not pit Boeing against Lockheed. Rather, it is the Boeing team, comprised of dozens of suppliers (e.g., Pratt Whitney, Raytheon, BAE Systems, Messier-Dowty) and their entire set of skills and capabilities, compared with the Lockheed team and its key partners, as well as the set of first- and second-tier suppliers.

Calling the constellation of firms a *team* implies that, for buyer and supplier, this is not business as usual. Although the aerospace industry has long assembled project teams, these have been very product-focused and were managed under the umbrella of traditional subcontractors and prime contractor relationships. The reporting relationships were clear, and the power in all aspects of decision making rested solely with the prime contractor. There were manuals governing the nature of the prime sub-contractor relationship that tried to leave no stone unturned and attempted to adjudicate any dispute that might arise. There existed a natural tension between contractual relations and working relationships.

During the early stages of the competition, both teams used the terms *partner* and *partnering behavior* to describe the manner in which members would interact. Contracts are still written but they are not used on a daily basis to dictate interaction and set the tone of the relationship among the team members. This does not minimize the importance of contract management as much as it changes the emphasis of living by the contract to managing a set of working relationships that must be flexible and adaptive. Simply, all team members are given voice and are valued beyond the materials/systems purchased; they are acknowledged for the expertise and capabilities they bring to the relationships.

Important to the new relationships is the role of trust that is often lost within the context of contractual relationships. This is not to say that in the past companies mistrusted one another. Previously, trust tended to be limited to the letter of the contract and reinforced the arm's-length contractual relationship.

The View from Procurement   At the level of the procurement function, there are new behaviors that must be developed and adaptations in mindset that must occur to accommodate the change in perspective to the extended enterprise. Table 1.2 summarizes the different expectations and roles associated with procurement and shows how those new roles reflect a more strategic view of the relationship among the members of the extended enterprise. Procurement now takes a more proactive role in orchestrating a networkwide response to customer needs, as well as in looking for opportunities to leverage the capabilities of its partners. The total enterprise is the relevant competitive entity. This perspective belies the past, where buyers were rewarded on variance to purchase price and on the quality and timely delivery of goods purchased.

From Table 1.2 it is clear that the focus becomes less transactional and short term. Procurement is now actively involved in developing suppliers for the long term who complement the buying firm's existing skills and whose capabilities bring value to the marketplace. Change must happen quickly because

TABLE 1.2 Procurement's New Role in the New Competition

EVOLUTIONARY CHANGE	REVOLUTIONARY CHANGE
Primary point of supplier contact	Acts as a facilitator to enable multifunction, multilevel interaction
Administers the contract and manages the supplier base	Manages relationships among supply chain partners to maximize market acceptance
Reacts to the market and minimizes risk to the firm	
Tends to be transaction-focused	Proactively looks for opportunities to leverage skills and bring value to customers
Sees the flow of information to be one-way and into its own firm	Thinks long term and is willing to sacrifice in the short term for the long-term win
Engages in some cross-functional coordination but tries to be the main point of contact	Information flows are simultaneous and two-way
	Seeks functional integration by managing and leveraging the skills of partners

movement at a snail's pace is totally inadequate for the task at hand. Revolutionary change reflects the fact that suppliers offer opportunities for cost reduction and revenue enhancement. They provide an opportunity for the entire enterprise to learn from its members because information flows openly among them, and they contribute to systemwide innovation and technology development through early involvement in design and other processes that enable idea sharing. Procurement activities now include management of internal relationships that integrates across functions/units and externally with supply chain partners. Suppliers are chosen because they are problem solvers and can use their experience/capabilities toward mutually beneficial solutions.

Mercer Management[9] isolated key characteristics of the firms most prepared to embrace the notions of the extended enterprise. Among these characteristics are:

■ Customer alignment—the process begins with customers, and they drive the process.

- Collaboration—partners are linked through trust and respect, and roles are assigned by virtue of comparative advantage.
- Flexibility and speed—partners are quick to respond to change and are able to make adaptations quickly. Information replaces inventory, and information is a shared resource. Sustained advantage is a function of information that is transformed into knowledge from which the set of supply chain partners benefit.

In an attempt to facilitate such interaction, several software vendors have collaborated to provide a product management solution that links product development and strategic sourcing. An alliance between SDRC and i2 will allow users strategically to source, collaboratively design, engage in Web-based negotiations, manage the request for proposal (RFP) process, and link all supply chain partners to a common product view.

Challenges Brought on by Working Closely   Think about the challenges of integrating activities, information, and processes among independent firms that come together to compete against other extended enterprises while maintaining their own separate identities. There is an inherent tension in that firms come together to work jointly but each retains its own autonomy, and the default option is to act in its own self-interest.

One source of tension is the awkwardness between competing and partnering that is exacerbated by trade-offs between trust/opportunistic behavior and teamwork/self-serving behavior. Another source of tension is related to the role of suppliers and the functions they perform in the supply chain. If activities are not seen as complementary, it is likely that conflict will surface as supply chain partners argue over how much value they create and who performs a particular task more effectively. This debate becomes more heated and often results in discussions regarding equitable treatment and the sharing of risk and reward.

Still another source of tension is the unintended flow of information. Consider that the assets held by the supplier are of two kinds: tangible and intangible. Tangible assets are accounted for on the balance sheet, and intangible assets are not. Employee know-how is one of the firm's intangible assets. Explicit knowledge is codified and can be observed and copied. Tacit knowledge is not codified and is not easily copied. By working closely and spending considerable time with its supply chain partner, a firm can begin to learn and absorb this knowledge. To be resolved is how much tacit knowledge a supplier (or buyer) can transfer to the partner without jeopardizing its core expertise through the unintended leakage of information.

To be more competitive, Motorola, a pioneer in the market, has taken a second look at its personal communications sector (PCS) and has developed a strategy to lower costs and raise profits, in part, by more strategic purchasing. Motorola will simplify its product portfolio and, as a consequence, will simplify the way it designs and purchases materials. Central to this strategy is the selection of suppliers that are technologically superior. These gains could not be achieved without longer term supply agreements based on performance guidelines, not "specs"; a mutual commitment to work closely over a period of years; and an implied expectation that best practices will be shared and technology will be jointly developed. Of concern is the unintended leakage of information that might affect Motorola's future competitive advantage.

Rather than rely on integration processes as a vehicle to leverage technology, integration is also used to learn how much a company buys what from whom and how these discrete purchases can be rolled up to gain the full advantage of size. Raytheon estimates that it could save 5 percent annually on the $5.1 billion it currently spends by sorting out where its leverage points are.[10] Supplier integration occurs by knowing which divisions the same suppliers serve. Focusing on leverage to reduce costs fails to appreciate the other gains afforded by leverage, such as exchanging engineering data to improve the product development cycle.

LIFE AFTER PRICE LEVERAGE

Extended enterprise members must develop norms that support and extend the principles of the supply chain partnership.

When problems arise, they are treated as joint problems, rather than belonging to the individual responsible. Instead of having formal communications where information follows the chain of command, communications are more balanced and informal. Planning efforts include consideration for the relationship *and* the business.

Equally as important is the level of senior management commitment that requires visibility and transparency in operations among the members. The full benefits of an integrated supply chain cannot be achieved without access to an unprecedented amount of data and financial information. For all the talk in support of the extended enterprise, barriers are still in place that impede the level of collaboration required. Where barriers exist, a recent *Industry Week* survey suggests that a lack of leadership followed by a lack of strategic direction were viewed as the key impediments.[11]

Arvin-Meritor Corporation, a major supplier to the automotive industry, has developed a close cadre of suppliers that work with it globally. Arvin and its partners work hard to develop a sense of shared destiny. These companies are linked by trust and a belief that one partner will not act opportunistically at the other's expense. William Hunt, CEO, has taken the position that what is good for Arvin is good for its supply base and has rolled out several key programs to Arvin's key partners. Now the lean production systems that worked internally for Arvin are shared with its suppliers. A senior executive at Thyssen Steel, a major provider, buys the concept and states that it is exploiting the word *partnerships*. Both parties recognize that the better each treats the other, the longer the relationship will be successful and profitable. Recall that Arvin sells to automobile manufacturers, and we would be hard pressed to find a more cost-obsessed set of customers.

At an intellectual level, it is fairly simple to understand the benefits gained from such collaborative behavior. Yet at an operational level, reality sets in. Customers must provide accurate and reliable forecasts and must share data with suppliers who then must provide timely delivery, reliable quality, and responsiveness to changes that might occur. The ability to provide data integrity is important but the true challenge is a process that is based on a willingness to communicate openly and share sensitive information. As information replaces inventory, firms that are either unable or unwilling to share internal information will have higher costs and will not be viewed as potentially strong partners.

To be sure, technology is an enabler that facilitates interaction among levels in the extended enterprise. Cross-system compatibility is enhanced by advanced protocols that link customer requests directly to the shop floor production schedule. Cisco Systems reports that improved accuracy in communications within its supply chain has saved hundreds of millions of dollars. Access to information has become an expected part of the total product offering. The implications are:

1. Trust must lie at the core of the relationship.
2. Cross-functional integration is essential because the requisite information is located in different parts of the firm.
3. Products and services are bundled as part of the total value-added package, thereby solidifying the need for heightened cooperation internally and across the different supply chain members.

BEGINNING THE CONVERSATION NEEDED FOR THE EXTENDED ENTERPRISE

Despite the perceived gains and positive words, in the background is the skepticism that what people really want is price concession. The same *Industry Week* survey cited earlier reveals that pricing pressure is also a major barrier to achieving the goals of the extended enterprise. As criteria shift away from price to considerations of time saving, reliability, leverage, and end-use customer satisfaction, we witness an emerging conversation among trading partners. This conversation is relatively new, and many companies lack both the vocabulary and vision for this important dialogue.

A recently published study[12] reveals an interesting difference between buyers and sellers that supports the *Industry*

TABLE 1.3 Different Perspectives Required to Begin the Dialogue: How Buyers and Sellers See the World Differently

SELLER'S PERSPECTIVE	BUYER'S PERSPECTIVE
Sellers engage in SCM to: ■ increase end-use customer satisfaction ■ gain a strategic market position Sellers see the relationship as critical to success.	Buyers engage in SCM to: ■ gain better pricing ■ reduce lead times Buyers see the relationship as one where supply chain members can be easily replaced.
Sellers select supply chain partners who: ■ are reliable and consistent ■ have strong reputations ■ offer both economic benefit	Buyers select supply chain partners who: ■ are trustworthy ■ have integrity ■ know Buyer's business ■ are committed
Sellers describe the relationship: ■ lasting a long time ■ willing to devote extra effort ■ willing to share technical information ■ customers to this customer are important	Buyers describe the relationship: ■ have faith in partner ■ have sense of fair play ■ focus mainly on price ■ tend to use fewer criteria to evaluate

Week survey. Table 1.3 summarizes the findings and highlights the different perspectives of buyers and sellers.

Although buyer and seller seem to mouth the right words, it should be apparent that buyer and seller do not share compatible views in practice. Telling differences lie in the findings that:

■ Buyers see the relationship as commodity-like, where sellers can be easily replaced. Sellers see buyers as critical to their success. Sellers value the unique contribution potentially offered by buyers who can affect end-use customer satisfaction. Buyers attribute no such uniqueness and, in fact, are predisposed to short-term thinking.

- Buyers think very little about selection criteria beyond price and fail to consider a host of other factors that might lead to higher market share for the entire supply chain membership.
- Sellers talk about relationships, value-added capability, and supply chain-wide benefits. Buyers understand the importance of customer-driven supply chains but are uncomfortable with such talk. To demonstrate how stark the differences between buyer and seller can be, buyers and sellers were asked to describe their relationship using a sports analogy. Buyers referred to chess and focused on the mental exchange with the seller. Sellers, on the other hand, referred to rugby, roller derby, and football as games that best described the interaction with the buyer. It would be a mistake to look at the difference and respond that a little competition is healthy and keeps the seller honest and ensures a low price. Such an observation ignores the underlying premises that guides extended enterprise thinking.

DEFINING THE EXTENDED ENTERPRISE

Thus far, the discussion of the extended enterprise has not included a formal definition. The extended enterprise is the entire set of collaborating companies, both upstream and downstream, from raw material to end-use consumption, that work together to bring value to the marketplace. The advantages of the extended enterprise derive from a firm's ability to quickly utilize the entire network of suppliers, vendors, buyers, and customers. The flows of information that lie at the core of the coordination and collaboration among network members not only link disparate information sources, they also provide an opportunity to build knowledge-based tools. Companies engage in longer term partnering relationships built around mutual goals and accompanied by a very rich and deep exchange of information. Members' view that their destinies are interdependent. This serves to separate the extended enterprise from other loose confederations of buyers and suppliers. The fact that success is now a function of the collective performance of the enterprise and not individual firm actions signals a significant change: The important words implied by the above are seamless and transparent.

Extending the notion of an integrated supply chain, members are bound by a shared set of norms and social contracts that emphasizes a win-win philosophy such that each shares equitably in the gains and the risks inherent in any form of competitive arena. Through their collaborative efforts, partners recognize:

- The importance of maximizing value for the marketplace and the entire network of suppliers. The gains, benefits, and costs savings should be felt system-wide throughout the extended enterprise. The advantages should be equitable, not necessarily equal. Advantage should be realized in proportion to individual contribution made.
- To achieve these benefits, extended enterprise members must be willing to relinquish total control.
- The need to gain system-wide synergies such that 1 + 1 = 3 and not something less than 2, as is often the case. The challenge here is one of integration and combining the complementary skills of each member of the extended enterprise.
- Members develop a laser-like focus on achieving end-use customer satisfaction so that competitive advantage results. A litmus test is whether the extended enterprise is able to operate with greater effectiveness and efficiency than is the single firm.
- Development of product and process is enhanced because companies can strategically link their core competencies with the competencies of their partners. The level of analysis is now the extended enterprise, and the entire network benefits from this leverage. Speed to market is accelerated, costs are lowered, and new market opportunities are more easily accessed.

It is natural to draw similarities to the definition of value chains and supply chains when describing the extended enterprise. However, the differences are more profound. At one level, the *link and node* supply chain models of production are not adequate to capture the way information and materials flows are managed. This approach is best suited for the sequential production schedule where interaction is viewed more as handing off from one point of production to another. The differences bring the extended enterprise to a higher level of integration and collaboration. Rather than moving linearly, it would not be uncommon to find a complex web of interchange and not a straight-line flow, as is depicted in Figure 1.1.

One popular text[13] defines the extended supply chain as the integrated set of activities completed by full supply chain participants upstream and downstream. It is clear that in this text an underlying emphasis is given to managing the logistics of the process. The observation that a small number of firms have comprehensive channel integration capability is compelling but downplays the gains achieved beyond cost saving and customer service.

Value chain analysis is a method for decomposing the firm into strategically important activities to understand their impact on costs and value. The framework argues that competitive advantage is understood by disaggregating the value-creation process into its discrete parts that contribute to a firm's costs and create a basis for differential advantage.[14] In fact, one might argue that too much attention is directed to finding costs, and less energy is devoted to value creation and creation of competitive advantage. Conversations about the extended enterprise require a different perspective—a different world view.

At the extreme, we are sympathetic to the notions of a virtual corporation, where it is difficult to know where one firm ends and the other begins, by virtue of the permeable boundaries, the flows of information, and the level at which members jointly plan. Table 1.4 reflects the level of transformation needed to move from more traditional supply chain or value chain thinking to the extended enterprise mindset. In many value chain discussions, firms ask questions regarding where they should be to reap the greater value-added position. Despite an

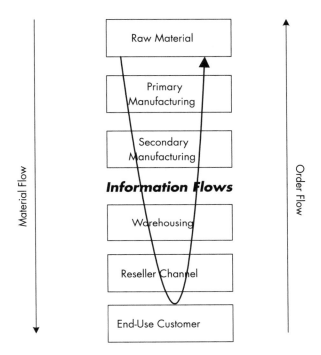

FIGURE 1.1
A typical supply chain.

element of joint action, value chain partners still retain some vestiges of self-serving behavior. In the extended enterprise, such behavior violates basic norms and rules of engagement.

Supply chain management tends to focus on supply or demand issues but rarely incorporates the two. In addition, the intent is often to maximize flows and assets based on manufacturing resource planning (MRP) systems or other inventory-/production-based systems. These are all-important and are part of extended enterprise thinking, but although these considerations are necessary, they are not sufficient for the full impact to be realized. Shared product development, providing a complete business solution, and integrated long-term planning are also part of the extended enterprise.

Another differentiating factor is the role of learning and knowledge sharing/creating. Extended enterprises are learning

TABLE 1.4 Comparison of Supply Chains, Value Chains, and the Extended Enterprise[15]

BUSINESS FACTOR	SUPPLY CHAINS/ VALUE CHAINS	EXTENDED ENTERPRISE
Environment	More stable and static	Dynamic and changing
Focus	Tends to be industry-centric	Finds partners who bring part of the business solution
Value-creation approach	Leverages own competencies, more self-sustaining	Leverages the competencies of all members
Relationship type	A teaming approach with some aspects of partnerlike behavior	Strong collaborative behavior with very solid partnering behavior
Infrastructure thrust	Cost-driven	Value-driven
Profit focus	Increasing own profit is the default	Increasing profits system-wide
Knowledge	Shared carefully but tends to look internally	Shared widely over the system
Orientation	Tends to emphasize workflows, etc.	Emphasizes also knowledge and learning

organizations where knowledge is viewed as a quasi-public good to be shared across the member firms. Not only must managers now share insights and knowledge, they must also develop mental models that espouse a systems view. Enterprise members search for system-wide leverage points that bestow competitive advantage throughout the network.

The extended enterprise recognizes that people are one of the most valued assets a firm can bring to the relationship. People are empowered to act, are trusted to use information as intended (i.e., for the good of the extended enterprise), and are trained to work well in teams and to support the notions of cooperative behavior. Learning is valued, and opportunities to learn are provided. Neither value chain nor supply chain analysis explicitly speaks of people as a valued resource. These competencies are the essential ingredient of the relationship that unleashes the value-creating ability of the extended enterprise. Many of these value-adding activities are less visible in the immediate term and can be related to measures such as return on assets, growth in market share and sales, and higher returns to stockholders.[16–18]

Table 1.5 further illustrates some of the unique characteristics of the extended enterprise by making comparisons with more traditional procurement thinking. By emphasizing a small set of criteria, we show that extended enterprise thinking is not business as usual and certainly is different from both a purchasing department perspective and a single firm perspective.

First, the focus of information technology is on cross-firm solutions and enables the free and honest flow of information to all partners in the supply chain.

Second, processes and structures emphasize decentralization and participation throughout the supply chain, with each partner given a say in how value is created and delivered to end-use customers. It is not possible to deliver a supply chain-wide solution if enabling mechanisms do not foster participation across all extended enterprise players. System-wide thinking replaces both a procurement function and a single firm orientation.

Third, people lie at the core of the extended enterprise. People trust, people share information, and people must be equipped to address the changes in perspective that are required. It is essential that we recognize that most managers do not currently possess the skills or mindset needed to operate in an extended enterprise environment.

Fourth, having enabling technology does not ensure that the right information is shared across companies. Workflow-related information is necessary to make the process work. However, the ability and willingness to share company-specific knowledge and expertise grant a competitive advantage to the extended enterprise.

The outcomes derived from the above do, in fact, differentiate winners from losers. Leverage is not seen as one firm's ability to gain concessions at another's expense; rather, it is the harnessing of complementary resources for the benefit of all members and especially for the end-use customer for whom the value proposition must be relevant.

TABLE 1.5 Comparisons across More Traditional Approaches to Procurement and the Extended Enterprise Framework

Business Factor	Traditional Procurement Focus	Firm-Level Perspective	Extended Enterprise Perspective
Information technology	Decision support is transaction-based Decision support and transactions internally focused Heavily transaction-oriented	Sourcing plus logistics, cross-disciplinary Decision support tools and transaction internally focus Some attempt to seek external opportunities	Seek cross-firm linkages to gain a competitive advantage Use of enterprise software and e-hubs Enterprise-wide is encouraged and includes partners
Focus of processes and re-design	Cost reduction and transaction-focused Risk avoidance to total cost of ownership Make vs. buy Operational silo-centric	Risk mitigation to reduce total cost of ownership EVA Outsource to lower costs Some cross-function/ processes Enterprise-centric	Total cost of ownership and revenue enhancement EVA and seek profits system-wide Core skills drive strategy to bundle product/service Encourage sharing risk-taking system-wide Learning system-wide to leverage skills of others Customer-centric

TABLE 1.5 Comparisons across More Traditional Approaches to Procurement and the Extended Enterprise Framework (Continued)

BUSINESS FACTOR	TRADITIONAL PROCUREMENT FOCUS	FIRM-LEVEL PERSPECTIVE	EXTENDED ENTERPRISE PERSPECTIVE
ORGANIZATIONAL STRUCTURE	Bureaucratic and hierarchical Hybrid centralized/decentralized Internally focused Encourages command and control	Bureaucratic but flatter Some empowerment Virtual under-utilization Multiple interactions upstream and downstream Shared services internally Mostly transaction efficiencies Some effectiveness measures	Our supply chain Unnatural alliances Non-bureaucratic and hierarchical Virtual ownership Complex networks Look to fill skills Does not seek only to reduce fixed costs by shifting to variable costs
PEOPLE	Focus on own company What do you do for me? Some shift from price variance to some strategic thinking	Less command and control, although it remains the default option Broader skills, more analytical with strong logistics to lower the cost for me	Win-win Relationship management Business/general management thinkers Enlightened self-interest Manage for good of the supply chain

TABLE 1.5 Comparisons across More Traditional Approaches to Procurement and the Extended Enterprise Framework (Continued)

BUSINESS FACTOR	TRADITIONAL PROCUREMENT FOCUS	FIRM-LEVEL PERSPECTIVE	EXTENDED ENTERPRISE PERSPECTIVE
INFORMATION CONTENT	Cross-organizationally focused but still internal Multiple sets of data Tries to find supply chain opportunities for firm	Some two-way exchanges and information sharing Linkages for just in time and electronic data interchange Mostly emphasizes workflow with some planning information	Widely shared and transparent Closed-loop system Share plans that are jointly developed Information and knowledge are key Value relationships and information
OUTCOMES	Rationalize supply base to leverage cost Gain efficiencies Turnover high because skill sets begin to change Transform role	Expand supply to gain efficient use of working capital and assets Increased opportunity/challenges for human capital Some chain-wide thinking and information sharing	Expand market access Leverage financial assets Operational excellence Velocity Look to customers to build networks Differentiated value chains Unleash human capital from the entire extended enterprise

Although there is still no consensus as to the correct set of metrics to use to measure the performance of the extended enterprise, it should:

- reflect qualitative and quantitative measures
- capture supply chainwide margins, return on investment (ROI), return on sales (ROS), and the like
- reveal competitive metrics related to other extended enterprises
- measure end-use customer satisfaction, repeat purchases, and loyalty
- reflect both short-term and longer term goals
- value learning as a viable outcome

SUMMARY

The transformation from SCM to extended enterprise thinking is more than just developing a new vocabulary and seeing this change as a fad. Firms that embrace this thinking have already acknowledged that the pace of change is such that speed and adaptability are critical to their future success and that they have no choice but to change.

There exists a strong rationale for why change is essential; nonetheless, change will come at a price in the short term as management grapples with the loss of old-fashioned control and the need for information-intense exchanges that are fundamental to the process. Seamless delivery, transparency in all aspects of logistics, and permeable boundaries are less problematic than is the need to trust other network members, especially in light of the historic nature of their relationships. Trust will build slowly but it must be built, for it is the bedrock of the extended enterprise's foundation.

If a company is to embrace the extended enterprise, senior management must be firmly behind it and must demonstrate a consistent and clear commitment to the norms and values that guide behavior. Because trust is key to the success of these collaborative relationships, there can be no question as to the buyer's intentions. If senior management does not align its strategy with its systems and processes, there is room for confusion.

As stated previously, the extended enterprise is the entire set of both upstream and downstream collaborating companies, from raw material to end-use consumption, that work together to bring value to the marketplace. Its primary goal is to leverage the skills/capabilities of its members to achieve a sustainable competitive advantage relative to other competitive supply chain networks by better meeting and anticipating end-use customer needs. This goal can be achieved only if:

- Each supply chain member is valued, given voice, and is taken into consideration when short- and long-term plans are developed.
- Reward and risk are shared equitably across the entire supply chain, and performance is measured at both the firm and the extended enterprise levels.
- All members value learning and share their knowledge such that all members benefit from new product innovation, as well as innovative processes, systems, and procedures that transcend the entire network and serve to link all the members.

2

TRADITIONAL
VIEWS
AND WHERE
WE HAVE BEEN

I n Chapter 1, you explored the extended enterprise and considered its growth as a direct response to the demands of new competition. The extended enterprise represents a major transformation in how businesses conduct themselves and how they cooperate and compete with other businesses. In particular, the level of competitive analysis now encompasses the entire network of companies that collaborate to battle for global success against other extended enterprises. You saw how truly difficult it is for companies to enact the many changes needed to transform the firm and its other supply chain members to embrace the notions of the extended enterprise. To truly appreciate the challenges facing companies that are beginning to embrace extended enterprise thinking, it is best to view the extended enterprise from a historical perspective.

Cooperation between buyer and supplier and among channel intermediaries, manufacturers, and other members of the distribution channel has never been easily managed. In fact, if you look back 20 years or so, you find that these different levels of the supply chain rarely cooperated and, with few exceptions, had little reason to do so. More recently, a report sponsored by the Distribution Research and Educational Foundation (DREF) simply stated that the relationship among manufacturers and their distribution system no longer works.[1] Tension regarding different views of how channel-wide policy is determined and performance is assessed has contributed to higher levels of conflict among downstream supply chain members. Poor communications are among the central issues to be resolved because channel parties acknowledge openly that they do not adequately share information. These tensions exist today and give little indication of abatement.

In The Beer Game, a management simulation, it becomes quite obvious what happens when channel members do not share information. Backlogs accumulate, out of stocks occur, and excess inventory builds throughout the supply pipeline. Referred to as the *bullwhip effect*, variability increases for supply chain members located farther upstream. Similarly, Procter & Gamble noticed that retail demand for its diapers was reasonably constant but over time the variability in orders placed with some of its suppliers was quite pronounced. These problems exist despite the findings that a managerial philosophy in support of supply chain management (SCM) improves customer satisfaction by improving product/service offerings at lower costs.[2]

As responsibility shifts between supply chain members, there is often an attempt to wrestle back power so that one firm can take control of the supply chain. Home Depot, SYSCO, Grainger, and a host of dominant companies attempt to maintain leverage over their suppliers through their buying power, independent of their position in the supply chain. In addition, they try to develop specific cooperative programs that cannot be used by others with whom they compete. Such power plays often run counter to any enlightened view of supply chain cooperation.

The automotive industry is replete with examples of behaviors that reflect the purchasing muscle of the major manufactures. Unfortunately, this behavior continues in light of the evidence that cooperative behavior leads to greater product quality, lower development costs, and faster time to market for new models. In the United States, where the top five car producers account for 90 percent of the sales,[3] OEMs often talk cooperation but are driven by power and control instead of win-win intentions. General Motors works very hard to shed its command and control mentality when dealing with its suppliers. Yet it cannot fully seem to reverse old bad habits, because there is still a tendency to pull the price card when times get tough. Ignacio Lopez created some of these tensions* during the early 1990s at GM. Chrysler, too, appears to have reversed its long-standing cooperative programs (its SCORE program) with its suppliers when Daimler seized control of senior management positions in Detroit. There seems to be a disconnect between what supply chain members recognize as smart business practices and what they actually do.

One explanation for this disconnect is the lack of trust regarding how sensitive information will be shared. When the manufacturer's intent is not clear, supply chain members are more likely to withhold critical market data. Without key market data, those farther away from the end-use customer cannot make intelligent decisions. This observation is well understood by Wal-Mart, demonstrated by its relationship with key suppliers, where point-of-purchase information is fed directly to its key suppliers' manufacturing processes. Expanding this linkage between information and inventory can be seen in the increasing reliance on vendor-managed inventory, where the supplier takes responsibility for ensuring in-stock positions while minimizing the costs of excess inventory. Nonetheless, the genesis for managerial action that restricts the flow of

---

* Mr. Lopez asked suppliers to produce, at their expense, proprietary designs for components/subassemblies in upcoming models. The expectation was that the chosen vendor would supply the entire model run. Instead, Mr. Lopez shopped these designs to the competition in search of lower prices. Legal considerations aside, such action violated any degree of trust between GM and its suppliers.

information can be traced to behaviors and beliefs that have long been held in the supply chain. That is, when there is no trust or credibility established among trading parties, there is no incentive to share information.

During the early 1990s, Tom Stallkamp, then chief procurement officer for Chrysler, turned the U.S. auto industry on its ear by developing close supplier relationships, sharing cost savings with suppliers rather than beating price concessions out of them. Although outsourcing has continued among the big three, the incentives are gone, and the door swings only one way. As president of MSX International, Stallkamp is again trying to transform conventional wisdom. The new business model is one in which MSX serves as an aggregator and supply chain manager for the smaller manufacturers who ship parts and components that become larger subassemblies. MSX is a supply chain broker, advocate and integrator that coordinates and orchestrates close, collaborative relationships with third-tier suppliers who do not have the clout or voice to work with the much larger OEMs.

Achieving these collaborative networks entails far more than synchronizing information systems and linking up production data. To remediate these problems, supply chain partners need higher degrees of collaboration, better joint decision making, and better and more frequent information sharing. When sharing information that goes to the core of business, managers must be assured that the partner will act in their best interests. Such thinking goes far beyond retail examples of inventory management and lie at the heart of e-commerce.

For some, the automotive exchange, Covisint, is seen as a barometer of the success of business-to-business e-commerce. Its success is ultimately linked more to collaborative processes than to e-commerce technology. This exchange completed 1,500 auctions in 2001, accounting for $51 billion in goods and contracts. Whether success can be proclaimed for Covisint is still undecided. Although it is true that the principals have saved millions of dollars through reduced costs, others argue that true success will come through the use of collaborative product development. One supplier noted that, "I am waiting for the day when an OEM wants my brains on the Internet for product development, not just my lowest price."[4] To understand the genesis of these issues better, let's begin by examining the nature of buyer-seller relationships over time.

TRACING SHIFTING PRIORITIES

TRADITIONAL BUYER-SUPPLIER RELATIONSHIPS: THE DARK AGES

During the late 1960s and early 1970s, the United States was nearing the end of an era of unprecedented growth and insatiable consumer demand. Given the focus on meeting consumer needs, companies were slow to recognize the true impact of the purchasing function, as is evidenced by the lack of professional talent that occupied the buying offices of major corporations worldwide. Buyers were charged with three major tasks: Buy at a low price, ensure timely delivery, and guarantee an agreed-upon level of quality. Three bids were the typical number of requests for proposals sought, and suppliers were selected mainly on the basis of price. The procurement function was viewed as a reactive, almost passive participant in the buying process. The function received little attention and, at best, was treated with benign neglect by senior management. Any bonus to compensation was based on low purchase price and variance to stated price. Given that the average U.S. manufacturing company purchased goods and services worth close to 50 percent of total revenue, the effect of any savings in purchase price on profits was far more meaningful than a comparable percentage of increase in sales. Yet the level of professionalism lagged behind other function units.

Buyers were encouraged to shop their bids and under no circumstance to become dependent on a single supplier. Sole or single-source contracts were taboo because they threatened the firm's independence and ability to control its destiny. Buyers would ask questions regarding the infamous *what ifs*: What if there is a strike? A fire, a natural disaster? What if the buyer decides to raise the price? Restrict the number of units available? The list would grow depending on the richness of the buyer's imagination and level of paranoia.

Buyers were trained and warned never willingly to become dependent on a single source of supply. In instances where only one supplier existed, buyers looked for a second source or stocked enough inventory to protect against whatever contingency might halt production. They would actively promote a second source that received only a small share of the purchasing volume as a check on the primary supplier. Interestingly, these games of playing suppliers against each other only created resentment and often detracted from any hopes of synergy. These games are probably the source of much distrust that exists today.

Suppliers were the enemy; they were opportunistic and thought only of themselves (as did buyers, but that was good business practice). Buyers viewed all purchases as commodity-like, such that price became the key determinant to winning a bid, and all suppliers were easily substitutable. Such behavior led to gamesmanship, and to prevent price from being the only criteria that mattered, suppliers attempted to *backdoor* the buyer and go directly to the engineer who had the authority to specify a particular product, subsystem, or assembly. If specified, the buyer had no choice beyond expediting the flow of paperwork and goods and services through the system. Suppliers also worked hard to create fear, uncertainty, and doubt in the minds of the purchasing organization (recall the admonition that "no one gets shot for buying IBM"). The purchasing function had little status and was seen mainly as a clerical function. Clearly, a great deal would have to change before purchasing would be recognized as a serious contributor to a firm's planning process.

Enter the shortages of the mid-1970s, and the procurement function slowly began to appear on the corporate radar screen. Whether as a response to higher commodity prices, an economy of shortages, or greater competition for suppliers on a global scale, purchasing achieved greater visibility. Two developments occurred as companies planned for their future supply needs: Senior management paid more attention to procurement, and purchasing managers broadened their heretofore limited horizons to play a more active role in non-purchasing corporate decisions.

One reason for the greater attention from senior management was a result of the dramatic rises in raw material prices, beginning in the mid-1970s. As purchasing's share of the manufacturing cost pie increased to over 50 percent for most major industries and competition put pressure on prices, financial managers began to recognize the leverage inherent in purchasing cost reductions, compared with sales increases. It is fairly straightforward to demonstrate how a 5 percent reduction in materials cost translates into a 13 percent increase in ROI.[5]

ENTER MATERIAL MANAGEMENT: THE BEGINNING OF THE AGE OF ENLIGHTENMENT

The term *materials management* connotes the importance of combining a number of purchasing-related activities in one function with the intent of gaining system-wide efficiencies. Under this concept, purchasing would be joined with logistics, inventory control, and other related activities. The logic stems from the fact that each of these activities is interrelated and, therefore, should be linked. However, calling a duck a swan does not make it a swan. It is true that placing these previously independent areas under one roof eliminated many problems resulting from the impact that one decision in an area had on other parts of the business. Although this was a first step in achieving cross-functional interaction, it would not be unusual to find that buyers who bought large volumes of materials at steep discounts often did not consider the inventory carrying costs. At the other extreme, attempts to reduce inventory levels might have led to out-of-stock conditions that shut production lines, and the use of slower (and cheaper) modes of transportation might have resulted in either higher carrying costs for safety stock or lost sales because the product was unavailable as the parts or components from off-shore sat in port, waiting for clearance.

To best minimize these mistakes, it made sense to develop processes that took a system-wide perspective and attempted to balance the requirements of the previously independent departments under the same roof. Purchasing (now Materials Management) could take a more proactive stance and potentially eliminate the deleterious effects of silo thinking* among departments that impact the flow, delivery, and use of materials. Figure 2.1 illustrates the integration of purchasing with other key areas. To implement such an approach successfully, you must first understand how different departments and activities affect purchasing-related decisions, then you must build a business case for the gains resulting from the integration of these areas under the umbrella of materials management; finally, you must ensure senior management's buy-in. Given where purchasing has been in the past, this effort is often non-trivial.

Along with the corporate migration to materials management thinking came software systems that linked the various departments, allowing greater visibility and enabling better system-wide decisions. However, the Center for Advanced Purchasing Studies found that those responsible for materials management activities were decentralized and reported through different managers.[6] Through decentralization, structural silos were inadvertently created that inhibited these newly found technology enablers (e.g., MRP, MRPII)** from reaching their full potential. The lack of coordination is a serious enough problem and it is exacerbated by the reality that different areas might be in conflict regarding objectives and goals. Silos breed narrow focus and a singular concern for "what is good for my function/ department" mentality. Once again, the potential for suboptimization looms in the background as purchasing attempts to find its strategic voice.

More fundamentally, these problems indicated a lack of commitment from senior management to articulate a vision

---

*Silo thinking happens when managers cannot think beyond their own functional area or department and tend not to appreciate the enterprise-wide effects that actions in one area have on another.

**Material requirements planning and its successor, manufacturing resources planning, (MRP and MRPII), are variants of a process for estimating supplier requirements for delivery of parts in specified periods to satisfy the master production schedule. The process begins with customer demand and works back through the system to the supply of materials, as explained in Chapter 3.

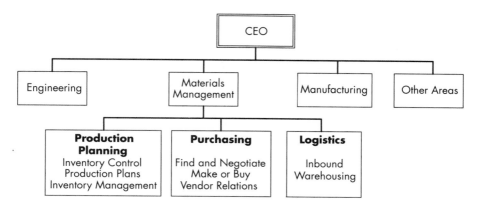

FIGURE 2.1
Materials management as part of the organizational structure: An illustration of how the function might be organized.

that supported this more coordinated view of the supply chain. In part, the rationale for such behavior can be explained by neglect. The idea of competitive advantage had not encompassed fully the supply side of the equation. In fact, as late as 1998, a study by Deloitte Consulting[7] revealed that only 70 percent of companies interviewed thought such integration was critical to their future success. To think that many firms still believe they can be successful in the long term by acting alone defies all sense of logic.

Strategic Sourcing   An interim stage between materials management and SCM was strategic sourcing, whereby buyers attempted to define and find world-class suppliers with whom to work. Sellers were no longer seen as equal (substitutable), and some were acknowledged to be better than others in terms of quality, delivery, and other key criteria. A notable difference in buyers' perspective of price was that the emphasis had begun to shift to a concern for the total cost of ownership. Buyers were now encouraged to seek longer term relationships with fewer suppliers from whom real benefits could be achieved. Closer ties were not sought with all suppliers; where appropriate, spot-market-based transactions were maintained. Where closer ties could be formed, however, buyers found that in some cases the costs of total purchasing could be reduced by 15 percent or more.[8]

Note that the objective was not a random decision to reduce a firm's supply base, although even the most rudimentary analysis would be expected to show that a large number of suppliers could be dropped by virtue of poor performance. In fact, many consulting engagements around this time entailed a supply base rationalization plan where the consultants asked for a percentage of the savings generated, not the standard fee. Dropping underperforming suppliers is not the hard part; finding the world's best is. To begin the process, firms first needed to understand the relative strategic importance of the goods and services they purchased. For example, imagine a continuum of goods and services ranging from those strategically critical to the business to those necessary for daily business needs. Table 2.1 illustrates the range of goods and services you might consider in trying to prioritize the tens of thousands of items a firm might buy. The major difference between the two extremes has been highlighted, as have some of the key distinctions in selection criteria.

Simply, firms are now forced to develop screening methodologies that move away from price-based criteria to other performance criteria. For some firms, the shift was half-hearted and misinformed, in that the criteria changed but the basic approach to the supply base was still adversarial. The effect of such screening was that a threshold performance level was established, and any supplier below that level was not considered for a more strategic role. Too few companies understood that the standard criteria of quality, price, and delivery were necessary but not sufficient conditions.

As selection criteria changed, it became apparent that the questions being asked were often hard to answer because data were not easily attainable. Moreover, the nature of the questions was such that a quantitative response was inappropriate, and "softer" data became more relevant to the supplier selection process. For example, if you wished to understand a potential supplier's level of commitment, you were faced with responses that could not be easily quantified, as could the variance to stated price. Numbers-oriented, hard-data managers found these responses to be less than compelling.

TABLE 2.1   A Continuum of Goods/Services Purchased: Understanding Differences in the Types of Goods Purchased

very important   mundane

Mission Critical	Daily Requirements
■ Supports the strategic goals of the firm	■ Affects the day-to-day operations
■ Provides a competitive advantage	■ Typical considered commodity like and consumable items
■ Threatens the business if not available	■ Supports the goals of the firm but are not linked to them
■ Essential to the final product/service	■ Not instrumental in running the business
■ Has a significant financial impact	
Selection Process	**Selection Process**
■ World-class supplier	■ Meets minimal acceptable criteria
■ Focus on total cost of ownership	■ Focus on purchase price and ease of doing business
■ Involves a complex procurement process involving a number of departments and people	■ Could be ordered through computer-based model according to inventory needs
■ Closer, more interdependent relationships	■ Durable arms-length relationships
■ High degrees of coordination require working with one supplier	■ Maintain competition among suppliers
■ Levels of commitment needed raise tensions around pricing	■ Longer term contracts but buyer reserves the right to open bids
■ Value-adding capability essential	■ Lower price is the driver

FedEx has developed a screening mechanism for ascertaining a potential partner's willingness to work with it. Its selection process takes willingness as a sign of potential commitment and is a primary criterion in its partner selection decision-making process. To gain a more complete picture, FedEx also attempts to understand the degree of fit relative to goals, values, and strategic direction.

The following set of questions illustrates the range of information needed. These questions reflect the tone of this line of inquiry. Such information is very different from more traditional approaches to supplier selection in that it focuses on commitment and a willingness to work together now and into the future versus only cost, availability, and quality issues.

- How has the supplier communicated commitment? To which degree have unique resources been dedicated to this relationship?
- Is the supplier willing to be involved early in the design stage? What skills does the supplier bring to the relationship?
- Is there recognition of the fact that we both contribute to competitive advantage? Or that our fates are linked?
- Will the supplier be able to grow with us and offer value-adding capabilities over the life of our relationship?
- Does the supplier offer true innovation? Is it sustainable? What if the market changes; how adaptable is the supplier?
- Does the supplier look at problems and see them as "our problem" or "my problem"?
- Do communications flow formally or informally, both within the supplier's organization and between our two organizations?
- How well does the supplier know my business?

From these questions, it should be clear that not all good suppliers are candidates for strategic sourcing. A good supplier might fulfill the requirements as set out in the request for bid/proposal but might fall short in its willingness to work closely with the buyer or to share its technology and the like. Strategic suppliers are much more than good suppliers who deliver the right quantity at the right time for the right price. Just-in-time (JIT) programs and other systems that link firms electronically address only some of the issues that guide supplier selection. That is, being linked electronically is a necessary but not sufficient condition for selecting a strategic source of supply. To be sure, there are transaction efficiencies that are realized but there are other important benefits that are more difficult to ascertain, such as trust and credibility. When there is transparency between buyer and supplier and the flow of information is reciprocal and reliable, value is greater.

Knowing that it is possible to segment sellers on their performance, good suppliers were suddenly in high demand. In order to align with these better suppliers, many buyers found themselves having to seek and recruit suppliers actively. Buyers developed proactive strategies to attract these world-class suppliers. *Reverse Marketing*[9] is an aggressive approach to achieving supply objectives through the buyer's efforts to secure supply from a particular supplier or set of mission-critical suppliers. These efforts might be viewed as an early foray into supplier development programs. In instances where a supplier has lost its edge, the buyer might present a program for improvement that entails greater commitment than had previously been the case. Toyota and Nissan in recent years have marketed to suppliers the importance of innovative processes and have urged them to attend intensive training at their respective universities.

Honda of America has a staff of 400 purchasing professionals, with 70–100 working solely on supplier development programs, teaching them problem-solving techniques and helping them improve quality, cut costs, and reduce lead times. In the late 1990s, John Deere Co. added 100 new professionals to its strategic purchasing staff for similar supplier development programs.[10] Such efforts result in a win-win because the supplier improves, and the end product is more competitive in the marketplace. Certainly, the ability to leverage both costs savings and capabilities have enormous payback. Although the bottom-line effects of leveraging skills are less easily quantified, the indirect effect on cost savings can be attributable to overhead savings, labor costs, more efficient processes, and other factors that reduce the cost of doing business.

It is worth noting that the processes that drive strategic sourcing also lend themselves to linking these decisions more closely to the strategic planning process of the firm. Because the sourcing decision-making process is based on an attempt to triage the type of product/service under consideration, procurement professionals were forced to evaluate suppliers and products by the importance of the product to the firm. Although the link to business strategy should have always existed, it has now been made explicit. Priorities were established, buyers differentiated among materials and allocated resources and effort in proportion to the importance of the materials/services being bought. During the transition to SCM, the linkage of purchasing strategy to business strategy became more obvious, and buyers slowly began to fill the previously unfilled gap.

FROM MATERIALS MANAGEMENT TO SUPPLY CHAIN MANAGEMENT

Supply chain management is an integrated management approach for planning and controlling the flow of materials through the entire distribution system.[11] To a large extent, SCM describes a set of interrelated processes that are intended to increase the overall efficiency of the system. Closely knit supply chains tend to exhibit behaviors in which sourcing cuts across company boundaries with a focus on reducing costs and improving quality. Reflected here is a shift from denominator management (i.e., a focus on cost reductions) to an attempt to affect the numerator—corporate revenue. Recall that materials management is focused mainly on the internal processes, the need to reduce costs for the firm and manage more efficiently all aspects of its procurement function.

The difference between managing costs and growing the top-line revenue is illustrated in Figure 2.2. The different components of return on equity are decomposed and traced back to their root elements. Rather than reduce the cost side of the equation only, the exhibit demonstrates that by leveraging the supplier's skills, an impact can be felt at the level of revenue and profits. For example, Chrysler Corporation's well-known

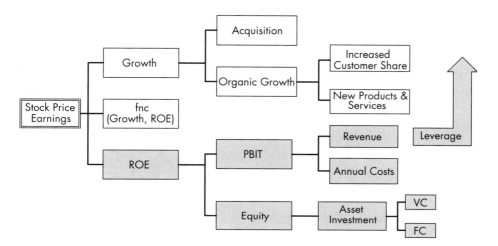

FIGURE 2.2
Supply chain optimization: Comparing cost saving to revenue growth.

"SCORE" program, which motivated suppliers to reduce costs and improve quality through an innovative shared-savings program, produced a series of documented savings for Chrysler over a several-year period that amounted to multiple billions of dollars.[12] For companies where cost cutting has become a way of life, management is often limited in its ability to think creatively about top-line growth and how the supply base can contribute to end-use customer satisfaction.

Supply chain management progressed into the 1990s with firms extending their best practices to include their most trusted and strategic suppliers. Supplier efficiency included taking over redundant value-chain activities, such as logistics, so that goods are received either directly at store locations or through cross-docking without inspection. In other instances we find that suppliers are sought to contribute to product development.[13]

You can manage a supply chain for your own benefit or for the benefit of the entire network. Although the objective of SCM is to maximize value to the customer, it is not always clear as to whose profits and costs are of major consideration. If the supply chain is transparent, then the creation, nurturing, and delivery of value is of mutual benefit for all. This inequity in benefits and risks has implications for the difference between cooperation and collaboration among supply chain partners. This distinction also highlights the difference between supplier compliance and commitment. Partners are committed to the relationship, and traditional buyers and sellers are compliant and work together until a better alternative comes along. Among the key requirements for SCM to succeed is a shared culture that deemphasizes short-term, company-specific gains in favor of the network of supply chain partners.

Figure 2.3 illustrates the different stages through which companies progress in forming close relationships. Ignoring open market transactions because they symbolize the most adversarial form of buyer-seller relationships, SCM behaviors can range from cooperation to coordination, to collaboration. As firms approach collaboration, the thinking and behaviors espoused by the extended enterprise become more relevant. Given that SCM encompasses several interrelated processes (i.e., customer order cycle, replenishment cycle, manufacturing cycle, and procurement cycle), the goals of each can be

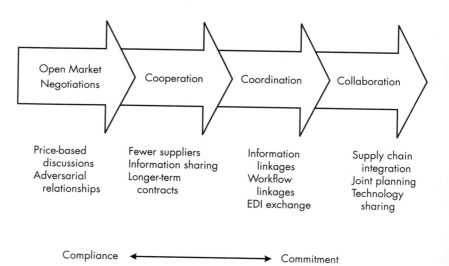

FIGURE 2.3

The key transition from open-market negotiations to collaboration: Knowing the difference between compliance and commitment.

achieved only if the members of the supply chain cooperate. Commitment is achieved through a reduction in the number of suppliers that operate under longer term, often evergreen contracts in which parties agree to a rolling five-year relationship.

Through supply chain cooperation, goods can be received on time at a specified level of quality at a price agreed to by contract. In all likelihood, costs are expected to fall over the life of the contract, due to learning effects, volume commitments, and/or mutual cost-reduction efforts. However, cooperation does not ensure that the amount of information shared extends much beyond the terms of the contract. Also, in many cases suppliers do not commit resources and managerial talent to the buyer beyond what has been formally agreed to. Compliance should not be confused with commitment, and a supply chain can operationally achieve high levels of efficiency; however, it might not be the most competitive, relative to other supply chains where commitment has been fostered. Note that cooperative supply chains can be competitive but the extended enterprise can achieve a sustainable competitive advantage.

Figure 2.4 examines the range of buyer-supplier relationships on two dimensions: strategic importance and financial/commercial complexity. Strategic importance conveys a concern for how critical the component is to the final product, such as the "engine" supplied by Canon in HP's laser printers. Complexity captures a concern for how difficult or relationship-specific the buying process is for the partners. Firms might cooperate because of the complex processes surrounding the purchase of the product. In the aerospace industry, there are often demands made for local content as part of the buying process when dealing with foreign governments. These commercial offset programs require that a portion of the product be assembled in the foreign country with local labor or that parts of the final product be sourced with locally produced parts. These programs are very tailored to the purchasing government and the need to establish relationship-specific systems and/or processes for payment, information flows, and the movement of goods that have no applicability to other suppliers. These transaction-specific investments are in effect nonfungible and must be managed carefully within the supply base.

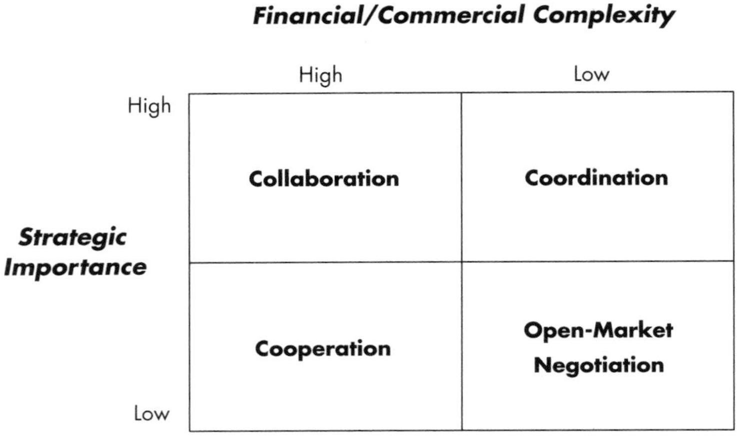

Financial/Commercial Complexity

	High	Low
High	**Collaboration**	**Coordination**
Low	**Cooperation**	**Open-Market Negotiation**

(Strategic Importance — vertical axis, High to Low)

FIGURE 2.4

Supply chain management strategy: Relating importance and complexity to the type of relationship.

Complexity examined at a more fundamental level reflects three primary dimensions.[14] One dimension is uncertainty, which captures the degree of variability in the series of tasks that comprise the workflow and information flow in the system. Uncertainty in the system affects the reliability of consistent and on-time delivery, manufacturing performance, and the collective performance of the entire system. The second dimension addresses the technological intricacies of the product, such as the number of parts, the related services, and the connectedness of the product to other components or parts. If the purchased product must be used with specialized software and is part of a larger subsystem, it would be considered fairly complex. A third dimension affects the number of contact points required to purchase the product/service. If the product requires a great deal of cross-functional integration, the involvement of different internal departments, and a number of specialized external firms, it is deemed to be complex.

When parties in a supply chain agree to coordinate their activities, additional gains are realized. One simple example is the decision to purchase just in time or to go to a paperless ordering system. Yet it is not enough simply to coordinate activities or standardize billing systems. Technology links the firms more seamlessly but technology alone does not breed closer relationships. Many companies (and their procurement managers) openly fear becoming too reliant on suppliers and worry that these so-called partners might take advantage based on that dependence. Opportunistic behavior can be held in check through bilateral information exchange. However, the willingness to share information must be built on a foundation of trust.

Achieving a more integrated supply chain integration requires an understanding of the organizational drivers that lead to greater information sharing, developing trust, and encouraging personal relationships. Practically, it means integrating suppliers by pursuing leading-edge practices and incorporating key sourcing dimensions in strategy, systems or processes, and operations concurrently with the supply base. The process of developing the technological capability for intensive information exchange through JIT, electronic data interchange, and point-of-sale systems or even the Internet is not the major hurdle confronting supply chain partners. The basic problem hinges on the issue of trust and incentive/reward systems that are operationally successful across organizational boundaries. As will be shown in later chapters of this book, a number of companies are successfully integrating their business processes across organizational boundaries with impressive results. These companies have established both the technological capability and the level of trust necessary for this type of close relationship. But experience also shows that, absent trust, the likelihood exists that self-serving behavior will emerge and partners will be unable to leverage each other's skills/capabilities. Absent trust, transaction costs are increased! It all boils down to the belief that if your supply chain partners are to act responsibly, there must exist alignment in both norms and expectations that explicitly state what is acceptable behavior.

Alignment Matters   Many businesses claim to have adopted a "customer facing" organization, although the results often fall short. One reason is the failure of the organization to align itself internally. Companies have unfortunately developed a silo mentality in which functional turf battles occur among these internal fiefdoms. Silo thinking is bad enough. Compounding this problem is that buyers and sellers have traditionally viewed the buy-sell process from different perspectives. Supply chain management requires multidisciplinary actions. When problems arise, it is not unusual to find that the weak link is directly attributed to the misalignment of perceptions, goals, and objectives, both within and between companies. Be cautioned that a company cannot approach SCM as though it were the sole benefactor!

A.T. Kearney[15] argues that to achieve integrated procurement, leaders must implement processes to direct and coordinate supply chain-relevant activities throughout the organization. At the heart of this process is an attempt to align procurement structures with organizational structures, an investment in improving the skills/competencies of the firm's procurement professionals, and recognition that procurement's impact should reach senior-level decision-making. Externally, it emphasizes the active participation of suppliers in processes and decisions that extend to business planning, new supply chain initiatives, and proposed changes in company policies. Simply, process is facilitated when there is a shared vision that transcends the supply chain.

FROM SUPPLY CHAIN MANAGEMENT TO EXTENDED ENTERPRISE THINKING

The seeds of extended enterprise thinking were planted with the use of terms such as *trust, shared vision, alignment*, and *commitments* to describe the characteristics of an integrated supply chain. Current supply chain thinking tends to fall short of the expectations of the extended enterprise because there is little alignment in processes and procedures that permit the full power of collaboration among supply chain partners to emerge. Firms still balk at the importance of giving consideration to all members of the supply chain, because managers are still rewarded for efficiency gains and outcomes that lend advantage their firms to the detriment of the rest of the supply chain. Yet the idea of the extended enterprise is very much alive. In practice, it symbolizes a future world that is right around the corner for the more enlightened firm that accepts the tenets and principles that will be developed in the book. For the majority of companies, however, the underlying thinking and requisite mindset is far too different from current practice. These firms will surely be laggards in adopting extended enterprise thinking. There are a small number of companies that quietly adopt the principles of the extended enterprise and have begun to implement it with their best suppliers. These firms view such a change in thinking and behavior as a competitive weapon. These exemplars will be highlighted in future chapters.

The movement from the dark ages to the age of enlightenment has presented a series of radical changes in how purchasing managers approach their jobs and how they think about the entire procurement process. Just so you understand the severity of these changes, Table 2.2 attempts to capture some of the highlights. You can see that beyond the more comprehensive change in viewpoint (from the firm to the supply chain), the differences convey a recognition and acceptance of interdependence among supply chain members, as well as a focus on performance measures that emphasize both the

TABLE 2.2 Comparisons of Supply Chain Management and More Traditional Buying[16]: A Step Toward Extended Enterprise Thinking

MANAGEMENT PROCESS	SUPPLY CHAIN PERSPECTIVE	TRADITIONAL BUYING PERSPECTIVE
Overall perspective	Externally oriented on processes, systems, and metrics for the chain	Internally oriented on products, sales, and revenue for the firm
Key performance targets	Value creation in the marketplace	Department-level targets
Business goals/ objectives	Alignment across the supply chain	Alignment across departments and functions inside the firm
Business process improvements	Look and implement what works system-wide	Costs and internal processes are emphasized
Relationships	Cross-system relationships	Cross functional relationships

firm and the supply chain. Each one of these changes brings us closer to appreciating better the importance of extended enterprise thinking and the differences between it and SCM.

SUMMARY

In this chapter, you traced the different stages of developmental growth in the area of procurement, from early efforts to manage costs and efficiencies internal to the firm to more serious efforts to gain systemwide effects and provide benefits across the entire supply chain. It has been repeatedly suggested that the transition requires far more than a change in behavior and the manner in which buyer and seller interact. Implicit in this discussion has been recognition that there are certain competencies[17] that enable the change process to accelerate and make a difference in how chain members think, act, and engage one another. Managers should possess strong functional skills that cover both depth of skill and high levels of integration. These integration skills must be effective under conditions of high uncertainty and complexity. Also, the companies in which these managers work should possess world-class information technology that enables coordination and integration.

3

SUPPLY CHAIN PLANNING: FROM PAST TO PRESENT

Chapter 2 described the progression of management focus and changes in behavior from traditional, adversarial buyer-supplier relations up through supply chain management (SCM) and extended enterprise thinking. Those changes did not happen spontaneously or of their own accord but were driven by a number of external and internal factors, such as: competition, technological change, and changes in corporate organizational structure and management practices, including team-oriented approaches and new performance measurements. Two of the most important aspects are information technology and supply chain planning/scheduling/coordination methodologies and systems. Although it is difficult to separate the two (information technology and planning/scheduling), the purpose of this chapter is to look primarily at the role of the latter. The overall topic is referred to as *supply chain planning* (SCP) but it subsumes the related activities of scheduling and coordination. Over the years, a large number of different methodological approaches have been developed for attacking the challenges of supply chain planning/scheduling. For example, Figure 3.1 shows the acronyms of the major methodologies positioned roughly on a timeline of the major periods mentioned in Chapter 2.

One framework for thinking about this topic and gaining a better understanding of the significance and role of the different methodologies is suggested by Figure 3.2, which subdivides the overall topic into the categories of SCP, supply chain execution (SCE), and supply chain transaction (SCT). This framework has been popularized recently by some vendors of computer software programs and systems to help

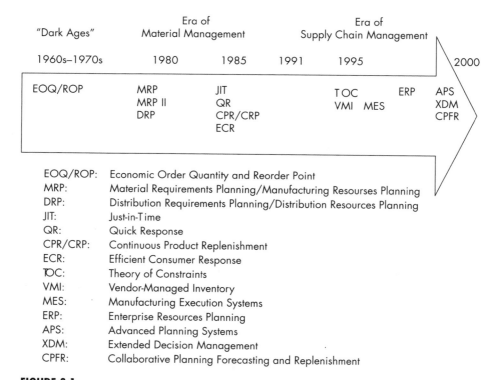

EOQ/ROP:	Economic Order Quantity and Reorder Point
MRP:	Material Requirements Planning/Manufacturing Resources Planning
DRP:	Distribution Requirements Planning/Distribution Resources Planning
JIT:	Just-in-Time
QR:	Quick Response
CPR/CRP:	Continuous Product Replenishment
ECR:	Efficient Consumer Response
TOC:	Theory of Constraints
VMI:	Vendor-Managed Inventory
MES:	Manufacturing Execution Systems
ERP:	Enterprise Resources Planning
APS:	Advanced Planning Systems
XDM:	Extended Decision Management
CPFR:	Collaborative Planning Forecasting and Replenishment

FIGURE 3.1
Supply chain planning/scheduling methodologies.

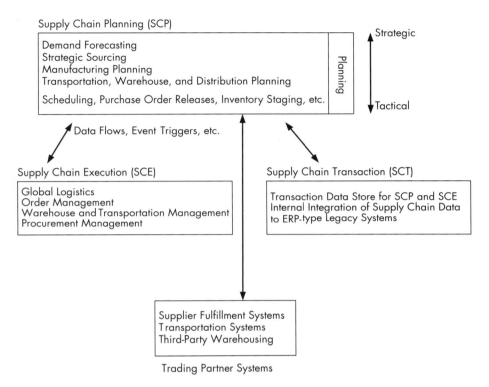

FIGURE 3.2
Supply chain planning approaches. Source: Adapted from R. Reddy and S. Reddy, *Supply Chains to Virtual Integration* (New York: McGraw-Hill, 2001).

potential customers better understand the positioning of the varied software packages and systems, which have proliferated greatly in recent years.

IN THE DARK AGES: ECONOMIC ORDER QUANTITY AND REORDER POINT

For example, during the "dark ages" of buyer-supplier relations mentioned in Chapter 2—the 1960s until about the early to mid-1970s—most manufacturing firms operated independently, with a "command and control" hierarchical organizational structure focused on potential high-volume mass markets and planned and scheduled their production based on a demand forecast ("make to stock"). Products were "pushed" out of the factory based on the demand forecast, with manufacturing efficiency and lowest cost as prime operation objectives. Purchasing was generally regarded as a low-level activity, responsible for executing and processing orders initiated elsewhere in the organization. Purchasing's main role was to obtain any needed resources at the lowest possible cost from the supplier. Communications with customers and suppliers were relatively infrequent and often slow. Information technology (IT) systems were largely mainframe-based, and different sites within the same company often had incompatible operating systems or software. Supply chain planning was site-dedicated and focused on the site's inventory and shop floor control via the use of such techniques as the economic order quantity (EOQ), reorder point (ROP), Gantt charts, and relatively unsophisticated priority sequencing rules. Supply chain transaction systems were similarly site-oriented, with little or no cross-functional communication (e.g., manufacturing systems were unable to interface with finance systems, etc.). Supply chain execution systems were less calculation- and algorithm-oriented than SCP or SCT systems (as they typically still are); the printed outputs from these systems generally had to be communicated to other sites and other companies via mail or telegraph lines.

MATERIAL REQUIREMENTS PLANNING: MORE "PUSH" FOR MATERIALS MANAGEMENT

Developments in computing technology around the early 1970s ushered in the era of materials management, which saw the flowering of material requirements planning (MRP). The general category of MRP-generic systems represents the most widely adopted factory planning/control paradigm, particularly among medium and large companies. In practice, MRP is driven by a *master production schedule* (MPS) showing the quantity and timing of end item production. The individual end items of the MPS are "exploded" into component part requirements via their engineering bills of material (BOM) and summed across end items to determine gross requirements of each part for each time period, which are compared with on-hand inventory to determine net requirements. The lead times of the component parts are then used, working backward in time from the MPS time periods, to determine the time points at which purchase orders or shop manufacturing orders should be issued for the component parts. These parts are thus "pushed" onto the shop floor or into inventory or shipping in accord with the manufacturing schedule. These simple but powerful concepts are ideally suited for computer application, and MRP enjoyed great popularity beginning in the early 1970s, as computers became cheaper and more powerful.[1]

The initial versions of MRP, which focused on material only, produced a schedule of shop order manufacturing dates (and purchase order release dates) without imposing any constraints on shop manufacturing capacity (e.g., labor and machines). The resulting "infinite capacity" manufacturing schedules were often infeasible or unrealistic, because MRP ignored these other resources; its scope was subsequently expanded to address machine and labor resources, and MRP evolved into manufacturing resources planning (MRPII). This exists in many different versions but typically includes some form of capacity requirements planning ("rough-cut capacity planning" and/or capacity requirements planning [CRP]) to produce feasible component part schedules. Figure 3.3 illustrates a sample version of such an MRPII system.[2]

Some variants of MRPII embodied the concept of sharing information from a centralized database with other functional departments outside the operations area, thus foreshadowing some key ideas of enterprise resources planning (ERP; discussed below).[3] However, despite the popularity of MRPII, other MRP-generic weaknesses (e.g., the use of fixed lead times in calculating schedules and system "nervousness" or sensitivity to demand changes) attracted much criticism in

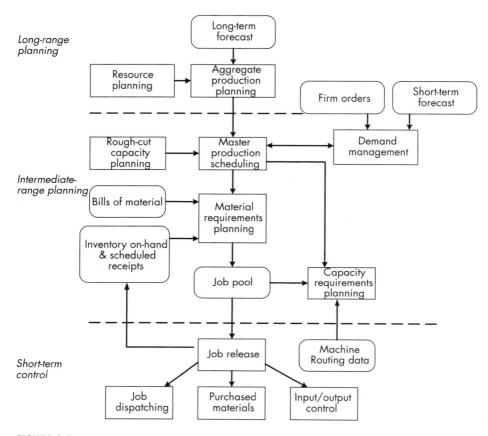

FIGURE 3.3

Manufacturing resources planning hierarchy. *Source:* Adapted from W. J. Hopp and M. L. Spearman, *Factory Physics*, 2nd edition (New York: Irwin McGraw-Hill, 2001).

the late 1970s and 1980s. This came at a time when interest in Japanese production methods was peaking, resulting in an anti-MRP "backlash" and heightened interest in Japanese techniques, such as the Toyota production method, also known as just-in-time (JIT) production control, which is discussed below.

DISTRIBUTION RESOURCES PLANNING = MATERIAL REQUIREMENTS PLANNING FOR DISTRIBUTION

Distribution resources planning (DRP) extends the concepts of MRP to multitier warehouse/distribution inventories. Developed in the late 1970s and using basic MRP logic, the calculation approach begins with demand at the end of the distribution channel and works backward through the distribution system to produce time-phased replenishment schedules for moving inventory through the warehousing/distribution network. Thus, DRP is a technique for planning and coordinating warehousing and transportation, including equipment, personnel, and financial flows. It has fundamental advantages over ROP techniques in these applications, yet it has not been nearly so widely adopted as MRP.[4]

JUST-IN-TIME: "PULL" SYSTEMS

JIT takes its name from the idea of replenishing inventory only in the quantity needed, as close to the time of actual need as possible, with material being "pulled" through the production system by end-item demand. For example, Sun Microsystems attributed 50% of its $350 million inventory reduction in 2001 to the adoption of a new "pull" system in which parts are delivered to Sun by its suppliers only when a customer order is logged at Sun. The new system was implemented after two years of devising the game plan, reengineering processes, and hammering out contractual requirements. According to Sun management, the new program represents a significant change in the way Sun does business with its supply chain partners. Sun previously relied on a "push" approach, in which suppliers reacted to forecasts and sent components into the channel.[5]

JIT is actually much broader than its name suggests; its goal is to eliminate all types of waste, including unneeded inventory, machines, space, scrap, time, etc. Because there is no excess inventory allowed, delivery due dates are more critical, which in turn implies a planning system capable of developing accurate plans that can be reliably implemented, either by the firm's own internal manufacturing function or outside suppliers. JIT's primary emphasis is on execution activities, but experts such as Vollman, Berry, and Whybark emphasize that intelligent planning is an important ingredient in JIT implementation.[6] JIT-generic systems have a host of names, including *continuous flow manufacturing, stockless production, repetitive manufacturing, short-cycle manufacturing,* and *Toyota production system;* three names increasingly used are *lean manufacturing, make-to-order* (MTO), and *build-to-order* (BTO).[7]

The widespread popularity of JIT concepts beginning in the late 1970s ushered in a new, fundamentally different emphasis on buyer-supplier relations, as noted in Chapter 2. The extension of JIT principles from internal factory activities to external suppliers—sometimes referred to as *JIT purchasing*—requires close relationships with suppliers ("coproducers") to facilitate delivery of exact quantities of near-perfect items exactly when they are needed (typically more frequently and in smaller amounts than with reorder point or MRP approaches). The principles of JIT purchasing also include long-term supply contracts with a smaller number of suppliers and supplier development programs involving sharing of sensitive information, when necessary, for improvements in price, quality, or delivery performance. Furthermore, supplier evaluation includes an increased importance on delivery performance, quality, and other factors, as opposed to price. Under this scenario, the nature of relationships obviously shifts from adversarial to cooperative, with mutual trust and cooperation becoming main factors in supplier selection, rather than lowest price.

As noted above, the fundamental objective of a JIT system is to eliminate waste and redundancy in the production-delivery system. Cost reduction is a second-order outcome because the true gains come from improved quality. A production line supervisor cannot consistently receive the exact quantity of materials needed on a JIT basis and *not* have an expectation of "zero defects." Firms define and structure these JIT relationships differently; therefore, the ultimate benefits vary in impact and strategic significance. At one extreme, JIT relationships can be collaborative. However, many JIT relationships are merely coordinated exchanges and do not reach the level of joint interaction and mutual gain that they might. The typical focus of JIT is the timely flow of goods, with little consideration given to the value-added services that can be derived or to the level of differentiation achieved in the minds of the end-user. However, in some instances, JIT relationships are more intimate and involve joint design, product development, and dedicated resources. In these cases, firms exchange technological and managerial skills and begin to exploit synergies far beyond merely coordinating the flow of materials and products.

JIT relationships can be structured to achieve different goals based on expectations, the nature of the actual agreement, and past experience. More formal agreements are less likely to encompass the full range of benefits that might accrue as a result of joint planning and shared resources. Agreements based on trust and commitment are more likely to be more expansive and cover an array of joint initiatives. The critical issue is alignment of goals, because the partners should have similar expectations and desires.

MORE "PULL" ALONG THE CHAIN

There are four approaches that represent attempts at improving supply chain performance by sharing end-customer demand/sales information backward along the chain. Although they are quasi-"pull"/JIT approaches, none of these incorporate analytic routines that might attempt to optimize supply chain decisions for the various parties involved.

- Quick response (QR) which began in the late 1970s as a cooperative effort between several major retailers and suppliers of selected products (mostly textile industry-related), was experimented with in several other industries into the mid-1990s.

- Continuous replenishment of products (CRP) is a modification of QR that eliminated the need for replenishment orders and was implemented by Procter & Gamble with a number of its major customers.
- With vendor-managed inventory (VMI), the supplier assumes more responsibility and actually manages inventory for the retailer.
- Efficient consumer response (ECR) is a grocery-industry-focused variation of QR that involves cooperating partnerships of manufacturers and grocery chains and attempts to achieve significant cost reductions in ways other than solely through improved inventory replenishment (e.g., better allocation of shelf space and fewer wasteful promotions and new product introductions).

TOC (Theory of Constraints): Focus on Bottlenecks   Among the more recent approaches developed, these techniques focus on "bottlenecks" (machines, operations, or stages of production or distribution) that constrain throughput. The primary body of knowledge for dealing with such bottlenecks, developed by Elihu Goldratt in the mid-1980s, is known as the *Theory of Constraints* (TOC). It is also known as *synchronous manufacturing*, because the approach involves all parts of an organization working together to achieve the goals of bottleneck elimination, operating expense reduction, and throughput and profit maximization.[8] The concepts and principles of TOC have attracted great attention and are considered among the more significant developments in operations planning/scheduling in the past several decades. From a supply chain perspective, it is pertinent to note that the developers of TOC observed that "the sum of the local optimum solutions is not equal to the global optimum,"[9] a notion that is incorporated in TOC-based planning/scheduling procedures.

MANUFACTURING EXECUTION SYSTEMS: FOR THE SHOP FLOOR AND MORE

A major weakness found in MRPII was its lack of precision and responsiveness, required for coordinating the thousands of simultaneous events occurring in a factory environment. In response, many manufacturing companies implemented factory floor information and communication systems that include functions such as resource allocation, operations scheduling, document control, data collection, labor management, and performance analysis. These manufacturing execution systems (MES) are designed to provide control of the factory floor and feedback on a real-time basis. Since the advent of ERP (discussed below), they often interface with or are included as part of an ERP system. There has, in fact, been a convergence of the two, because MES vendors have expanded their scope to include pre- and post-factory floor activities, and ERP vendors have expanded their applications to include both the supply chain and the factory floor.[10]

ENTERPRISE RESOURCES PLANNING: THE INTERCONNECTED ENTERPRISE

As Hopp and Spearman[11] note, the years following the development of MRPII saw a succession of attempts at improved planning/control systems, including MRPIII and business requirements planning (BRP). None of these approaches were widely adopted, and it was not until the early half of the 1990s that a new successor to MRPII emerged in the form of ERP. ERP's goal is to coordinate a firm's entire business activities, from suppliers through customer invoicing. Like some variants of MRPII, ERP utilizes a centralized database to facilitate the flow of information among the firm's various functions (represented by modules within ERP), including accounting and finance, logistics, purchasing, manufacturing, marketing, and human resources. The modules are linked together so that users in each function can monitor what is happening in other areas of the company. And, like MRPII, there is an MRP-generic module that does product explosions and gross-to-net material requirements planning. But ERP is much broader in scope, also emphasizing best practices and tying suppliers and distributors more closely to the user firm. ERP systems allow a company to automate processes as well as track transactions and items throughout the company. The explosive growth in distributed computer processing, the popularity of the business process reengineering movement, and increased globalization of supply chains are all factors cited by some observers as contributing to the popularity of ERP. These systems are very good at monitoring transactions; however, they generally lack the analytical capability to determine what transactions *ought* to happen.[12] Hopp and Spearman report that although total sales for MRPII software in 1989 ($1.2 billion) were about one-third of total software sales in the United States, worldwide sales of the top 10 ERP vendors alone were $2.8 billion in 1995, $4.2 billion in 1996, and $5.8 billion in 1997.[13] One company alone, SAP, sold more than $3.2 billion in ERP software in 1997, including some installations costing between $100 million and $250 million each.

PLANNING IN PIECES

As noted earlier, the dominant planning paradigm today is represented by MRPII (the basic logic of which is also embedded in ERP). As can be seen in Figure 3.3, the planning process based on this approach is both hierarchical and subdivided into modules, each of which represents a separate part of the problem (e.g., materials planning, capacity planning, aggregate planning, master scheduling, etc.). When MRP was developed in the 1970s, there was no computer software or hardware capable of handling the entire planning problem. The subdivision of the planning process simplified the overall computational problem and allowed use of available technology. However, one result of subdividing a problem in this fashion is that poor results in one module may not be detected until the results are transferred to another module (e.g., a material plan with poor capacity features calculated by the MRP module is not detected until the results are evaluated by the CRP module, etc.). Thus, iteration is required between some of the modules. Also, decisions made in the factory planning process may impact the distribution plan and vice versa, requiring iterations between the MRP and DRP processes. Despite the increased speed from newer computers, which allows more iterations in a given time period, the problems addressed are so complex that relatively few iterations can be achieved, and human planners still have difficulty seeing "the big picture" necessary to arrive at a global optimum solution, as noted by Peter Senge[14] in *The Fifth Discipline*:

> "From a very early age, we are taught to break apart problems. . . . This makes complex tasks more manageable, but we pay a hidden price. We can no longer see consequences of our actions; we lose our intrinsic sense of connection to a larger whole. . . . When we try to "see the big picture," we try to reassemble the fragments in our minds . . .but the task is futile. . . . Thus, after awhile we give up trying to see the whole altogether.

The difficulties of "seeing the big picture" are increased in supply chain planning, even for a relatively simple network such as that shown in Figure 3.4, because each stage of the network may involve one or more different organizations. In a business environment of traditional arm's-length relationships, each of the separate organizations must forecast what it believes the other organizations in its supply chain will do. Each must carry its own safety stocks, with the net effect that total inventory in the chain is higher than necessary, and competitiveness of companies in the chain suffers.

INTERFACING ALONE IS NOT INTEGRATION

The concepts of "integrated" planning and an "integrated" supply chain have been around for decades, with hundreds of related books and software packages in existence. However, most of these address issues associated with merely connecting

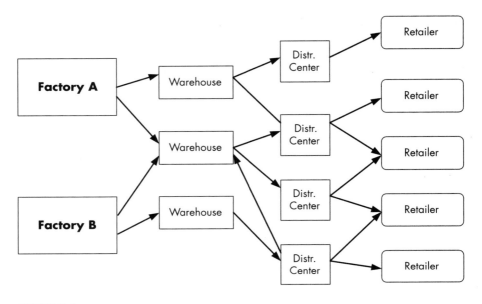

FIGURE 3.4
Possible supply chain flows in a simple network.

the various planning modules, or *interfacing* them, so as to allow information exchange and access of shared data among modules in the same or different organizations. ERP is a prime example of this. Although these efforts may represent an improvement over earlier, stand-alone approaches, this type of interfacing is not true integration insofar as supply chain planning is concerned, because the interfaced modules don't work together analytically to create the "big picture" necessary for a global optimum solution. For example, Chopra and Meindl observe, "ERP systems are great at telling a company what is going on in the company, because they are operationally focused, but fall short in helping a company determine what *ought* to be going on in the supply chain because they do not have sufficient analytic capability."[15]

ADVANCED PLANNING SYSTEMS: BRAINS FOR ENTERPRISE RESOURCE PLANNING

It should be clear by now that ERP systems are good at enabling the sharing of transaction-oriented business data across the entire enterprise in a real-time manner, (i.e., helping managers keep up with what is going on, when, and where). They capture and produce large amounts of data. But, as noted, they generally lack capabilities for helping managers decide what activities *should* be done. Advanced planning systems (APS) are intended to fill this gap. They interface with ERP or MES systems and use advanced algorithms to model supply chain constraints and enable intelligent supply chain planning and decision making. In one sense, an APS is like the brain over the ERP body; it extracts massive amounts of data from the ERP software and analyzes it to determine the best course of action. APS software uses extremely sophisticated mathematical algorithms and other approaches to analyze all aspects of a particular supply chain decision issue and develop plans that offer the best solution, given all the factors involved. The solution algorithms and approaches include linear programming, TOC modeling, simulation, and heuristics. The solution output may be either a true mathematical optimum (e.g., how a supplier can ship all orders on time and maximize gross profit) or merely a feasible solution (such as how the supplier can ship all orders on time). APS systems require large amounts of computer memory and high processing speeds to attack realistically sized business problems; it is only fairly recently that they have become cost-effective.[16]

As one example, companies in many industries are trying to move away from the traditional make-to-stock business model to a make-to-order (MTO) business model, which is much more difficult to execute well. In order to serve customers with a single shipment of mixed goods under the MTO model, it is often necessary to abandon large distribution centers and employ "mixing center" warehouses that serve as merge sites for factory shipments. In these mixing centers, products arrive, are staged temporarily until all portions of an order arrive, then are combined and shipped out together in one shipment. However, it is not unusual for manufacturers switching to this approach to find that their on-time delivery performance from the warehouse to the customer drops dramatically, even though their performance from factory to warehouse may be excellent. HON Industries of Muscatine, Iowa (a leader in wood and steel office furniture, with sales of about $2 billion) found itself in this situation when it shifted to an MTO model in 1999. HON has 15 factory sites and was employing 6 mixing center sites. Although HON's "complete orders on time" (COT) metric from factory to warehouse was 98 percent, COT from warehouse to customer was only 64 percent. In looking for solutions, HON managers found that traditional supply chain planning solutions didn't model warehouse constraints. HON subsequently adopted an APS package that uses TOC concepts in modeling order fulfillment constraints both at the factories and warehouses, and was able to provide a solution in one computer run, which provided the lowest overall cost for fulfilling an order. Previously, two separate runs that sequentially analyzed transportation and distribution inventory costs were required, and the lowest-cost solution was not always obtained. HON's COT metric from the mixing centers on all product lines jumped to over 97 percent and was 99.0 percent on some product lines. Both customer satisfaction and market share increased; savings were reportedly in thousands of dollars per day, mostly in transportation cost savings but also some inventory cost savings. The APS package had a payback period of less than one year.[17]

Analog Devices Inc., a Massachusetts company, implemented an APS to overcome deficiencies in its MRP system after customers, complaining about uneven service levels, began to lose confidence in the company's ability to meet delivery promises. Analog's MRP system was unable to readily adjust available capacity to actual incoming orders; when customers demanded more than the system had scheduled for production, Analog didn't have the needed inventory to deliver by the dates it promised, causing some customers to seek other suppliers. Analog's new APS system allows scheduling of orders on a real-time basis instead of according to a planned forecast; once scheduled, the orders are executed against remaining unused capacity to give customers a firm delivery date.[18]

Although APS systems are extremely powerful decision-aiding tools, they are, like ERP systems, designed for operation within a particular firm's organizational boundaries, rather than across boundaries along the supply chain. For example, inventory-oriented APS systems have typically been focused on planning OEM finished good inventories. But, in a situation of outsourced manufacturing (increasingly popular in a number of industries today), inventories across the supply base impact the OEM's bottom line. These OEM's need visibility into the finished goods and raw material inventories at their contract manufacturers and suppliers. Because traditional APS systems fall short of providing this type of capability, some observers have called for the development of a new category of "extended decision management" (XDM) applications, which will provide visibility across the extended supply chain to help measure and manage the extended enterprise and help streamline demand and supply.[19]

APS systems exist today to address a broad range of within-firm supply chain problems, including production planning and scheduling, supply chain planning, demand planning, and transportation planning. As the HON example shows, APS implementations can produce a fast return on investment and help companies build competitive advantage. Despite this, the rate of APS implementations has lagged other applications. A February 2002 report by J.D. Edwards company, for example, indicated that of the firm's 6,400 worldwide customers, fewer than 10 percent had installed APS software from any vendor. However, the report also stated that 70 percent of the companies intended to install either APS or customer relationship management (CRM) software in the next 24 months, concluding that APS and CRM were "tremendous growth areas" for J.D. Edwards.[20] This finding agrees with the author's own experience, which strongly indicates that successful implementation of new supply chain software applications requires much more than simply acquiring the new technology. This is in line with other findings that real success in this arena requires effective change management procedures dealing with people, processes and policies, on both an intra- and an intercompany basis.[21]

THE INTERNET
AND E-MANUFACTURING

The Internet has had significant impact on supply chain planning and scheduling practices, not simply because of improved communication between all links in the supply chain. For example, numerous companies today routinely use e-procurement systems to communicate changing market demand in real time and adjust supply needs. One example—of many that could be cited like this—is Honeywell's Garrett Turbochargers Division, the world's largest maker of turbochargers for autos, trucks, and light aircraft. Garrett deals regularly with about 125 key suppliers in the United States, Europe, and Asia. Until recently, Garrett communicated with these suppliers by EDI (electronic data interchange), fax, and e-mail to get production information to them and solicit firm order commitments from them. In 2001, to foster quicker connections with suppliers, Garrett implemented an Internet-based system that allows suppliers to view current inventory levels at the turbocharger firm, fill consignment levels, make firm delivery commitments to orders, and set up payment procedures by accessing Honeywell Garrett's accounts payable systems.[22]

Another well-known example of a company that has used the Internet in managing its supply chain is Dell Computer. The more obvious virtues of the Dell business model are well known. Dell's combination of direct-to-consumer sales and build-to-order/JIT manufacturing means practically no inventory and unparalleled success in matching product offerings to customer demand. No computer is ever built without a specific customer order. The company's Web site allows customers to specify the configurations of their computers; over half of

Dell's sales, totaling more than $50 million per day, were booked over the Internet in 2001. In addition to its publicly available Dell.com Web site for individual consumer orders, Dell has created special "premier page" Web sites for its business customers to facilitate procurement of company-approved choices of PCs and IT equipment. In 2001, there were more than 12,000 of these premier pages on Dell's system. But in addition to this widely known "front-end" use of the Internet, Dell has also created a "back-end" intranet (valuechain.dell.com) with Internet connections to most of its suppliers. These connections link Dell's material planners directly to supplier inventories, and orders for parts are placed electronically. Dell also uses these supplier connections to share a wide variety of real-time information from its customers and its own plants, including inventory data, quality data, and technology plans. For example, incoming order information is shared immediately with Dell's suppliers, who deliver inventory to Dell plants from supplier-owned "hubs" (warehouses) located near the plants in less than 90 minutes after receiving a replenishment order. The suppliers also use this information to improve the accuracy of their forecasts, because some of their components have long delivery lead times from second-and third-tier suppliers. At Dell's end, from the time a customer order gets to the factory, a finished PC can go to shipping in less than four hours (which is about the length of time Dell owns the inventory), and the computer can be on the customer doorstep or at the customer's loading dock the next day.[23]

Until 2001, Dell's several factories around the world operated essentially the same but independently of each other, with separate planning and scheduling groups and separate databases for each factory. However, the company recently implemented a Web-based centralized planning/scheduling system incorporating components from i2 Technologies that connects all factories. The new system provides global visibility of demand and supply for 150 material planners who manage Dell's approximately $20 billion annual global buy.[24]

Dell's new global planning/scheduling system is an example of how manufacturing companies are currently involved in a "second wave" of enterprise improvement activities that involve Internet-based applications and are much more decision- and analysis-oriented than before. The first wave of supply chain-related Internet applications focused mostly on automation of internal work flow (including ERP systems) and procurement-related transactional activity, such as placing catalogs online and buying goods and services. Some of these applications followed—and complemented—business improvement initiatives, such as reengineering, business process analysis, lean manufacturing, and lean thinking.

These new applications include dramatic advances in decentralized manufacturing and control involving "E-manufacturing"—the marriage of the digital factory and the Internet. E-manufacturing uses electronically transmitted knowledge to design products, transmit orders, procure components, drive production machines, and follow it up with remote product maintenance in the field. It links factories to one another, to their supply chains, and to dealers and customers. For example, Arctic Cat, a maker of snowmobiles in Thief River Falls, Minnesota, linked up with suppliers in Asia who make the molds for its snowmobile parts. Now when an engineer in Thief River Falls changes a windshield's configuration, the modification is entered automatically in the mold-making equipment halfway around the world. A process that once took weeks has been reduced to minutes. Similarly, IBM's storage systems division in San Jose, California uses new software to make changes automatically in manufacturing processes at its eight worldwide plants from Mainz, Germany to Shenzhen, China. The changes are stored in a server at each plant; machines at the plants constantly query the servers for changes and automatically incorporate them into their runs. Before the implementation of this E-manufacturing system, IBM had to maintain IT staffers at each plant to write new computer code for each change—an activity that typically took days or weeks.[25]

With sales of over $2 billion per month conducted electronically, Intel may be the world's top E-business company. Intel has expanded into E-manufacturing not only for itself but also for other companies, with a dozen space mission control-like centers that help other manufacturers run their plants. But, as *Fortune Magazine* noted, the new phenomena of E-manufacturing is not limited to high-tech companies such as Intel; what some industry observers refer to as the "easy-dot-com, easy-dot-go" collapse of the dot-com "bubble" has obscured real advances by smart manufacturers that are using the Net to generate real value in so-called old economy companies.

Cutler-Hammer, a $1.4 billion division of Eaton Corp. located near Pittsburgh, makes complex assembled electrical and electronic products such as electric panels and motor controls for residential and industrial equipment. The company has dramatically boosted its competitiveness as well as sales and profits since launching its e-factory effort several years ago. Cutler-Hammer's new system allows a customer, a distributor, or one of the company's sales engineers in the field easily to configure the characteristics of hundreds of complex products with intricate wiring patterns and precise placement of dozens of electrical and electronic components. What differentiates Cutler-Hammer's new system from other Internet-based configuration programs used by companies such as Dell Computer and Cisco is its sophistication and its direct connection to production equipment in Cutler-Hammer factories. Now, minutes after a field sales engineer, distributor, or customer in California or elsewhere completes the customized specifications for a product, machines at two almost identical Cutler-Hammer factories in Fayetteville, North Carolina and Sumter, South Carolina begin automatically producing the product. The program automatically takes care of even the smallest but significant detail, such as labels that specify the speed and power of motors and components. After composing the labels, the program directs the nameplate engraver to print the label. In the past, a technician would type the information for the nameplate, increasing the possibility of errors and slowing the process. The two factories also run a total of 17 satellite assembly operations; an additional 14 assembly plants in the United States and Mexico are connected to the new system. Company executives say the move to E-manufacturing has helped motivate the streamlining of internal processes and business practices. For example, Cutler-Hammer has standardized its products and models, slimming down the number of steel enclosure sizes from more than 400 to only 100. In 2001, more than 61,000 orders were processed electronically, and Cutler-Hammer's CEO credited the new system with increasing sales of some products by 20 percent, doubling profits, increasing productivity by 35 percent, and reducing quality costs by 26 percent.[26]

The importance of the Internet can be judged from the fact that most new factory equipment today comes with a built-in Net connection to allow machines to be monitored and controlled from a remote location just as easily as from a control room overlooking the shop floor.[27] For example, Unifi Inc., a producer of textile fibers, runs 22 plants from its headquarters in Greensboro, North Carolina. With a system like Unifi's, data from the various shop floors can also be plugged in to company ERP systems to keep tab on everything from SCM to customer service and accounting.

A major factor relating to the importance of the Internet for supply chain applications is the relatively recent development of new software standards, such as extensible markup language (XML). This new tool allows the "tagging" of groups of data to smash the language barriers that have segregated different breeds of computers, different business-process software, and different database formats. The XML tags make it much easier for program and system developers to integrate data from business partners with back-end systems—a critical point for Internet marketplaces forging relationships with numerous trading partners, as well as companies building corporate "extranets," such as Dell Computer. For example, in 2001, Eastman Chemical Co. was expecting to conduct 30 percent of its $5.3 billion in sales on its private exchange, using XML computer-to-computer transactions or manually via its Web site.[28]

A different type of example exists at Maytag Corporation. Before that company began using XML, getting the specifications of a new dishwasher or other appliance to retailers was traditionally, according to Maytag managers, "a Herculean process" that involved downloading all the information from a Maytag company mainframe computer and retyping the information into an Excel spreadsheet. Now Maytag uses XML to permit the specifications to be transmitted directly from their mainframe computer to the computers of their retailers and trading partners. The new process has dramatically decreased both the time and error rate associated with this process and will eventually cut Maytag's cost of catalogue production as much as 80 percent.[29]

PLANNING AND SCHEDULING INTEGRATION ACROSS COMPANY BOUNDARIES

Companies such as Cutler-Hammer, IBM, and Unifi have made great strides in using the Internet to help improve their competitiveness and profitability. But the Internet has been only one of several factors responsible for these improvements, which have typically also been driven by streamlining of internal business processes, breaking down traditional "walls" between functional units, and other "lean" business practices. And, as impressive as some of these efforts and results are, they have largely been confined to individual companies instead of being widely shared across supply chains. Because of this, most supply chains today contain unnecessary waste and cost in the form of duplicated business processes and inefficient practices. A company's buying/procurement process, for example, is likely to be a mirror image of its supplier's sales and order-fulfillment process. Even though the two companies may exchange data/information electronically (and thus be "integrated" in the eyes of many software vendor marketers), workers in each company end up doing essentially the same work, with similar forms and documentation, and similar checks and balances.

Recognizing the gains to be obtained by simplifying and truly integrating such company-to-company processes, a few leading companies have moved ahead in restructuring and combining some of them. For example, Michael Hammer tells how Hewlett Packard has done this with its supply chain for computer monitors, which stretches back through an electronic contract manufacturer (ECM) who buys the case for the monitor from an injection molder, who acquires the material for the case from a plastics compounder, who in turn buys the compound material from a resin maker.[30] According to Hammer, this supply chain was fairly easy to describe but almost impossible to manage well, for a variety of reasons. HP assumed responsibility for ensuring that all parties would work together, share information, and operate in a way that guarantees the lowest costs and highest levels of product availability throughout the chain. HP set up a computer system to share information among all the participants and posted its demand forecasts and revisions for its first-tier partners to use in their own forecasting. The partners also began to post their plans and schedules and to use the system to communicate with their own suppliers and customers. HP's procurement staff manages the entire process, monitoring upstream suppliers, resolving disputes, and helping keep materials and product flowing. Because it coordinates the entire process, HP can order all required resin directly from the resin supplier, at considerably lower prices than the numerous small compounders involved were able to get. According to Hammer, cost for the resin dropped significantly, the number of HP people involved in managing the supply chain was cut by 50 percent, time to fill an order dropped by 25 percent, and sales increased for the products managed by this process.

Another example of cross-company process integration involves PolyOne Chemicals Corporation. PolyOne was created by a merger of Geon and M. Hanna Company in 2000. Geon had long been recognized as an industry leader in adopting and leveraging IT for competitive advantage, and the new company is continuing these practices. For example, PolyOne's E-procurement software is used by employees at its 60-odd facilities in North America to purchase everything from production machinery to paper clips, at an estimated saving of $10–$20 million per year. PolyOne recently implemented a new procurement system with its 10 largest suppliers of production materials. The company now runs integrated transactions in real time with these suppliers via a custom-made XML-based system.[31] What's unique is that ERP transactions on the buyer side are immediately entered directly into the supplier's ERP system, i.e., a purchase order from PolyOne automatically turns into an order entered at OxyVinyls or one of the other nine supplier companies without a person seeing the transaction. The system was developed and tested with the largest supplier for about a year before expanding to the top 10. With that one supplier, involving purchases of $250 million per year, inventory levels dropped by about 8 percent, and 40 rail cars used for transfer and storage of materials (at a cost of $10,000 each) were eliminated. The new system has reduced the cost of each of PolyOne's 17,000 monthly purchase transactions from $110 to $75, saving over $595,000 per month.[32]

Finally, a different type of example of cross-company integration involves Lucent Technologies. Lucent's services group consists largely of 8,000–10,000 installers of telecommunications equipment who move from project to project. An average installation involves 200–250 individual items, some sourced from a variety of distributors and some manufactured by groups within Lucent, as well as Lucent's contract manufacturers and OEMs. Traditionally, the materials required for an installation were ordered from suppliers and staged at one of Lucent's 200 installation warehouses, from which they were pulled as needed for the project. Lack of visibility across the supply chain was a major problem: "We had virtually no visibility on the Lucent side and were completely blind to what was going on outside of our organization," stated Lucent's director of SCM. Inefficiencies in the supply chain were costing Lucent $150 million annually in installation productivity losses alone.[33] In 2001, Lucent installed a "collaborative execution" software system to gain real-time visibility across its supply network. Lucent connected its leading suppliers, such as Anixter and Graybar, and its third-party logistics provider, Ryder Logistics. Now a customer order coming into Lucent from field sales representatives or customers is fed into Lucent's Tradestream system. All changes, cancellations, deletions, shipments, receipts, and other transactions associated with that particular order are also entered into the system, regardless of whether the data come from supplier, customer, Lucent, or Ryder. Lucent's system converts all incoming data into XML format, moving the data via the Internet as encrypted proprietary XML messages. Now, according to Lucent management, suppliers can synchronize their forecasting and demand planning with Lucent. Also, Lucent's system personalizes display screens for each individual user and allows users to write rules designating the events they want to monitor. When something falls outside of established parameters, an alert message is automatically sent. Rules can also be written to help spot opportunities as well as problems, such as order quantity price breaks and shipment consolidations. Ryder Logistics has used the new system effectively to manage Lucent's shipment schedules so that delays and disruptions are minimized.[34, 35]

SUMMARY

These examples show that some companies today are achieving a high level of cross-company integration of supply chain planning and scheduling. They are sharing product and production plans with suppliers, collaborating with customers to improve prediction of demand and plan production, and using Web-based systems to speed both planning and execution. Where implemented, such initiatives have resulted in significant supply chain improvements. However, examples are still few, with only a relative handful of companies able to approach the vision of a seamless extended enterprise working together to meet end-user requirements. A major reason for this, we believe, is that "integration" has been viewed primarily as an information technology challenge instead of what it really is: a broad-based process change and management challenge.

4

DEVELOPING
EXTENDED
ENTERPRISE
THINKING

I n this chapter, you consider the model for the extended enterprise by examining in greater detail the set of characteristics and factors that distinguish the extended enterprise from other supply-chain relationships. Few companies currently exemplify the extended enterprise because these networks are just now on the horizon. In addition, not every company will embrace its tenets or be convinced that the advantages are worth the perceived loss of control or loss of independence that a firm must sacrifice.

In Chapter 2, you first explored the notion of the extended enterprise and traced its development from an historical perspective. Figure 4.1 shows how the idea of the extended enterprise has emerged over time. There have been a number of inflection points that mark progressive stages in the

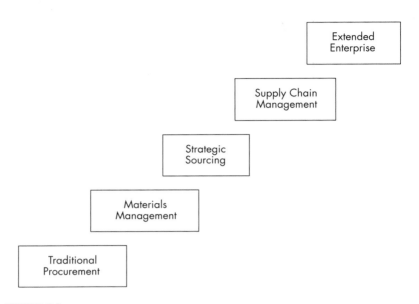

FIGURE 4.1
Toward the implementation of the extended enterprise: Documenting the journey.

development of the procurement function as it transformed from the role of expeditor/buyer to the manager of supplier development and supply chain coordinator. In Chapter 3, you saw that a number of firms and their supply chains are beginning to embrace the tenets of the extended enterprise. Technology has enabled this transformation. Advanced planning and scheduling tools serve to connect levels of the supply chain as though these separate firms were vertically integrated. Note that technology alone cannot complete the transformation. Changes in organizational processes and managerial mindsets are at the core of developing extended enterprise thinking and behavior.

An extended enterprise perspective sees the entire supply chain as the central focus in gaining a competitive advantage. New product development decisions, strategic planning, and elements of competitive advantage are all viewed at a supply chain level, and the chain is as strong as its weakest link. Laws of comparative advantage help direct the allocation of resources, and performance is based on systemwide metrics and outcomes. Functional considerations are now raised to supply chain-level issues. Managers throughout the system now ask what is good for the whole and what benefits the end-use customer?

TOWARD THE IMPLEMENTATION OF THE EXTENDED ENTERPRISE

Traditional procurement activities that were linked to adversarial buyer-seller relationships gave way to materials management, where suppliers and buyers entered a period of detente. The fear of self-serving behavior seemed to fade to the background, and buyer and seller began to better appreciate the importance of a more coordinated approach in dealing with each other. Longer term contracts existed among supply chain members, and some integration was achieved between purchasing and the other support functions (e.g., logistics). The key objective was to improve the efficient flow of goods from supplier to buyer. Price, quality, and delivery were the buyer's major response to competitive pressures.

These linkages became stronger under the period of strategic sourcing. Tying the incremental gains in volume given to this much-reduced set of suppliers was typically contingent on cost reductions, better service, and other value-added activities where buyers could leverage their size. Control was still a primary driver, and the buying firm was motivated mainly by its own needs. The current age of supply chain management (SCM) represents a first step away from exercising control to building strategic relationships with key suppliers. Leverage is now based on competence, and buyers look for suppliers who have critical skills/capabilities that bring value to the marketplace.

Despite the potential supply chainwide gains, procurement performance metrics still were internally focused and only rarely showed a consideration for other members of the supply chain. As you will see in Chapter 9, what gets measured gets done, and people will perform to the compensation plan.

Competitive realities, the globalization of markets, and the rising costs of doing business, along with other factors have caused managers to reevaluate all their relationships, not just how they interact with key suppliers and customers.

In response to competitive pressures, Bose Corporation has empowered key suppliers (e.g., cabinetry and electronics vendors) to spend money on parts as needed. Based on more than information sharing, these changes encompass changing roles and responsibility, and are intended to improve partners' competitive advantage. Akin to vendor management inventory, these actions begin to represent the level of collaboration we advocate. Yet not all companies would allow such latitude on the part of their suppliers. Reluctance is tied to the fear of letting another company get too close. The key to supply chain improvements lies in cross-functional and interenterprise improvements such that all parties share the same data and view of the world, and recognize their interdependence.[1] Software is not the glue that holds collaboration together; it is the catalyst.

Competitive pressures not withstanding, the costs associated with weak coordination and cooperation in the supply chain are quite profound. A recent study[2] has shown that breakdowns in SCM lead to shareholder wealth destruction. Using a critical event* of the public announcement surrounding a supply chain problem, these glitches result in a production or shipping delay, which in turn affect the market-adjusted stock price. During the period from 1989 to 1998, 861 glitches were reported. The average change in a firm's stock value was around $120 million. This observation alone should be incentive enough to improve supply chain performance. Other research has tried to link supply chain performance with returns to stockholders.[3] To assess the level of returns, companies were first assigned to pools of above average, average, and below average on a measure of total return to

---

*A critical events methodology typically tracks the changes in one variable (here, stock price) hypothesized to be caused by another (an announcement of a supply chain glitch) and measures the effects both before and after the event happens. This approach is used in finance to track the market's reaction, as measured by stock price, to merger announcements across a range of firm's and industries.

stockholders. (Total return was based on Compustat data using average monthly closing stock prices adjusted to account for dividends.) Firms that were placed in the above average pool tended to form more collaborative relationships, shared more new ideas, had greater tendency to share risks and rewards, and acknowledged that collaboration was critical to success. It should not be surprising that less than average performers focused almost solely on strategic cost management practices. This unilateral focus on expenses to improve returns could come at the expense of other strategic considerations.

It could be argued that these shorter term solutions highlight a lack of appreciation for the true benefits of collaborative action. It is important to note that many actions that result in better supply chain performance really describe a change process that cannot be implemented overnight. For example, in the mid 1990s, Cessna reviewed its competitive position and came to the realization that it could not compete against the major companies in the aviation market. Its size placed it at a disadvantage relative to GE, Honeywell, and others. Management believed that greater alignment within the supply chain could become a source of competitive advantage. They found that on-time delivery was poor; quality suffered, and redundant activities added costs; costs and pricing were escalating; and the entire supply chain was out of control.

A new supply chain initiative was started to bring Cessna from a materials management mentality to a more integrated supply chain focus. They knew that the answer was not to push cost savings back on the supplier. Forcing a supplier to cut into margins to reduce costs merely shifts responsibility and does not make the added costs go away. Instead, working with suppliers and sharing information through EDI and other enabling systems forced integration to reduce inventories systemwide. Ordering parts and components through a transparent material resource planning (MRP) system also encouraged greater joint planning. Accuracy and visibility became the hallmarks of its supply chain strategy.

To begin the process of transformation, extended enterprise thinking must flow from the firm's strategic plan. It is the strategic plan that translates senior management's view of the future into a reality. Yet this future state must be understood within a larger context. It would be helpful to understand on a more global level the future trends that will affect the development and acceptance of extended enterprise thinking.

A VIEW TO THE FUTURE

Each of the trends described below supports our notions of the extended enterprise and are illustrative of a number of changes that we have seen evolve in recent years.*

- Longer term relationships will continue to grow with greater reliance on purchasing more from fewer suppliers.
- Consolidation of the supply base will extend to suppliers who evidence an ability to serve on a global basis. Thus, we will see a greater reliance on fewer, albeit larger, global suppliers.
- Customer relevance will become increasingly important and will drive relationship-centric supply chains.
- Contractual relationships will grow in importance and will be a key mechanism for linking supply chain members. Contract management can help reduce costs and improve internal efficiency. By automating the process, it is possible to construct a reporting tool to monitor performance and to contribute to further cost reduction. Companies such as Oracle and i2 have added modules to their e-commerce suites in hopes of expanding the range of information available to both internal customers and suppliers. No doubt such tools are important and help ensure the timely execution of terms and conditions. At the same time, within the extended enterprise context, many companies will recognize that strict contractual

*This discussion is based on Donald Bowersox, David Closs, and Theodore Stank, "Ten Mega-Trends that Will Revolutionize Supply Chain Logistics," *Journal of Business Logistics* 21, no. 2 (2000): 1B16 and work presented in Chapter 21 of Robert Monczka, Robert Trent, and Robert Handfield, *Purchasing and Supply Chain Management* (Cincinnati, OH: South-Western College Publishing, 2002): 688 et seq.

relationships will be too confining for certain types of supply chain relationships.

■ The migration from functional to process integration will continue with specific emphasis on the use of service providers as part of the external supply chain.

■ With the challenge of managing a more diverse work-force will come a transition from training to knowledge-based learning. This implies that managers will need to think systemwide and understand how all the pieces fit in providing value to customers.

■ Suppliers and the sourcing process will receive greater attention from senior management and will be incorporated in strategic goals. Attention will first be focused on attaining cost savings, then will incorporate issues related to achieving top-line growth.

■ Procurement will begin to take a more strategic role in developing, working with, and planning with key suppliers. At the same time, their involvement in the more mundane, tactical activities will decrease. The use of technology will eliminate much of the mundane workflow-related activities.

■ Leveraging the supply base and building on its skills and competencies will become more important.

■ Outsourcing will grow as firms concentrate on what they do well and abandon what is not core to their future competitive success.

■ Supply chainwide information sharing, planning, and performance metrics will take on greater importance.

■ Performance metrics will reflect the contribution of suppliers to corporate goals and objectives.

Supply chains could easily resemble virtual corporations, where boundaries blur and all partner firms strive to bring value to the marketplace. These trends imply closer ties among buyers and key suppliers so that the supply network can achieve greater competitive success on a local and global basis. In addition, planning and performance metrics will extend to the entire extended enterprise, and in the process, both risks and rewards will be shared systemwide.

STRATEGIC INTENT DRIVES EXTENDED ENTERPRISE THINKING

You can think of strategy development partially as the process of bringing innovation and change to the firm. A firm's strategy directs the organization over time and helps managers navigate the uncertain waters of change in pursuit of its objectives and goals. Strategy is future focused and cascades from the corporate level to the business unit then to the functional department. Any strategy that guides managerial action at these different levels in the organization must be aligned so that there are no mixed signals, conflicting plans, or incompatible execution of these plans. Figure 4.2 illustrates the cascading effects of a firm that selects a strategy of low cost or differentiation.*

Building on this simple example for a moment, a firm focusing solely on a low-cost strategy makes very different demands on its supply base than a firm that competes through differentiation. A low-cost strategy drives suppliers to continuously lower prices, either through productivity gains, economies of scale, or business processes that remove waste, inefficiencies, and/or redundancy from the system. Depending on the buyer's level of self-interest, the burden for cost reduction would fall proportionately on the supply base, and the related performance metrics would be driven by cost-related factors. Although greater efficiencies are achieved; the sole focus on costs might lead to behaviors that are detrimental in the long term. For instance, if your suppliers are constantly under pressure to reduce costs, where is innovation likely to fit into the equation? Why would a supplier invest on the buyer's behalf if, at the end of the day, it is the purchase price that counts? Value in use or total cost of ownership might not be reflected in the metrics employed to gain price concessions. More critical is the observation that firms that emphasize cost

---

*This example is based on Michael Porter's discussion in *Competitive Strategy* (New York: Free Press, 1980). In many instances, firms cannot select one approach or the other. That is, it is more common to find that firms must have low costs and must differentiate their products to compete on a global scale.

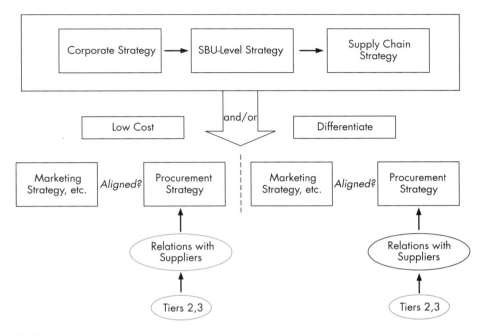

FIGURE 4.2
Strategy cascades and must be aligned.

reduction over long periods of time appear to lose the ability to think about and execute plans that are customer-centric.

If, on the other hand, the firm selects a differentiation strategy, cost is still a concern but the focus is on bringing value to end-use customers through innovation, value-adding capabilities, and/or an intimate understanding of customer requirements, processes, and the like. If the firm espouses differentiation but encourages key suppliers to participate in reverse auctions, which tend to be cost-based, there is a potential misalignment. The criteria established for selecting the set of suppliers to include in the reverse auction can include measures that capture characteristics other than price; however, most of the time price emerges as the dominant criteria used to differentiate among potential suppliers. Nonetheless, Dell and Motorola get high marks for supplier development and for the use of non–price-related criteria. Dell's quarterly supplier-rating scheme measures four key criteria: Technology is number one, and price/cost is number four.

One large multinational company sends such mixed signals and has caused a great deal of skepticism among its suppliers. Simply, suppliers *hear* one thing and experience contradictory behavior. This confusion results in more tentative suppliers who are reluctant to make commitments on behalf of the buyer. As a direct result, the buyer is unable to achieve the full benefit of the expertise, skills, and experience that the supplier could bring to the table. Suppliers hear that the buyer wishes to develop closer ties with its key suppliers and wants to work with them to improve product design/development processes, etc. At the same time, they *experience* buyer behaviors that show that partnerships must be developed with caution because, despite words to the contrary, costs rule! Cost pressures and earning demands have caused the disconnect between what the firm says and what it does.

It is perfectly fine to triage one's supply base and use auctions for some commodity purchases, long-term cost-indexed contractual relationships for other relationships, and more collaborative relationships for a handful of strategic relationships. Difficulties arise when the selection criteria are not clearly communicated, and potential suppliers have no clue as to what to expect. Consistency is fundamental to the trust-building process. Given this lack of alignment; the ability to implement a coherent supply chain strategy suffers. Supplier development tends to be less focused on skills and capabilities, and the emphasis on meeting present cost targets trumps any consideration of a future vision.

Strategic intent[4] is the process of linking business goals with an understanding of the key relationships, skills, and competencies that are essential to future success. Managers must confront questions such as, What are the present and future needs of the marketplace and what changes must be enacted now by the members of the supply chain to be prepared for the future? Some of these changes require different resources, and others require different skills. Among the skills that might be needed are ones that help partners more effectively manage a new set of relationships among members of the supply chain. To prepare for these changes and to guide attempts to narrow this gap, the following kinds of questions should be addressed:

- What role does the buyer-seller relationship play in the competitive arena?
- What are the goals and objectives of the relationship? Short-term? Long-term?
- Is there alignment between our strategy and our suppliers' strategies?
- What is the value brought to the market? Does it result in a sustainable competitive advantage? If not, explain.
- Which partner is responsible for what component of the value equation?
- Each supplier partner will fill what gaps?
- Where does competitive advantage lie in the future? What skills will be needed? Are we preparing for the future now?

Within an extended enterprise context, supplier evaluation is driven by the value proposition for the entire supply chain and what the present and future needs in the marketplace are. Strategic gaps are filled by the members of the supply chain, and their potential membership is determined, in large measure, by the strength of their skills and how they contribute to the overall supply chain's competitive success. The essence of strategic intent hinges on core competencies,* not on products, resources, or tangible assets. An understanding of competencies comes from the accumulated intellectual capital of the firm and is the sum of its technology, expertise, experience, and management processes. Many of these skills might not be resident in the firm but will come from the firm's closest suppliers and partners. So extended enterprise thinking broadens the notion of competencies to the entire supply chain and looks to where the skills lie, attempting to harness them for the improvement of the entire enterprise as it strives to meet the needs of its present and future customer base.

One key strategic capability is the ability to leverage a partner's skills/expertise beyond tangible assets and explicit knowledge. There are central (i.e., core) skills/assets that are less easily transferred among supply chain partners. Employee

---

*Ideally, these competencies should be unique, create value, and not be easily imitated.

know-how and reputation, for instance, are resident in the cultural fabric of the firm, are not easily codified, and are often not immediately recognized. To understand what gives rise to such core competencies is to understand the *genetic structure* of the firm. These competencies are the essential ingredients of the relationship that unleashes the value-creating ability of the supply chain.

In some industries, it is not uncommon to find such partnerships built to enable a transfer of knowledge and/or technology among firms in the supply chain network. High-tech firms find knowledge transfer essential by virtue of the fast-paced, highly uncertain nature of their industry.[5] The type of knowledge exchanged between partners is partly a function of the extent that knowledge is easily communicated and understood. Information technology is not a panacea, and the ability to learn from your supply chain partners requires far more than new and improved systems.

For example, Nike's highly publicized inability to integrate a SAP enterprise solution, a Siebel CRM application, and an i2 SCM application highlights some of the pitfalls of large-scale supply chain software integration efforts. This effort cost over $400 million, and its failure was attributable to an inability to link to Nike with its hundreds of suppliers. Bank of America implemented an enterprise resources planning (ERP) system that involved standardizing systems in 23 countries as part of a reengineering of its global cash management processes.[6] Not only was the task of integrating internally a challenge, but the need to interface flawlessly with customers presented an even greater challenge. To help the implementation of the system, several key steps were critical. Among these were:

- Getting senior management buy-in and support
- Creating a strong cross-functional and interdisciplinary implementation team
- Establishing communication networks to ensure the timely flows of information within and across the boundaries of the bank
- Achieving total agreement on the implementation plan. Once differences of opinion were aired and resolved, all parties gave their support to the agreed-upon plan of attack.

Although technology implementation might, in and of itself, appear to be a serious challenge, the key success factors hinge on the people and their ability to work in a collaborative environment. There is no question that major challenges in implementing ERP systems arise from the massive scale of these projects. These issues are independent of whether the system comes from SAP, Oracle, or PeopleSoft. The data appear to be very clear—about 50 percent of information systems projects fail.[7] Nonetheless, ERP systems are alive and well. One estimate suggests that the ERP market will grow at a rate of 32 percent through 2004.[8] A concern is whether managers overestimate the power of the software and neglect the role played by the people in these massive reengineering projects.

FROM INTENT TO INTEGRATION

Consider a future vision that establishes a set of goals and objectives for the company. One of Ford's goals is to improve its productivity and continue to develop processes that lead to faster cycle times, shorter lead times, and better quality. The ultimate goal is to move to a make-to-order manufacturing process. To facilitate the process, Ford has taken an equity stake in Executive Manufacturing Technologies (EMT), a firm that provides software for tracking real-time shop floor production. Two points are worth making: First, Ford recognized that it could not achieve its objectives by relying on internally generated capabilities because its core skills are not in ERP-related software. Second, it acknowledged that these skills were important enough to take a partial ownership stake in the firm. An equity position gives them access and, thus, makes it easier for Ford to learn. In addition, partial ownership brings the skills and capabilities offered by EMT closer to Ford's sphere of influence.

In part, Ford's strategy is motivated by a desire to become more nimble in order to adapt more quickly to changes in the marketplace. The key to agility is a change in mindset that now focuses on the customer, leverages resources, and co-operates to compete. These supply chain partnerships are driven by a very pragmatic decision to fulfill customers' needs by providing solutions that use the skills of more competent firms when the expertise is not resident in the firm. However, the supplier selection process extends beyond the obvious evaluation of requisite skills or capabilities. Not all competent suppliers are candidates for supplier partnerships, and the due diligence conducted should take this distinction into account.

In 2001, Nokia was the only cellular phone manufacturer that was profitable; to stay that way, it has been working to gain greater visibility in collaborative forecasting. Adding to the profit pressure is the need to ensure that its inventory levels and those of its partners are not an unnecessary burden. With quickly changing technology, it is critical to minimize the amount of inventory in the system. "Old technology" results in unplanned obsolescence that must be driven from the system, often resulting in markdowns or write-offs. The key to Nokia's approach is to coordinate forecasting for both supply and demand. Central to this program's success is that supply chain partners must be comfortable with transparency and trust that the information provided, both upstream and downstream, is reliable.

Raytheon has taken a slightly different path to supplier integration and relies heavily on early supply involvement in product development and reengineering. This planned involvement comes after efforts to rationalize its supply base and consolidate its own purchases to benefit from Raytheon's purchasing leverage. For instance, early involvement helped to reduce the manufacturing costs and scale down the functionality of an infrared camera that was designed originally for the military. The camera is now offered as an option on certain models of Cadillac.

To manage this process successfully, procurement's role expands to include relationship management. Communication is key to the integration process that entails involving both external suppliers and procurement in activities that heretofore resided with developers, engineers, and technical and marketing people. Questions arise as to how to include purchasing in the process, given its limited past contribution to any decisions that are strategic in nature. Beyond the question of how to involve purchasing is a related set of issues regarding what kind of skills are needed to have procurement successfully fill its new role. Again, the strategy development process entails far more than creating a future vision. Structures and processes must enable the execution of this vision, and the future skill sets and capabilities of key players must be assessed.

SUPPLIER RELATIONSHIP MANAGEMENT

As seen in Chapter 3, supplier relationship management has emerged as an extension of attempts to automate the procurement function. Firms such as PeopleSoft, and Ariba, SAP have introduced applications that span the suite of procurement activities. One challenge is that the range of supplier interactions is both broad and deep; thus, the ability to manage the entire set of relationships is quite difficult. Even the term *strategic sourcing* spans all the prework needed for supplier selection, negotiations and contract signing, performance and milestone monitoring, and supplier development. The challenge again rests in integrating these different components.[9]

Apexon, a software company, provides via the Internet visibility between manufacturers and suppliers to ensure that orders can be fulfilled. The premise on which the company was built is that the supplier is really an extension of the manufacturer. Through a suite of products ranging from supplier assessment to planning, production, procurement, and quality tools, buyer and seller do not work at arm's length but instead, the supplier is the manufacturer's arm.[10]

MAPPING THE PROCESS FROM STRATEGIC INTENT TO PARTNER SELECTION

Figure 4.3 depicts a decision-making process that flows from strategic intent and incorporates the parameters into the supplier partner selection decision. At this juncture, the analysis is rather general but the flow should be quite logical and should emphasize the importance of tying the entire selection process back to what vision management has for the future. It is interesting to note that in smaller companies the linkage between the strategic plan and SCM is much more overt.[11] For the smaller firm this linkage is often critical to the firm's overall performance because smaller companies tend to be very dependent on the outsourcing of nonessential tasks. In addition, smaller firms more directly demonstrate the role played by senior management in shaping both strategic intent of the firm and the strategic sourcing decisions that follow.

The first set of decisions fixes the strategic direction of the firm and forces an analysis of how value is created for the marketplace and where in the value chain the capabilities and/or skills required to produce value reside. Implicit here is the recognition that the skills might lay outside the firm and that these capabilities must be harnessed. Throughout this process, questions must be answered that ensure that the skills being sought are not critical for the firm in the future. Skills that are deemed essential for future success are often brought internally or some assurances must be in place to guarantee access. For example, Ford took an equity stake in EMT to ensure access to that company's skills.

Once managers determine what is core and what is nonessential, they engage in both a reaffirmation that the strategy makes sense (fits) and a capabilities gap analysis. Fit and alignment force a discussion around issues germane to making the business case and is illustrated by the following set of questions:

- What is the value proposition? Is there relative advantage conveyed? To whom?
- What are the goals and objectives? Are they measurable?
- What are the business risks? Of the supply chain partnership? Of going it alone?
- What happens if the partnership fails?
- Are the linkages needed between our partner and us known? Appreciated? Are there adequate resources?

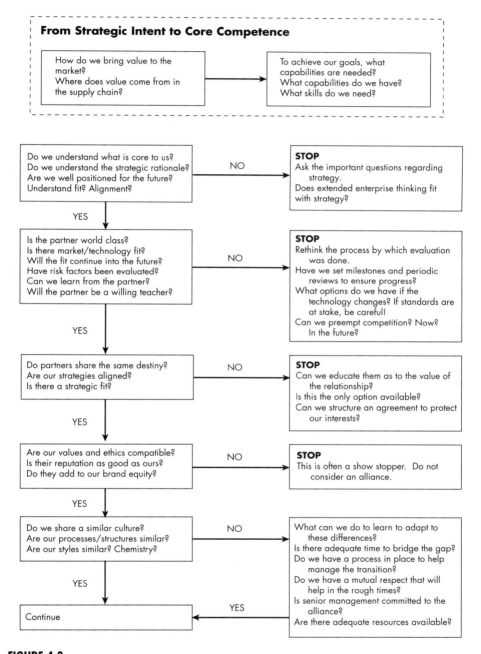

FIGURE 4.3
From due diligence to the beginning of the partner search process.

- What are the performance expectations for you and for your partner?
- What is the timeline? Milestones? Checkpoints?
- Do we have senior management's support? Are ample resources dedicated to managing the relationship?
- What are each partner's rights and obligations? Is there agreement?
- What information do we share? What do we hold dear?

From the gap analysis, you can ascertain which skills are resident in the supply chain and how the current supply base will fill gaps in the desired state (what skills are needed in the future). Then compare this with the current state (where you are now). If you need to develop certain skills, what is the plan for learning or acquiring the skill? If a new potential partner is needed to fill a gap, you need to understand the potential dynamics of adding a new partner. In the software arena, particularly in the enterprise software marketplace, there are very few, if any, firms that offer an end-to-end or complete solution. Adding modules from one firm might affect the relationship with another firm due to previous history and past dealing, as well as the current competitive landscape. At a minimum, the problems could be problems of compatibility.

The Garrett Engine division of Honeywell has a wide variety of customers, and its 350 suppliers provide about 90,000 different parts. There can be order fluctuations on the order of 20 percent up or down. The challenge is to ensure parts so that Garrett can meet a customer's order. Rather than negotiate for a number of parts on such a day, management has chosen to gain as much visibility as it can, both up- and downstream. By coordinating the ends of the supply chain, Garrett can better manage exceptions, stay lean, and utilize its suppliers as though they were an extension of Garrett. It is easy to imagine the cultural changes required to avoid the hedging and rely on honest data. Despite the number of vendors (e.g., Manugistics, i2, J.D. Edwards) whose software supports collaborative commerce solutions, problems often arise because people cannot get beyond the *I win, you lose* mentality of the past.

PARALLEL PROCESSING: UNDERSTANDING HOW TO MANAGE THE GAP

The gap analysis occurs on two separate but related levels. On one level, managers first determine the difference between the present state and the future state as it relates to market needs. The second-level gap analysis examines characteristics of the partners that must change so that the value-creation process continues to reap benefits for customers. The two equations below illustrate what the different gap analyses are. Equation 1 represents a relationship where a manufacturer (A) works with a supplier (B) to fulfill a market need that A does not have, nor does it seem reasonable that A develop that skill because B is more capable and has more experience, etc. You can easily imagine both partners working together but separately, using their competencies to create value but not attempting to leverage any of the potential synergies that might truly lead to a sustainable competitive advantage. Equation 2 represents a higher level of interaction between partners where they attempt to leverage their individual talents and jointly create a value proposition that results in a superior product/service that would be difficult to imitate. Imitation is difficult because partners combined their unique skills and expertise, and this tacit knowledge cannot be easily duplicated.

$$A + B = \text{competitive advantage} \tag{1}$$

$$A + B + (A \times B) = \text{sustainable competitive advantage} \tag{2}$$

There are two dynamics at work. On one level, the supply chain partners interact to create value in the marketplace. Here, skills are joined either in tandem or in sequence to meet the requirements of the market. For instance, you can develop a set of order-winning criteria and make decisions to make, buy, or borrow the skills or resources needed to compete. On another level, the way in which supply chain members interact will either enable or inhibit the value-creation process. Now focus on the nature of the interaction between partners and how well they implement the elements of extended enterprise thinking.

CREATING VALUE

Previously, you considered only the question of what skills are needed to create value. The answer to this question is relatively straightforward and entails understanding of the value proposition, what is important for customers, and how one extended enterprise can gain a differential advantage over competing extended enterprises. A sampling of the questions managers might ask is:

- What is it like to do business with my company (and my supply chain partners)?
- Describe a customer interaction. How does it vary by segment?
- In the minds of our customers, my company (and supply chain) equals?
- How is the combined value conveyed? Where do (can) we add value? Where do our partners add value?
- How does this align with customer needs?
- How does it differentiate our extended enterprise from the competition?
- What can we do better? Where do we have weaknesses that need improvement?
- What do competing supply chains do to better meet customers' priorities?
- What can we do to provide value to our customers' customers?

The goal here is to gain insight into the needs of the customer and how best to meet those needs through the skills and capabilities that lie throughout the supply chain. Although these questions present a less formal approach, there are more formal methods by which such information can be gleaned, such as conjoint analysis and focus group interviews. In addition, it is possible to ascertain *value in use* from direct observation of how customers use the product in the field. Notice that the questions above begin with the customer and focus the energy of the supply chain on solving problems for the end-use customer. Cost saving is still important; however, supply chain members now recognize that they must all sit at the table and design products and services that bring the supply chain a competitive advantage over other supply chains.

GE's small electric motor division provided parts for Carrier's residential air conditioning units.[12] Although the two firms worked together for approximately 15 years, the relationship never seemed to develop to become a true partnership. There were numerous performance characteristics that drove the relationship; each of the successive memoranda of agreement specifying the relationship emphasized productivity gains that were tied to cost targets and price reductions. Eventually, the 15-year relationship was modified, and Carrier now works with a competitor. Both companies missed an opportunity to truly be innovative and utilize their respective expertise to develop new technology jointly that could have created a differential advantage for Carrier and improve the profitability of both companies.

In part, Carrier's motivation for cost savings was dictated by a corporate mandate to achieve supply chainwide savings of $250 million in the three years ending in 2000. First, the goal was to leverage its buying power, then Carrier would look to developing deeper alliances with key suppliers. To the informed observer, it became clear that Carrier looked mainly internally for innovation and drove its suppliers to provide cost savings. Figure 4.4 illustrates how one might envision the information-gathering process and the importance of focusing on market segments because the array of product/service characteristics and the different value-adding attributes are likely to vary by market segments. For instance, transparency of information, speed of delivery, and service response time have been used effectively to segment markets.

Certainly from this template, it is possible to match current skills and capabilities with needs in the marketplace

Segment:

Customer Value	We Bring to the Market	Our Key Suppliers Bring	Our Key Competitors Bring
Order-Winning Criteria: Core Attributes Value Added	Resources? Competencies?	Resources? Competencies?	

FIGURE 4.4

Beginning to understand value creation by market segment.

and to understand whether there is alignment, then to begin the process of narrowing the gap, should one exist. This process results in understanding the different opportunities that confront both the individual supply chain firms and the entire extended enterprise. In pursuit of a market opportunity, it is possible that a new business model emerges that reconfigures the supply chain in order to gain efficiencies.

One such example is Cisco, which changed the traditional business model for telecom equipment because it is not a manufacturer in the mold of Nortel or Lucent. John Chambers had challenged the firm to achieve fast and profitable growth with minimal internal infrastructure. Under Chambers, Cisco began to rely heavily on third parties and contract manufacturers to produce for them. In fact, many products are shipped by the contract manufacturer directly to the customer. Relying heavily on the Internet, Cisco communicates with suppliers and customers who, in many instances, configure their own equipment on line.

Yet the mere fact that there are important components of value resident within the members of the supply chain does not guarantee that these skills will be effectively leveraged for the benefit of the customer. Very often, the synergies that are expected never materialize. As is the case with a number of mergers and acquisitions, the hoped for $1 + 1 = 3$ is often $1 + 1 < 2$. Changing the business model is necessary, but not alone sufficient to achieve the system-wide goals. In an extended enterprise context, we refer to these other changes as reflecting the spirit of the supply chain relationship.

Enabling Value Creation   A second gap that exists examines the different changes that must occur in how supply chain partners engage each other to achieve the value creation they both espouse. In some instances it might be required that skeptical parties lower their guard and truly work together to gain the unique benefits that accrue when partners combine their special talents and skills. Returning to the Carrier and GE example, the two partners failed to realize significant advantage by working together on new air conditioning technology such that the results would truly leverage the skills of both. Suppose that the marketing research data revealed that consumers preferred quieter units or higher energy efficiency, or that they wanted a unit that lasted twice as long as current models. These two great companies could have addressed these challenges through joint projects, thereby distancing themselves from Trane, York, or other competitors. Yet it appears that they viewed the market as primarily commodity-like and were unable to change this orientation. The two companies continued to work in sequence and were never able to work effectively in ways that might have built on skills possessed by the other. Another explanation is that they were so caught up in the true price-driven nature of the relationship that no hope of collaboration could occur with the current management on both sides responsible for the relationship. Neither party chose to engage the other in a truly collaborative manner for several reasons:

1. Incentives did not support such activities; metrics were mostly cost reduction-based.
2. The rules of engagement as defined in the memoranda of agreement contained very little language about collaborative action, particularly as it related to joint product development.
3. The parties could not get beyond a relationship in which information flows were controlled and monitored, and trust was limited.

Although not an explicit concern, Carrier's relationship with GE was (and is) very complex and, in other parts of the business, is somewhat contentious. Not only was GE United Technologies' (UTC) third-largest supplier, but GE and Pratt Whitney, another UTC division, also compete very aggressively in both the commercial and military markets for the sale of jet engines worldwide.)

THE THREE CS

The essence of the extended enterprise can be captured in the three Cs—connectivity, community, and collaboration—that serve to show the true distinctions between ordinary supply chain thinking and the systemswide view that is required by the extended enterprise.

Connectivity Connectivity illustrates the extent to which members of the extended enterprise are linked and the nature of the bonds that unite them for a common purpose. As noted elsewhere, supply chain *integration* is about information technology linkages and the different types and modules of enterprise software that connect buyer and supplier. From vendor-managed inventory to visibility throughout the different levels of the supply chain to demand and supply forecasting and other tools to remove the guesswork and waste found in logistics and other aspects of inventory management and replenishment, much has been written about providing information to the full set of supply chain partners. Again, the Beer Game provides a simple but powerful illustration of the point that the further a supply chain member is separated from actual customer demand, the higher the probability is that unnecessary levels of inventory will be carried in the pipeline.

Connectivity in the automotive industry varies from manufacturer to manufacturer, and the variance is quite large. For some tier-1 OEM manufacturers, connectivity is viewed mainly as being e-commerce-capable. That is, effort is directed first to consolidation of the supply base, then to deciding which lower tier suppliers will become electronically connected and will communicate computer to computer. It is interesting to note that tier-1 suppliers have low expectations and indicate that less than 20 percent of their second-tier suppliers are e-commerce-savvy.[13] Unfortunately, most of the time connectivity relates solely to achieving operational excellence and emphasizes inventory turns, order-to-delivery cycle time, order fulfillment, and so on. Yet for the extended enterprise, these are necessary but not sufficient points of focus.

Effective supply chain partners are linked through a rich array of data and information. Although it is essential to monitor issues of efficiency; the extended enterprise is more interested in questions of effectiveness. Beginning with information about achieving higher levels of customer service, a number of other considerations refocus the communications and information exchange to meet the following kinds of principles:[14]

- Customer feedback should be shared systemwide, and a formal mechanism should exist.
- Demand forecasts should be shared with suppliers, as should information about product development/obsolescence.
- Quality issues dealing with products and processes are the concern of all the supply chain members and should be shared in real time.
- Visibility is essential throughout the system and should be accomplished in real time.

As an example of these principals, Cisco Systems has long understood the importance of information visibility and its link to manufacturing and product quality. Cisco monitors quality (defect rates) at the source and shares customer feedback with these same suppliers. This ability to monitor at the source also enables better performance metrics and criteria for partner selection.

Envision a set of strategies that share common elements or accommodate the intent of other extended enterprise members. First, each member acknowledges the interdependence among all the partners. As a result of this recognized dependence, information flows more freely, joint actions become more predictable, and supply chain partners look to other supply chains as their key competitive threats.

Community The extended enterprise is truly a community of interest where firms with a set of compatible goals and objectives willingly work together to achieve a common vision or set of objectives. Similar to a community, there must be a set of norms, expectations, and shared values that establish how firms interact and what roles supply chain members play and that define the boundaries for what is considered acceptable behavior. These norms and values develop over time and are part of the social fabric (not the business relationship) that binds the members of the extended enterprise. A strong indicator of whether supply chain members can work together is the level of cultural compatibility. Earlier, you considered the spirit of the relationship and what supply chain members' value and hold dear as common principles that guide their behaviors and set expectations of how others should act.

Many companies hold supplier council meetings where information is shared and expectations around performance are developed. As a social structure, members of a supply chain develop expectations around issues related to information flows and the sharing of data. There are more subtle issues related to expectations surrounding investments, risk sharing and reward, problem solving, and the like. For instance, less harmonious supply chains might share information on a need-to-know basis only, and suppliers are kept in the dark. Implicit here is a desire for the buyer to leverage his or her position because information is power. Other supply chains are transparent, and each member understands the risk management process, where value is created, and the contribution each member makes. Information sharing is, to some degree, a metaphor for the level of respect given to the supply chain members based on their role and position in the value chain. Is there a defined pecking order with lower tier suppliers being viewed as second-class citizens? Do all members treat each other with respect? Do suppliers have a voice in the decision-making process? These questions speak to the social fabric of the supply chain and say a great deal about how members will relate to each other when problems and/or crises arise.

Collaboration   At the heart of the extended enterprise is a set of principles, processes, and structures that foster collaboration among the supply chain members. Collaboration occurs when firms share compatible goals and work jointly to achieve results that each could not achieve easily alone. Implied here is a recognized mutual interdependence where each party recognizes that their fates are linked and that there is no room for one to act in its own self-interest to the detriment of the other. Also, there is a shared understanding that contractual agreements cannot specify in detail the full nature of the relationship over time.

Recall that earlier we made a distinction between coordination, cooperation, and collaboration. Collaboration entails more formal processes than either of the other two, because processes and structures are put into place to accommodate joint planning, richer communications, and shared decision making. Although each partner maintains its own identity and autonomy, firms join to accomplish their shared objectives and goals. Collaboration requires a more durable and profound relationship due to their shared vision and motivations to achieve mutually beneficial outcomes. If there are equity interests to consider, the voting rights tend to split by the size of a partner's investment. What is essential is to realize that the process is open, all members' concerns are taken into account, and all are given voice. Motivation for such close ties can range from pure altruism to a concern about a common threat. It is rare that companies will join together for pure altruism because opportunistic behavior is often seen as the default option. In many instances, firms join together to block or counter the moves of a common rival. It is safe to say that most firms are motivated to collaborate by enlightened self-interest. Simply, it makes good business sense to partner, given the advantaged gained.

Aerospace/defense suppliers often engage in collaborative product commerce where engineering data are shared in real time. These data are generated from CAD, ERP, and other planning systems, and they span the life cycle of the project. This approach is in response to the increasingly complex requirements of new products, the expense associated with these efforts, and the need to reduce cycle time from idea to finished product. Although such a program appears to be a version of early supplier involvement in design, it does require a cultural shift away from the mentality that the prime contractor rules and the subs merely dance to the tune that is being played. Lockheed Martin was an early adopter of this program and used it effectively on the Joint Striker Fighter program.

Despite the positive press regarding collaboration, there are many issues to resolve around such important issues as relinquishing control, shared governance, and performance metrics. Given the past arms-length relationships that were prevalent across all business sectors, there are a number of challenges facing potential supply chain partners. You encounter in detail these issues in Chapter 7. It will suffice to say here that it is one thing to espouse collaboration and quite another to implement it in practice. All too often, supplier collaboration is a code word for price reduction and cost control.

SUMMARY

It should be apparent that although the extended enterprise offers a great many advantages over other forms of relationships, its tenets and principles have not been accepted universally, nor have they been adopted without much consideration and concern. First, these relationships must flow from the strategy of the firm and must be tied to the future intent of the firm. Second, these relationships are intended for only the most critical and essential components, subassemblies, or services. Third, not all qualified suppliers make good extended enterprise partners; supplier selection is based on understanding the gap between market needs and present capabilities and competencies.

Although you can easily appreciate the need to find partners who have complementary skills and allow partners to leverage the skills and resources of the entire supply chain, value creation is not enough. There are other factors that enable value creation. Among these factors are relational characteristics that foster collaborative behavior, supply chainwide learning, and information sharing up and down the supply chain. There is a natural tension that all supply chain partnerships face: the dilemma of cooperation versus competition.

What captures the notion of the extended enterprise are the 3 Cs—connectivity, community, and collaboration. Connectivity is far more than ensuring that the workflow is transparent and seamless in its efficiency. Linkages among extended enterprise partners should run the full corporate hierarchy where firms are linked for logistics and related activities *and* are involved in jointly planning, goal setting, and measuring performance utilizing systemwide metrics. Community reflects the fact that the extended enterprise is guided by a set of systemwide norms and values that develop over time and establish roles and set expectations regarding what is acceptable behavior. Collaboration captures the essence of the extended enterprise and builds from the sense of community. Supply chain members acknowledge that their fates and destinies are linked and actions that advantage one member to the detriment of others make no sense and, in fact, diminish the effectiveness of the enterprise.

5

OUTSOURCING IN THE EXTENDED ENTERPRISE

E arlier chapters of this book developed the notion that in the extended enterprise, the choice of suppliers and the management of relationships with suppliers should flow from the strategy of the firm and its recognition of what is of core importance and what is not. Outsourcing, as it has evolved today, provides a good example of this process. Before illustrating this, it might be helpful to review briefly the history of outsourcing and its recent trends.

BACKGROUND AND TRENDS

Outsourcing—the shifting of work to organizations or individuals outside the firm—is not a new phenomenon. Construction companies have always subcontracted large portions of their project work to outside contractors, and the federal government has long used contractors and subcontractors in the development of military equipment and weapons systems. In the general business area, Automatic Data Processing Inc. (ADP) began taking over companies' payroll functions, and EDS (Electronic Data Systems) began handling computer and data management for clients in the 1950s; Aramark Corporation has been running cafeterias for business organizations, colleges, and hospitals since the 1960s.

Outsourcing has been expanding rapidly since about the mid-1980s, as confirmed in a number of studies by both academics and consultants.[1–3] By 1991, the trend was so pronounced that Charles Handy predicted in his book, *The Age of Unreason*, that by the beginning of the twenty-first century, less than half of the workforce in the industrialized world would be in "proper" full-time jobs in organizations.[4]

Handy's prediction has not been verified in terms of percentage of workers but it seems to have come true, at least for some major industries, in terms of volume and variety of work outsourced. Experts estimate, for example, that today about two-thirds of the North American auto industry's $750 billion in value is created by suppliers to the OEMs, and the average electronics OEM was in 2002 expecting to outsource over 70 percent of its manufacturing.[5] McKinsey & Co. consultants report that the pharmaceuticals industry has seen the emergence of a $30 billion contract drug development and manufacturing market with annual growth rates of 17–20 percent,[6] and Dun and Bradstreet estimates outsourcing to be a $1 trillion global market.[7]

Forrester Research, the widely respected technology forecasting firm, identifies and analyzes emerging trends in technology and their impact on business. The high-tech sector has been shown to be a leading-edge industry in many respects, and Forrester regularly reports on outsourcing activities and trends in that sector. A recent Forrester report predicts that the U.S. outsourcing market in high-tech firms will top $226 billion by 2006—up from $103 billion in 2002. Forrester notes that long-term business pressures are driving U.S. companies to more outsourcing, with outsourcers steadily assuming responsibility for more and more business processes of the

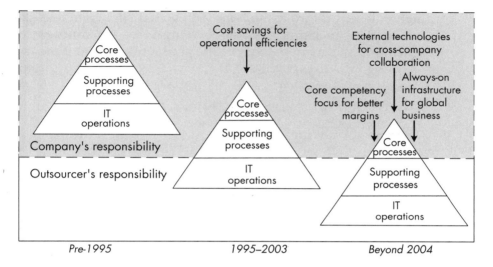

FIGURE 5.1
Long-term business pressures drive more outsourcing. *Source:* Forrester Research, Inc., March 2002.

typical large high-tech company ($1 billion-plus sales).[8] As illustrated in Figure 5.1, the dominant pressures are changing from cost savings to a focus on core competencies, cross-company collaboration, and global operations.

One factor contributing to the shifting pressures indicated in Figure 5.1 has been the increasing adoption of "lean manufacturing" and "lean thinking" principles in a number of manufacturing industries over the past decade. Lean manufacturing is another driver of increased outsourcing and cross-company collaboration. Lean enterprises outsource a high percentage of value-added of their products (sometimes more than 70 percent) yet have fewer suppliers than do traditionally organized firms. The higher level of outsourcing by lean manufacturers is driven by a focus on core competencies and a desire to reduce assets and costs. The heavy reliance on a smaller number of suppliers forces lean producers to develop close relationships with their suppliers because the firms are tightly connected through their production and new product development processes. Compared with traditional manufacturing practice, there is a higher degree of interdependence, higher levels of trust, and more blurring of organizational boundaries, including sharing of employees and increased sharing of information about costs, product design, and manufacturing processes.[9]

TRADITIONAL VERSUS NEW REASONS FOR OUTSOURCING

In the past, companies looked at outsourcing decisions as tactical decisions, with the primary emphasis on cutting costs in areas such as labor and overhead expenses. Although other reasons, such as access to new skills and technology, were important, the traditional main driver for outsourcing has been cost control. Management's outsourcing attention was typically focused on moving out parts, components, and portions of an activity or function to reduce costs as quickly as possible. Many companies continue to adopt a short-term perspective, as indicated by some recent studies that found cost savings still to be the number one motivation, particularly for manufacturing companies.[10,11] However, other recent surveys indicate that cost saving has been displaced by strategic factors as the primary reason for outsourcing. For example, the Outsourcing Institute's Fifth Annual Outsourcing Index, an online survey conducted in 2002 of 1,110 buyers of outsourcing services, indicates that more respondents (55 percent) singled out "improving company focus" than any other factor, with "reducing and controlling operating costs" running a close second (54 percent). Figure 5.2 shows the top 10 reasons for outsourcing, as reported by the survey respondents.[12]

BUSINESS PROCESS OUTSOURCING

The Outsourcing Institute's 2002 report suggests that the diminished role of cost cutting in the outsourcing process reflects the rise in popularity of business process outsourcing (BPO), along with an increase in emphasis on strategic reasons for outsourcing. As the report notes, the major trend in outsourcing since the mid-1990s has been toward increased outsourcing of entire business functions, products, and

FIGURE 5.2
Top 10 reasons companies outsource. *Source:* Outsourcing Institute, 2002.

processes, such as procurement, logistics, human resources, manufacturing, finance, and accounting. Although the information technology (IT) function ranked most popular in the 2002 study for all respondents, as shown in Figure 5.3, other functions, such as administration, ranked higher than did IT for small- and medium-sized companies.

Further documenting the increased popularity of BPO, another 2002 survey of European and North American business executives revealed that almost 90 percent of the companies surveyed outsourced IT or some key business function in the past five years, and 80 percent intended to spend either the same or more on business process outsourcing in the next three years. The study predicted that the BPO market will reach $1.2 trillion by 2006.[13]

Business process outsourcing is the vehicle by which a firm achieves improvements that affect enterprise-level performance. With BPO, the purpose of outsourcing extends to gaining competitive skills, improving service levels, and increasing the

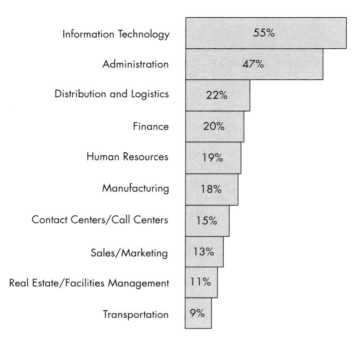

FIGURE 5.3
What's being outsourced today. *Source:* Outsourcing Institiute, 2002.

firm's ability to respond to changing business conditions. For example, a study by Accenture that examined active business process outsource firms revealed that many companies were engaging in collaborative relationships with outsourcing partners to create high-performance operations based on industry best practices.[14]

This approach to outsourcing is very consistent with the tenets of the extended enterprise on a number of dimensions and represents a departure from the more traditional forms of outsourcing. The differences are more than one of degree because there are distinctions that can be made between the decision to outsource ancillary services and the executive-level decision to transform the company through business process outsourcing. One of the major differences is the enterprise-wide focus that pervades managerial oversight, performance metrics, and the scope of decisions made. The outsourcing provider and the outsourcing firm must collaborate closely to ensure that the process works and that all interfaces are seamless; the intent is to push the envelope to drive value for the outsourcing firm. Fundamental to managing this relationship is a keen appreciation for the importance of the people involved and their ability to form and sustain a collaborative atmosphere, develop processes for shared risks and rewards, and foster a sense of joint commitment that begins at the highest levels of the firm and flows to the operational levels.

IBM: An Example of Transformation via Strategic Outsourcing Like component and parts outsourcing, BPO was traditionally employed in a straightforward manner typically involving the outsourcing of non-core activities to niche providers who could offer "best practice" processes in order to achieve cost savings and improve management's focus on more strategic issues. IBM's experience in the mid-1990s offers a good example of this approach. In 1994, IBM was a highly vertically integrated company that still made most of its own components for its computers. The company made 100 percent of its printed circuit boards (PCBs) and 85 percent of the memory chips used in its computers. It also made other components, such as keyboards and power supplies, and all of its PCs and laptop computers. Less than 45 percent of IBM's revenue was spent on outside suppliers, and there were no long-term supply contracts with its 4,900 production suppliers. With the high degree of vertical integration, there was also a great deal of secrecy. Gene Richter, IBM's head of purchasing, was brought in from Hewlett Packard in 1995 to effect significant change. As he put it:

> Everything at IBM was a secret; there was a feeling that everybody in the industry was trying to steal our technology and ideas, which was true 20 years ago. In procurement, we were the guardians of confidential information, the guard at the door who didn't let suppliers know anything. You couldn't have effective collaboration with suppliers because IBM didn't want suppliers to know what product their product was going to be used in. You couldn't develop volumes very well because the volumes planned were a secret. Parts would be shipped to central locations like Kansas City or St. Louis, and then we shipped them on from there so the supplier wouldn't know what plant it was going to.[15]

Under Richter's direction, the company dramatically changed its make-versus-buy policies and the way it viewed suppliers. Richter says that IBM realized that outside suppliers had technology that IBM needed and that competitors were reducing their costs by outsourcing. Although IBM could make many of its own critical components, so could other suppliers, often for less cost. So IBM began buying more from outside suppliers; by the end of 1999, the company was making only about 10 percent of its PCBs and 15 percent of its memory chips in house. In addition, the company introduced long-term supply contracts and dramatically reduced the production supply base, with 50 key suppliers providing about 85 percent of IBM's $17.1 billion (in 1999) in production purchases.

IBM's shift from manufacturing to outsourcing of non-core parts and components represents the traditional approach to BPO. But the IBM story also involves another aspect of BPO—strategic outsourcing. In addition to outsourcing parts and components, IBM also began outsourcing most or all of the manufacturing processes associated with some end products. Outsourcing of PCs and laptops to contract manufacturers began, to the tune of $3.5 billion per year, and workstations, mass-storage devices, and lower-end servers were also outsourced. IBM continued to build some high-end products, such as the System 390 enterprise server, because it was a complex product that required unique components and a sophisticated manufacturing process. The company's new philosophy was summed up by John Paterson, Vice President of Manufacturing: "Where we make a difference, we will build them ourselves; where we don't, we will buy them."[16]

The IBM story shows how strategic outsourcing can help transform a struggling, long-established manufacturing company into a competitive powerhouse. IBM dramatically redefined its core businesses, laid off or transferred from its payroll thousands of employees, and reconstructed its supply chain, in effect creating a different company. These efforts transformed the face of the company in that functions that were languishing were discontinued, focus shifted away from manufacturing to providing consulting services, and the traditional command and control/vertically integrated IBM repositioned itself as a more agile and responsive corporation. Ownership of computer hardware and component manufacturing is relatively minor at today's IBM, but the company's financial performance has catapulted from losses of $8.1 billion in 1993 to a net income of $8.2 billion in 2001 and $5.3 billion in 2002.

Dell and Nike: Leaders in Outsourcing   Dell Computer provides another well-known example in the same industry, but the Dell story shows how strategic outsourcing can revolutionize an entire industry. Dell concentrates its own resources on a superb customer knowledge and support system in the downstream portion of the value chain and a shared information system that strengthens its relationships with upstream suppliers. Dell relies on outside suppliers for essentially all component design and innovation and software, as well as all production except final assembly. By serving its customers directly, Dell captures vital market data and maintains a staff of dedicated managers for each major corporate customer. The suppliers, rather than Dell, provide both the scale of investment and depth of expertise needed to support innovations across a range of technologies and customer demands that Dell cannot satisfy alone. Dell grew at an 89 percent compounded rate for some years, achieving the highest sales productivity per employee in the industry. Dell continues to dominate its industry and achieved near-record financial performance for the 52 weeks ended January 31, 2003 of $35 billion sales and net income of $2.12 billion. Dell's competitors have tried to copy all or parts of the Dell model, and hundreds of managers from other companies in a variety of industries have visited Dell over the past several years to benchmark their operations and to study the Dell model for possible application to their own companies.

Nike is another company that has used strategic outsourcing to build a dominant position in its industry. Nike is one of the three largest athletic shoe companies in the world. Known as a shoe manufacturer, Nike outsources essentially 100 percent of shoe production and manufactures only a few key components of its patented Nike Air system. Nike creates maximum value by concentrating on pre- and postproduction processes (e.g., upstream: research and development; downstream: marketing, distribution, and sales). The company reportedly has the best marketing information system in the industry. Nike grew at a 20 percent growth rate and earned over 30 percent return on equity (ROE) for shareholders through most of the decade from the mid-1980s to the mid-1990s.[17]

STRATEGIC OUTSOURCING:
AN EXAMPLE OF THE
EXTENDED ENTERPRISE

IBM, Dell, and Nike are examples of companies that have implemented a "core competence with outsourcing" strategy to focus and flatten their own organizations so as to concentrate their resources on a relatively few core competencies and exploit the facilities, investments, and capabilities of outside partners. They are also examples of the fact that core competencies reside in key skills and knowledge, not products or functional departments. Core competencies involve activities and *processes*, such as new product development; and customer service, which cut across functions and should link with the processes of trading partners along the value chain, as noted elsewhere in this book and illustrated schematically in Figure 5.4. Recognition of this fact is why leading companies such as IBM, Dell, Nike, Toyota, and many others have put emphasis on developing highly effective cross-functional and cross-company processes that give them a competitive edge in selected dimensions of performance.

These companies also recognize that core competencies for any one firm are very limited in number. Some leading companies target no more than 2–3 core competencies in the value chain that are critical to future success, and they focus on those elements/activities that are important to the customers over the long run with unique sources of leverage where they can dominate. Some experts claim that 60–90 percent of most companies' in-house activities are services that are neither being performed at high levels nor contribute significantly to competitive edge, and can be outsourced at low risk if carefully managed.[18] This is one reason why successful

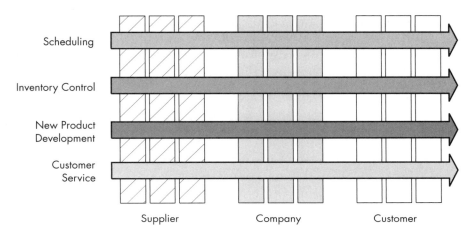

FIGURE 5.4
Process should link across partner firms.

companies in a variety of industries have been outsourcing non-core activities/processes, such as copying services, IT, etc. for which the firm has no special capabilities or advantages. Geoffrey Moore, in his book, *Living on the Fault Line*, terms these kinds of activities *context*, or background activities, in contrast to the core activities that directly impact the competitive advantage of the company in its targeted markets.[19]

Core value-creating processes determine the competitive capabilities of the firm; they may differ by industry and are critical to execute as perfectly as possible. Support, or enabling processes, on the other hand, indirectly or directly support value creation but don't help differentiate the firm. Enabling processes are prime candidates for outsourcing. Some value-creating processes may also be partially or fully outsourced if not found to be critical for competitive success. Past/current business pressures have been driving firms to increased outsourcing of non-core processes (enabling/support processes). New/future pressures are driving firms to outsource (partially or fully) some core processes also, to achieve rapid business transformation and improvement of internal processes. This will place increased emphasis on cross-company collaboration capabilities and new cross-company processes (which

Forrester Research aptly terms "intertwined BPO"), thus creating another version of the extended enterprise. To accomplish this transformational BPO, many extended enterprise capabilities will be required, including metrics and incentive/reward systems.

CHALLENGES TO GETTING THERE

Although outsourcing is prevalent today, evidence suggests that serious problems persist with some of these business partnerships. Dun and Bradstreet data on conventional outsourcing relationships show that 20–25 percent fail in any 2-year period, and 50 percent fail within 5 years.[20] Managers' fear of losing control—of their customers and their business—leads them to keep partners at arm's length. End customers suffer because this moves problems from one firm to another. According to some experts, today's partnerships tend to push inventory onto other partners along the supply chain, waste valuable information that could be useful to channel partners, and underserve end customers.[21] For example, in the automotive industry, some automotive OEMs' efforts to push inventory back onto their supply partners have hurt supplier performance; in the electronics industry, channel partners often block supplier visibility of end-user demand.

In the consumer packaged goods industry, retail companies often hoard customer information, which imposes costly data and process redundancy—costs that are passed on to customers.

One result of these situations is that some outsourcing firms have been stuck with excess inventory, as in the case of Cisco System's monumental $2.2 billion inventory write-down in 2001. Cisco, which became famous during the 1990s for being one of the most successful practitioners of outsourcing in the electronics industry, got into trouble because the company couldn't accurately interpret demand signals from its customers or communicate effectively with its lower-tier suppliers. To lock in supplies of scarce components during the boom years of the Internet, Cisco ordered—and agreed to pay for—large quantities well in advance of need, based on demand projections from the company's sales force. Cisco's customers, however, began placing multiple orders with Cisco's competitors, intending to accept only those orders that were delivered first. Suppliers—particularly at the second tier and beyond— would be swamped with multiple orders for the same key items. However, Cisco's supply chain management system couldn't show when spikes in demand at these tiers represented overlapping orders. Cisco became enmeshed in a vicious cycle of artificially inflated sales forecasts, artificially inflated demand for key components, and poor communication throughout parts of its supply chain.

Having learned from its costly mistakes, Cisco has begun to monitor the performance of its channels more closely. Working with software producer OneChannel, Cisco has dramatically reduced the variance in its ability to predict demand and take corrective action. OneChannel has developed predictive models that integrate and correlate leading demand signals and compare up-to-the-minute sales data with industry benchmarks through customized "dashboards" of key performance indicators. OneChannel's state-of-the-art ChannelMetrics software also alerts managers when demand is varying from the benchmarks and makes operational recommendations on how best to correct this variance. Members of Cisco management now indicate that the $2.2 billion write-down could have been significantly reduced with aid of the ChannelMetrics software.[22,23] Cisco has also radically improved its ability to communicate with its suppliers, implementing a new "e-hub" private exchange that connects Cisco with several tiers of suppliers and automates the flow of information using XML technology to simplify exchange of documents and information.[24]

The Cisco inventory write-down mentioned above is the most flagrant example of a number of problems suffered in the past three years by OEM companies in the electronics/telecommunications industry that have extensively outsourced their manufacturing activities to contract electronic manufacturers (CEMs). Sony, Apple Computer, Philips Electronics, Palm, and Compaq all had major product shortages; other OEMs were stuck with excess amounts of inventory that were either sold at losing prices or written off. Motorola, Ericsson, and others posted operating losses; Nortel laid off 10,000 employees, and Dell laid off 8,000. The aggregate loss in market value of 12 major OEMs, including Cisco, Dell, Compaq, Gateway, Motorola, and Nokia over the period from March 2000 to March 2001 exceeded a staggering $1.28 trillion.[25] Incidents such as these drew criticisms that the promise of outsourcing seems to be overstated and that outsourcing seems to have been carried too far.[26]

Subsequent analysis of the electronics industry problems by consultants from Booz-Allen-Hamilton revealed that many of the problems were due to misalignment of goals and poor communications between the OEMs and their CEM partners. The two parties had different inventory targets and different capabilities for—and attitudes about—surge capacity. OEMs were willing to pay for lower capacity utilizations and just-in-case capacity, whereas CEMs were tightly focused on lowest-unit-cost production. OEMs were committed to the end customer and would readily change production mixes to maximize production of fast-selling items, whereas CEMs were extremely reluctant to make schedule changes that might require purchase of materials at less-than-optimum bulk purchase prices.

The Booz-Allen analysis of the OEM-CEM conflicts concluded that the problems described were due to flaws in the practice of outsourcing, not with the theory, and noted that many of the OEMs failed to take time to understand the CEM's business model. Among the suggestions was the notion of "progressive" relationships between the OEMs and their CEM suppliers, which would allow flexibility of production changes over time. The Booz-Allen study concluded, "Outsourcing is here to stay. . . . For outsourcing to work, OEMs and CEMs must look beyond the deal. They need to step back and re-evaluate their relationship, realign the *processes, and evolve.*"[27]

Given the OEM-CEM problems cited above, it's not surprising that some outsourcing firms have compared their conventional outsourcing relationships with a marriage between the partners because of the difficulty of creating and maintaining frictionless working relationships. If this is true for these conventional outsourcing relationships, it's safe to assume that new, higher-collaboration levels of outsourcing will be equally or more challenging to manage for successful results.

One factor that will help improve the management of outsourcing relationships in the future is the increasing availability and use of new channel management and interenterprise management tools now being offered by software vendors such as Allegis, Bizgenics, Comergent, OneChannel, and WorldChain. Some of this new software combines business analytics, demand management, and supply chain execution to provide levels of cross-enterprise data visibility and event management not previously possible. The example cited earlier of OneChannel's enterprise ChannelMetrics implementation at Cisco is illustrative of this new category of IT tools. The focus of this new software is on letting all members of a supply chain, from manufacturer to distributor to plant to warehouse, access the same inventory and shipment data and work together to meet preset channel performance criteria. Having the capability to illuminate true demand, inventory buildup, channel performance, and profitability across the channel should enhance both partner performance and partner relationships.

Additionally, some guidelines for successful outsourcing relationships in the future can be gleaned from the world of lean manufacturing. As noted earlier, lean manufacturing firms typically outsource a very high percentage of their products' value-added content. In such cases, it's not enough to be the most efficient firm; what's important is to be part of the most efficient supply chain or network. Lean buyer-supplier relationships depend heavily on the nature of the product or services outsourced. The closest relationships are required when the buyer firm, i.e., the outsourcer, depends heavily on the supplier firm for innovation and design skills in the product or service being provided. Successful relationships are characterized by a high degree of interdependence; e.g., the buyer firm depends on the supplier firm for innovation and design content; the supplier firm depends on the buyer firm for both business and technical support. Although this interdependence is the glue that holds the lean buyer-supplier

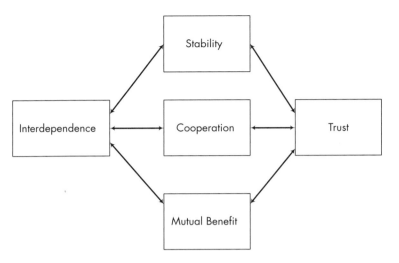

FIGURE 5.5
Factors in successful buyer-supplier relationships. *Source:* Cooper and Slagmulder, 1999.

relationship together, it is trust that enables the buyer and supplier firm to interact in closer, more sophisticated, and more mutually beneficial ways. As suggested in Figure 5.5, trust is created by the stability of the relationship and the high level of cooperation between the firms. Cooper and Slagmulder note that once the right level of relationship is established, the firms can begin to manage interorganizational costs and engage in practices such as employee sharing, shared research and development, dedicated equipment and facilities investments, and sharing of cost information.[28]

THE ISSUE OF CONTROL

The fear of loss of management control over outsourced products or services deserves special comment because of its continuing presence and impact on outsourcing results. In the past, vertical integration was the gold standard of control; all activities were housed under one corporate roof, and the chain of command (i.e., the organizational chart) was the indicator of who was responsible for what. As firms began to outsource activities, the organizational chart lost some relevance because control was now ceded to an organization outside the firm's boundaries. Suddenly, managers realized that they couldn't control what they don't legally own. In fact, for business process outsourcing to work, the outsourcer typically must assume legal, physical, and managerial control of the process. However, if control can be defined as the ability to influence or affect someone else's decision or the outcome of that decision, the issue of legal and physical ownership becomes less critical. If a firm can significantly impact the outcome of a decision made by another organization, it is not clear why that firm must own the process leading to the decision.

What is clear is that the manner in which the outsourcing firm's management affects the decision might well require skills that are not used in a more hierarchical setting. Skills such as, for example, open and honest communications, the ability to develop a shared vision, and the capability for achieving alignment in strategic direction and tactical execution might supplant the need for control (as in command and control). Numerous examples of successful outsourcing prove that it is quite possible, albeit initially uncomfortable for some managers, to maintain the essence of control without the physical ownership. The question really becomes, How does an outsourcer achieve the same level of comfort and assurance that comes with keeping the process and managing it internally? Asked another way: What is the nature of the relationship between the partner firms that reduces the psychic need for control and protects the concerns of the outsourcing firm? The evidence cited earlier from experience with lean manufacturing clearly highlights the overarching importance of trust, stability, and cooperation in the relationship. However, also implicit in the answer to these questions are several points that emerge from other observations[29,30] of successful outsourcing relationships:

- Understanding the culture and the values of both partners goes a long way toward bringing peace of mind to the outsourcing decision. Both the outsourcer and the outsourcing provider must take time to develop insights into each other's culture. If the outsourcing firm feels, for example, that the provider/supplier understands subtle issues that are woven into the fabric of the outsourcing firm that help guide behavior, outright control is less important.

- Trust building results in partners believing that one will not knowingly act in his or her self-interest to the detriment of another. In Chapter 7, trust is discussed in more detail; suffice it to say here that a key part of the outsourcing partner's selection process should focus on the character and trustworthiness of the supplier candidates. Additionally, flexibility in action and a willingness to adapt to changing circumstances despite contractual obligations go a long way toward building trust.
- Establishing jointly agreed-upon metrics (e.g., six sigma levels of customer satisfaction, improved cycle time, etc.) that remove or minimize uncertainty around outcomes serves to change the meaning of loss of control. Use of the new channel-tracking technology and the reporting of key performance metrics by the channel partner also can play an important role here.
- True competitive advantage and business transformation come only from continuous improvement and the push for leveraging new capabilities. Partners should agree to challenge the status quo and think strategically about their relationship. Conservative approaches that focus on risk minimization and cost reduction will never achieve the stretch goals.
- The outsourcing firm should not try to micromanage the process. This does not mean that management relinquishes oversight or does not set and communicate very clear expectations. The outsourcing partner should be clear as to what is expected and collaborate where necessary but otherwise stand back and let the mechanisms that are in place guide the process.
- Both parties should work diligently to establish a win-win environment. Managing to a set of contractual rights and obligations merely builds an attitude and standards of compliance with the contract. Innovation, continuous improvement, and

transformational activities do not come from partners who have no "skin in the game" and are merely following the contract.

■ Visibility and open processes substitute for control. The willingness to share sensitive data and information openly (on both sides) grows only if partners trust one another.

THE EXTENDED ENTERPRISE APPROACH TO OUTSOURCING

Table 5.1 outlines the approach to outsourcing in the extended enterprise and links it to the more general processes covered in Chapter 4. The entire process described below follows closely the path to effective extended enterprise thinking. This similarity should come as no surprise; transformational outsourcing symbolizes the potential of the extended enterprise and captures the best examples of it in practice. To begin, the decision to outsource (make vs. buy) must be tied to strategy and must link to the notion of core competence. What are the firm's goals? What is the desired future to meet the needs of key customers and to improve the firm's competitive position? What key skills and capabilities are needed to accomplish these goals? Should these skills/capabilities be kept in the firm or can they be resident with a partner? Leverage via partnering can provide cost advantages, new capabilities, and the opportunity to transform the business to bring it to the next level. Note that the approach delineated below does not address a total cost analysis or a methodology for determining relevant costs because the intent here is to bring focus to other aspects of outsourcing. Competitive cost performance is a necessary but far from sufficient condition for engaging in outsourcing. An extended enterprise framework implies that the outsourcing firm would establish outsourcing criteria that reflect a push to learn from the outsourcing provider, inculcate best practices, integrate business processes, and gain access to better skills and/or better technology.

TABLE 5.1 An Extended Enterprise Approach to Outsourcing

1. Establish a sense of strategic intent. Begin the conversation around future states.	**2.** Know what skills and capabilities are important for customers. Which ones provide a competitive advantage?	**3.** Compare those skills with your current set of competencies. Which processes are core and which are not?	**4.** If not core, should you develop them or can you rely on outsourcing to provide them?
5. If you develop a skill, do you buy it or grow it organically? What is the business case for each option?	**6.** If you outsource to gain access to the competencies needed, what criteria do you establish for selecting the best outsourcing partner?	**7.** Beyond cost, what other business-related criteria do you consider? How do you assign weights to each criteria? What is the final ranking?	**8.** How important are factors that affect the relationship? List the factors and establish rough guidelines for dealing with each.
9. Select and meet with partner and begin jointly to plan the future. Be assured that you share a common vision and have compatible cultures.	**10.** Negotiate from a win-win perspective. Build in checks and balances, maintain flexibility, and look for ways to build trust and commitment.	**11.** Be explicit about expectations and monitor performance according to jointly agreed-upon metrics that cover all aspects of performance.	**12.** Look for levers that build your business capabilities and capitalize on the strength of your partner. Encourage and reward performance improvements.

SUMMARY[31]

Business process outsourcing brings the outsourcing decision to a different level and should be seen as more complex and complicated than decisions to outsource ancillary services or to engage in contract manufacturing. The objective here is to change enterprise-level outcomes and to achieve payoffs that radically alter the existing business. The importance of a deep commitment between the parties has been addressed. In addition, there are other challenges to consider when embarking on this path. Successful companies:

1. Work hard to build relationships among managers assigned to the project. These more comprehensive outsourcing agreements cannot be at arm's length; they require that managers spend time together building personal relationships through both business and social interaction.

2. Attempt to broaden the scope of the outsourcing process so that both parties understand the importance of the enterprise-level thinking that drives these outsourcing projects. To think more narrowly might result in missing a critical integrative linkage.

3. Manage the change process so both sides acknowledge that, in part, these outsourcing relationships are a catalyst for change. Do not assume that either side will welcome change without some resistance. Plan for problems from the beginning.

4. Work to reduce misalignment at all steps during the process. Should any aspect of the outsourcing process begin to stray from the agreed-upon path or should the partners suddenly begin to waiver from previously stated commitments, goals, or performance metrics, swift action is required to resolve these differences.

6

INFORMATION SYSTEMS AND TECHNOLOGY ISSUES IN THE EXTENDED ENTERPRISE*

A key requirement of the extended enterprise is to achieve virtually seamless integration across organizational boundaries. As pointed out in Chapter 3, achieving this level of integration extends well beyond the challenge of information systems (IS) integration. The handful of companies that have achieved the vision of seamless integration have done so by meeting the broad challenges of process reengineering, change management, and supply chain collaboration. That said, the demands of today's global, customer-driven competitive environments have dramatically elevated the importance of IS—to the point that effective use of information technology (IT), IS, and the advanced business processes they enable is

*The majority of this chapter was provided by Steve Williams, President of DecisionPath Consulting, Inc., Gaithersburg, Maryland.

absolutely critical to achieving the business goals of the extended enterprise. Accordingly, effective use of IT must be a top priority for business executives within the extended enterprise so that IT initiatives are business-driven, not technology-driven.

Historically, IT has been important to the fields of purchasing, logistics, and supply chain management since the 1950s, initially for automating routine operating processes and subsequently for planning, controlling, and improving such processes. Many of these uses have been internally focused, due in no small measure to past technological obstacles to sharing data and software applications across organizational barriers. One such example is seen in the history of *electronic data interchange* (EDI), which began before the Internet and permits computer-to-computer exchange of business information and documents in a standard electronic format over dedicated or shared communication lines. EDI has produced significant productivity and efficiency benefits, including reduction of errors, reduction of response times, and reduced costs. In some industries (retail, for example), the percentage of transactions via EDI reached as high as 60 percent, but usage has plateaued overall at about 50 percent of transactions, according to some surveys. Although large manufacturers, distributors, and retailers adopted EDI as the standard means of information exchange with trading partners, the substantial setup costs and expertise required for trouble-free operation have limited its adoption by medium- and small-sized firms.[1] The advent of the Internet has essentially eliminated some of these technology barriers, creating new opportunities for trading partners to share information and to share and integrate business processes, all with a view toward improving overall supply chain performance.

The confluence of advances in IT capabilities, increased global competition, and elevated customer expectations has motivated industry leaders in a variety of industries to create systems and processes that facilitate cross-organizational delivery of information between members of the value chain. Those who have succeeded in using IS to help them compete as an extended enterprise have reaped a variety of business benefits, e.g., enhanced customer loyalty, increased revenues, reduced inventory, reduced time to market for new products, more effective business processes, reduced costs, and/or increased profits.

Earlier chapters have discussed the preconditions for achieving the goals of the extended enterprise, focusing primarily on non-IT relationship factors, such as trust, open communications, and alliance competencies. An assumption made in this chapter is that *these non-IT preconditions have been met or can be met.* Given that assumption, this discussion can then hone in on such strategic issues as the ways and means by which IT can be used to provide the infrastructure for seamless integration and the key management challenges faced in realizing the value of IT investments.

INFORMATION TECHNOLOGY AND ITS ROLE IN SUPPLY CHAIN INTEGRATION

For our purposes here, IT is defined broadly to include traditional IT infrastructure elements, traditional enterprise applications and legacy systems, the Internet, Internet-enabled applications, and business intelligence and analytic software.

The notion of virtually seamless information links within and between organizations is one of the essential elements of integrated supply chain management. As seen in some of the examples of Chapter 3, this means creating tight process and information linkages between functions within a firm (such as marketing, sales, finance, manufacturing, and distribution) and between firms, which allow the smooth, synchronized flow of both information and product between customers, suppliers, and transportation providers across the supply chain. However, any discussion of supply chain integration must move beyond high-level statements of strategic intent. Managers must move from generalizations such as "we will

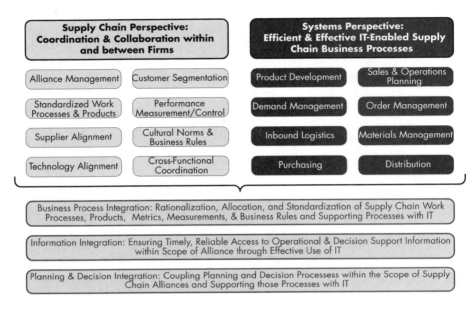

FIGURE 6.1
Elements of seamless integration. *Source:* DecisionPath Consulting research.

seamlessly integrate with our supply chain partners" to statements such as "we need to have the capability to allow our key raw materials vendors to access information about our inventory levels for their products on a real-time basis via a secure, access-controlled supply chain extranet." In the absence of such business-driven, process-specific require-ments statements, management simply can't ensure that the IT it deploys will enable seamless integration.

From a supply chain perspective, seamless integration is accomplished using relationship coordination and collabora-tion techniques to link business processes effectively. From a systems perspective, seamless integration is accomplished using *efficient and effective IT-enabled supply chain business processes* whose components work together correctly across the entire extended enterprise. The intersection between these perspectives emphasizes the use of IT to achieve deep and broad integration between companies, as suggested by Figure 6.1. This perspective is aligned with the higher level supply chain management objective of *optimizing the supply chain as a single system*, as opposed to each trading partner seeking local optimization, a path that has been shown to result in suboptimal supply chain performance.

Fundamentally, supply chain integration is about aligning and synchronizing the performance of the supply chain to meet the needs of end customers. To be completely effective, the collaboration to achieve this integration should be broad and strategic in scope. As shown in Figure 6.1, it should include integration of planning and decision-making processes, business operating processes, and information sharing for business performance management. There is considerable evidence that shows that this type of supply chain integration results in superior supply chain capabilities[2] and profits.[3] Furthermore, many of the strategic benefits of *vertical integration* can be achieved through *virtual integration* without the strategic costs of vertical integration. For example, Adaptec, Inc. of Milpitas, California is a "fab-less" semiconductor manufacturer whose products are marketed to the world's leading PC and server OEMs and to end users through more than 115 distributors and thousands of VARs (value-added resellers) worldwide. Products are designed and manufactured at Adaptec sites across the United States and Singapore and at various third-party fab locations around the world. Adaptec uses virtual integration software over the Internet to synchronize planning along its supply chain. Adaptec personnel at the company's geographically dispersed locations communicate in real time and exchange designs, test results, and production and shipment information. Inventory levels and lead times were reduced dramatically through use of the Internet-based collaboration.[4,5]

ENABLING SEAMLESS INTEGRATION WITH IT

Given the strategic business value of virtual integration, IT should be used to create *selectively permeable boundaries* among collaborating supply chain partners so that they can access the information and routines needed for specific functional applications as needed, yet not be flooded with

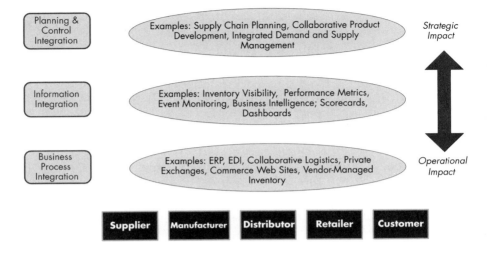

FIGURE 6.2
Supply chain view of seamless integration via IT. *Source:* Adapted from Sunil Chopra and Peter Meindl, *Supply Chain Management—Strategy, Planning, and Operation* (Upper Saddler River, NJ: Prentice Hall, 2001): 349.

unnecessary transaction data or unneeded analytical calculations. IT managers must partner with key business unit managers (internally and across firm boundaries) to define, develop, and deploy specific IT capabilities that promote planning, control, decision integration, information integration, and business process integration for the various members of the supply chain as needed. Different types of IT applications are needed, for example, for strategic versus operational planning, both at different levels within a firm and across all member firms of the supply chain, as suggested by Figure 6.2.

The horizontal axis of Figure 6.2 defines the scope, or range, of an IT system across the various partners or stages of the supply chain. There are IT systems throughout the supply chain, from end to end; some focus on only one stage, company, or function within a stage, but others cross multiple stages/partners and provide a broader scope of coverage. The vertical axis of the figure defines the type of decisions within a supply chain for which a particular IT system is used, such as strategic or tactical planning, or execution of operational plans. All three of these levels of decision making are necessary for each partner/stage in a supply chain.

Legacy systems tend to have narrow scope and focus on operational-level decisions for particular functions within an organization; they are typically built as independent entities with limited abilities for interaction and communication with other systems or stages. In contrast, enterprise requirements planning (ERP) systems span all functions within a particular partner/stage, have superior communication capabilities, and potentially can be expanded to include multiple partners/stages of the supply chain, as evidenced by some of the examples in Chapter 3. Obviously, not all supply chain members need all IT applications for every level of planning and control or access to all data across all stages of the supply chain. A key IT challenge in achieving effective supply chain integration is providing the right type of information to the right managers in the supply chain at the right time. Identifying the scope and boundaries of existing and needed IT systems is a necessary step in this direction.

PLANNING, CONTROL, AND DECISION INTEGRATION

Extended enterprise thinking is strategic, not ad hoc; thus, supply chain integration must include mechanisms that ensure that the extended enterprise is acting in concert over the long haul. This means that new product strategy, development, and introduction, as well as supply chain strategy, design, and operations should be done collaboratively. Further, decision pathways/architectures must be in place to ensure that joint strategic, tactical, and operational decisions can be made efficiently and effectively. Lastly, control mechanisms must be in place to detect and correct unfavorable variances from the grand plan. For example, the collaborative planning, forecasting, and replenishment (CPFR) approach being adopted in the grocery and consumer products industries encompass very specific business processes, enabled by IT, for preparing joint market-oriented plans, for translating those plans into forecasts and replenishment schedules, and for dealing with variance conditions.

INFORMATION INTEGRATION AND BUSINESS PROCESS INTEGRATION

Extended enterprise thinking takes a total system view of the supply chain, which requires timely information about the current state of operational processes up and down the supply chain, as well as business intelligence that enables forecasting, trend analysis, scorecarding, performance measurement, optimization modeling, and performance management. Extended enterprise thinking also takes the perspective of using IT and business process integration to create highly effective, customer-driven, and cost-efficient business process threads that are rationalized across the key supply chain partners. There are a variety of ways that IT can be used between companies to achieve business process redesign, including:[6]

1. Transforming unstructured processes into routinized transactions
2. Making processes independent of geography
3. Reducing the labor content of interfirm processes
4. Sharing information and analytical methods to speed and improve processes
5. Enabling parallel processing of tasks
6. Eliminating intermediate steps in a process
7. Providing the ability to track process status at a detailed level

Cisco Systems—A Case Study of Supply Chain Integration[7]   The wide retrenchment in the telecommunications industry has posed serious challenges to all manufacturers. Cisco Systems is among a select group in that industry that has bounced back from near disaster. After weathering a monumental $2.2 billion inventory write-off in 2001, Cisco returned to profitability for the year ending July 2002, despite a 15 percent drop in revenues. Cisco competes in the networking and communications equipment markets, offering products that help move voice, data, and video traffic across intranets, extranets, and the Internet. These markets are characterized by rapid technological innovation, convergence among key technologies, evolving industry standards, migration toward solutions (versus custom integration of systems), and changing customer requirements. Barriers to entry are relatively low because most of the products or solutions can be made from readily available components, and new ventures to offer competing products appear regularly. Cisco's competitors range from large multinationals, such as Fujitsu, Siemens AG, and Lucent, to focused competitors, such as 3COM and Nortel Networks.

To succeed in this environment, Cisco must bring innovative new products and solutions to market quickly and cost-effectively. The company's explosive growth during most of the 1990s led it to outsource heavily, as noted in Chapter 5, in order to have adequate manufacturing capacity. From a marketing strategy and product development perspective, Cisco has for years engaged in numerous strategic alliances to produce industry-leading products and accelerate market development. Cisco has alliances with partners such as EDS, IBM, Intel, Motorola, Oracle, and Sony, among others. Specific objectives and goals for these alliances include technology exchange, product and solution development, joint sales and marketing, and/or new market creation.

From an operating strategy perspective, Cisco collaborates with a variety of third-party contract manufacturers to obtain services for printed circuit board assembly, in-circuit tests, and installation of proprietary firmware on chips, product assembly, and product repair. For example, Solectron, an $18 billion electronics manufacturing services company, has core competencies in rapid introduction of new products, manufacturing, and supply management. Cisco capitalizes on Solectron's competencies and those of its other manufacturing partners to configure complex products to order that meet a wide variety of specific customer requirements.

As a means of supporting its strategy, Cisco created Cisco Connection Online (CCO) for customers and Manufacturing Connection Online (MCO), a business-to-business (B2B) supply chain portal for its contract manufacturers, suppliers, distributors, and logistics partners. Customers use CCO to diagnose network problems, find answers to technical questions, and order products. They can configure, price, route, and submit electronic orders to Cisco on an automated order-flow system. More than half of those orders go directly to Cisco's third-party suppliers, who in turn ship directly to customers. Cisco employees never touch the product. The site is also linked directly to Federal Express and UPS package trackers so customers can determine in real time the status of shipments. The use of CCO is not mandatory; customers can still have direct contact with live Cisco salespeople, a fact that gained Cisco a reputation as a leader in Web-based automated systems without having done away with the high-touch, personal face. The CCO portal shortened Cisco's order cycle by 70 percent (from 6–8 weeks to 1–3 weeks) and saved over $400 million in order processing and tracking costs in one year.[8]

The MCO portal was created to provide a central access point for manufacturing applications, reports, planning tools, forecast data, inventory information, and purchase orders. With the advent of MCO, Cisco's supply chain members didn't have to rely on faxes, email, or telephone calls. The Web-based applications implemented by Cisco allowed its first-tier contract manufacturers to interact with Cisco as though they were part of the company, creating in effect a *single enterprise*—the term that Cisco adopted for this external initiative.

MCO worked adequately until mid-2000, when a worldwide high-tech component shortage significantly affected Cisco and its manufacturing suppliers and customers. As noted in Chapter 5, a missing link in Cisco's supply chain management system caused second- and third-tier suppliers to overorder parts and components, for which Cisco was required to pay. The incident highlighted the need for increased visibility across the entire chain for all manufacturing supply chain partners. Cisco accelerated its "e-Hub" initiative to create a private e-marketplace that will provide seamless integration of interenterprise manufacturing supply chain planning, as well as execution processes. The primary goal is to deliver end-to-end visibility, optimization, event alerting, and performance, as well as other information beyond tier-1 manufacturing supply chain partners to tiers 2 and 3. By requiring all systems in the supply network to talk to each other, e-Hub ferrets out inventory shortfalls, production stoppages, and other problems almost as fast as they occur. By the end of 2002, Cisco had linked up about 150 suppliers and contract manufacturers, moving toward its ultimate goal of 650 manufacturing supply chain participant companies and about 2,000 total participant companies, including distribution and other units.

An interesting aspect of Cisco's e-Hub relates to the philosophy of information sharing and relationship management that has guided its development. Because of its commitment to long-term and mutually beneficial relationships, Cisco management wanted to create a manufacturing supply chain network focused on win-win manufacturing relationships, not on beating down suppliers for better prices through public auctions and automated supplier searches. Cisco encouraged the open sharing of information by creating extensive security measures that allow sharing among partners but prevent competitors from seeing each other's data. Users of the system feel that the level of information available through e-Hub "far exceeds that found in most manufacturing e-marketplaces in existence today."[9] Cisco's management indicates that such depth of information would not be possible without the strong security measures and the certainty that open sharing benefits all participants.

Cisco's single enterprise initiative—the combination of CCO, MCO, and e-Hub—provides a good example of how IT can be used to enable seamless integration within the extended enterprise. Figure 6.3 relates CCO and MCO capabilities to the elements of seamless integration described earlier—planning, control, decision integration, information integration, and business process integration.

> **Planning, Control, & Decision Integration: Coupling Extended Enterprise Planning, Control, & Decision Processes and Supporting these Processes with IT**
>
> ✓ Role-based supply chain event alerts based on defined decision rules
> ✓ Decision rules regarding inventory replenishment
> ✓ Collaborative product development

> **Information Integration: Ensuring Timely, Reliable Access to Operational, Planning, and Decision Support Information via Effective Use of IT**
>
> ✓ Forecast data
> ✓ Inventory data
> ✓ Open purchase orders
> ✓ Customer orders
> ✓ Customer order status
> ✓ Accounts payable information
> ✓ Application integration with trading partners

> **Business Process Integration: Rationalization, Allocation, and Standardization of Work Processes, Products, Business Rules, & Metrics and Supporting with IT**
>
> ✓ Access to Cisco ERP system integrates partners with Cisco MRP processes
> ✓ Automated routing of EDI data to suppliers
> ✓ Automated cross-organizational business processes, e.g., paperless POs and payments
> ✓ Collaborative new product development and introduction
> ✓ Real-time flow of customer orders to all partners
> ✓ Application integration with trading partners

FIGURE 6.3
Cisco Systems achieves seamless integration through effective use of IT.

Information technology enables Cisco and its contract manufacturers, suppliers, distributors, and logistics partners to *operate as an adaptive, market-sensing organism*, delivering a steady stream of innovative, customized product/service bundles on a make-to-order or configure-to-order basis. Through simultaneous availability of a variety of relevant information and IT applications, Cisco and its trading partners operate rationalized, parallel business processes that are standardized by agreed-upon business rules. All of the day-to-day operating processes, such as order management, demand management, purchasing, inventory replenishment, and logistics, are subject to codified business rules and cultural norms. For example, Teradyne knows that it has 4 hours from the time of a customer order to deliver finished backplane connectors to Solectron. Through the use of IT-enabled coordination mechanisms and collaborative processes, Cisco and its partners have achieved a level of cross-company operational effectiveness that results in a competitive advantage in meeting customers' needs and delivering shareholder value. This is the essence of what we mean by *seamless integration*, and it illustrates how IT can be used to enable the extended enterprise.

IT FOR THE EXTENDED ENTERPRISE

Prior to the commercialization of the Internet in the mid-1990s, establishing data communications linkages between geographically dispersed parts of a given company and/or between trading partners required substantial investment in specialized networking systems (e.g., wide area networks [WANs]). Further, the ability to share business applications between companies was limited and expensive.

An example of these technological limitations can be seen through the emergence in the early 1980s of EDI as a means of passing transactional information between trading partners. The ability to achieve this required the parties to the transaction to be connected, which created the value-added network (VAN) business whereby companies such as GE Information Services Company (GEISCO) and Sterling Commerce charged both trading partners annual subscription fees plus transaction charges to interconnect via their VANs. The fees involved were insignificant to large OEMs and their tier-1 suppliers but were out of reach for smaller suppliers, which limited adoption of EDI. Further, EDI as an application was batch-oriented, creating automatic time lags (order latency) between when an order was placed and when it was received. The cost of such order latency is pipeline inventory.

Today, the interconnections between companies are increasingly via the Internet. Transactional IT applications such as EDI have migrated to real-time Internet versions, and Internet-based business-to-business integration (B2Bi) technologies are being adopted to allow trading partners to create common applications that leverage each partner's prior investment in transactional IT, such as ERP systems and warehouse management systems. The Internet has changed the economics of sharing data, applications, and business processes within companies and between trading partners. Both the Internet and Internet-enabled applications software and business processes are "disruptive technologies" to some traditional businesses, but with demonstrated potential for enabling seamless integration and delivering differentiated supply chain performance that leads to competitive advantage.

STRATEGIC IT OPPORTUNITIES FOR THE EXTENDED ENTERPRISE

In formulating an IT strategy for the extended enterprise, the key question is how IT can be used within and between companies to enable, automate, improve, and/or inform the whole panoply of supply chain business processes (e.g., order management, distribution planning, production planning, capacity planning, invoicing, inventory management, product development, bills of materials management, customer service). A useful approach for looking at the types of IT used by companies is the IT portfolio framework proposed by Weill and Broadbent,[10] from which Figure 6.4 has been adapted to illustrate the types of IT investments that must be managed to enable the extended enterprise. The framework distinguishes between four main categories of IT investment. Strategic IT consists of applications that provide a competitive advantage to the first mover and is exemplified by Cisco's use of IT to outperform its competitors. Informational IT is used for planning and controlling the enterprise or extended enterprise. Transactional IT is used to automate, streamline, and integrate day-to-day transactional business processes, such as taking and fulfilling customer orders. Infrastructure IT provides the basic "plumbing" or "wiring" that allows the other categories of IT to work.

| **Strategic IT** |
| e.g., Collaborative Product Development, Customer Service, Integrated Demand and Supply Management |

| **Informational IT - Planning, Control, & Decision Support** |
| Business Intelligence & Analytical Applications: Data Marts, Dashboards, Trend Analysis, Metrics, Multidimensional Analysis, Balanced Scorecards, Customer Relationship Management; Business Performance Management; Spend Analytics |
| Supply Chain Planning/Advanced Planning & Scheduling, Demand Forecasting, Capacity Planning, Distribution Requirements Planning, Available -to-Promise, Capable-to-Promise, Inventory Planning, Inventory Visibility, Event Monitoring, Production Planning, Supply Network Design & Optimization |

| **Transactional IT—Business Processes** |
| Supply Chain Execution: EDI, Order Entry, Order Management, Transportation Management, Warehouse Management, e-Commerce, Inventory Visibility, ERP II |
| Enterprise Resources Planning (ERP): Financial & Management Accounting, Asset Management, Logistics, Material Management/MRP, Production Planning, Plant Maintenance, Quality, Sales & Distribution, Human Resources, Payroll, Others |
| Manufacturing Execution System (MES): Finite Scheduling, Material Movement, Work Orders, Inventory, Process Data, Process Control, Timeclock |

| **Infrastructure IT:** |
| Internet, Intranets, Extranets, Value-Added Networks, Workflow, Application Integration, Commerce Web Sites, Portals, Public Exchanges, Private Exchanges, XML, Web Services, Security, Wireless, Bar Code Scanners, RFID Tags, Servers, Mainframes, Data Warehouses, etc. |

FIGURE 6.4
IT portfolio for the extended enterprise. *Source:* Adapted from Peter Weill, and M. Broadbent, *Leveraging the New Infrastructure* (Boston: Harvard Business School Press, 1998).

IT INFRASTRUCTURE

Historically, *infrastructure* meant mainframe computing plus telecommunications, and in the 1990s it came to include client-server computing, as well. Today, infrastructure also includes commerce-enabled Web sites, extranets, intranets, private trade exchanges, portals, and public exchanges. Some say that the Internet is the infrastructure, and we cannot seriously consider achieving seamless integration without including the Internet as part of our IT infrastructure. This means that companies and their trading partners are facing or will face decisions about how to incorporate the Internet and emerging Internet computing technologies, such as Extensible Markup Language (XML), Web services, and B2Bi, into their legacy infrastructures. Some may elect to outsource the entire issue through traditional outsourcing deals with companies such as EDS or Computer Sciences Corporation, through the use of application service providers (ASPs), and/or through the use of public or private exchanges managed by third parties.

Because infrastructure can specifically affect such dimensions of organizational performance as revenue growth, return on assets, time to market, sales from new products, and product or service quality,[11] we prefer to think of infrastructure as the equivalent of the offensive linemen on a football team, whose effectiveness often determines the success or failure of the entire offensive unit. In other words, without an appropriate IT infrastructure, businesses have little chance of using IT as an offensive weapon and no chance of operating as an extended enterprise.

TRANSACTIONAL IT

The day-to-day workhorses in the IT portfolio are transactional applications, the most visible of which is often an ERP system. Other common transactional applications include manufacturing execution systems for shop floor control, warehouse management systems that track the locations of raw materials and finished goods, and commerce-enabled Web sites that allow customers to select and/or configure products and place orders. A fundamental IT strategic concern in an extended enterprise context is to link the transactional IT systems of the various trading partners. The goal is to achieve the kind of seamless integration recently being achieved by Cisco Systems with its e-Hub implementation and single enterprise concept.

There is a close similarity between transactional IT for the extended enterprise and the use of ERP within a single company. In the single-company context, ERP is used to make internal, interdepartmental transactional business process flows more efficient and effective. In the extended enterprise context, the Internet is used to link the transactional IT systems of the trading partners to achieve efficient intercompany business processes and more effective customer service. This similarity explains the use of the term *ERPII* by some in the IT industry to denote the use of

Internet-enabled transactional applications between trading partners. The similarity also presages some of the challenges that will be encountered along the path to seamless integration. One such challenge is the need for process reengineering across company boundaries.

INFORMATIONAL IT

Informational IT is oriented toward planning, analysis, control, information sharing, decision support, and performance improvement activities within a company and, increasingly, along the supply chain. A powerful example of an informational application for the extended enterprise is the ability to make inventory information available via the Internet so that suppliers can analyze when to replenish a customer's inventory of a product that they make. For example, regional grocery retailer H.E. Butt relays point-of-sale information on a near real-time basis to major food manufacturers' warehouses to allow the manufacturers to plan replenishment based on actual inventory positions and usage information.

In the extended enterprise context, informational IT supports planning integration, control integration, decision integration, and information integration. It is critical that the managers and operating personnel responsible for supply chain performance have the information and applications they need to:

- Make and act on joint plans
- Monitor and measure actual performance
- Compare actual performance with targets
- Take action to correct operating problems
- Direct continuous improvement initiatives
- Measure the results of improvement initiatives

Informational IT in the extended enterprise can be as simple as making retail point-of-sale information available to the entire trading community or as complex as implementing a closed-loop business performance management system across multiple companies.

STRATEGIC IT

Some IT investments are strategic applications designed to deliver a competitive advantage. This is especially true if competitors cannot easily replicate the application. Cisco's CCO and other Internet applications provided a competitive advantage that allowed Cisco to achieve higher growth and greater shareholder returns for a number of years in the 1990s. Another recent application is collaborative product development in industries such as automobiles or consumer electronics, where time to market is a competitive variable.

The fact that relatively few companies have thus far been able to achieve seamless integration presents a strategic opportunity. The commercialization of the Internet is relatively new, as are many of the Internet-oriented infrastructure technologies, such as XML, enterprise application integration (EAI) software, B2Bi software, and Web services. Further, many companies have yet to deploy robust informational IT internally, let alone among trading partners. So any group of companies that can make substantial progress toward planning, control, decision integration, information integration, and business process integration (collectively, seamless integration) stands a good chance of gaining a competitive edge in many industries.

REACH AND RANGE IN THE EXTENDED ENTERPRISE

The ability to select intelligently and deploy effectively the four categories of IT discussed above (infrastructure IT, transactional IT, informational IT, and strategic IT) can constitute a significant competitive advantage. By aligning the use of IT among trading partners and making IT applications accessible via the Internet, there is a dramatic increase in the possibilities for interfunctional, interfirm collaboration among supply chain partners. These kinds of shared applications are the essential building blocks of an IT strategy for the extended enterprise.

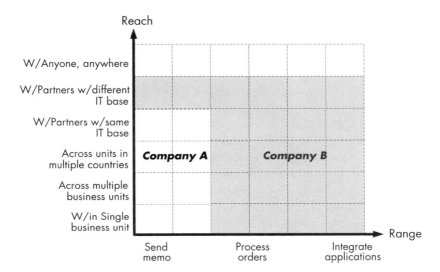

FIGURE 6.5
The concept of Reach and Range.

One useful construct for helping to think about shared IT applications is the notion of *Reach and Range*, introduced by Keen in 1991.[12] Reach is whether two parties can connect, and Range is what they can do together if they can connect. Figure 6.5 illustrates these concepts, showing the different capabilities of two hypothetical companies. Company A can connect with supply chain partners who have the same IT base but can perform only a limited range of actions. Company B can reach supply chain partners with different IT bases and can perform a broad range of business processes. Company B can reach more potential partners and can execute more business processes. In other words, Company B is further along the path to seamless integration.

In the pre-Internet days when Keen developed this framework, the ability to telecommunicate (Reach) within and between firms was far more difficult than it is today. One of the substantial impacts of the Internet has been its ability to extend and enrich Reach dramatically for all companies having access to it. More specifically, the Internet extends the ability of any company to communicate with its trading partners, and it enriches Reach by enabling more economical interoperability between the separate information systems of the extended enterprise. With such Reach comes the ability to deploy IT effectively to support planning, control, decision integration, information integration, and business process integration. These are necessary conditions for seamless integration.

Although effective Reach is crucial, experience in the IT industry suggests that it will become a commodity more quickly than Range. From an extended enterprise perspective, the potential for competitive advantage thus resides primarily in the Range dimension. The ability to connect to and achieve technical interoperability with customers and suppliers (Reach) is not likely to be a differentiator for long. Rather, it is more a matter of what being connected allows one to do (Range). For example, Dell has deployed IT that allows it to perform a broad range of tasks with its customers and suppliers via the Internet, including processing orders, placing purchase orders, providing order status information, and managing inventory. Compaq and Gateway have been able to reach the same customers via the Internet, but for years neither company could replicate the range of business services available at Dell's site.

CAPITALIZING ON IT OPPORTUNITIES FOR THE EXTENDED ENTERPRISE

The ideas and frameworks described thus far can be used to help guide the process of developing a coordinated strategy for IT in the extended enterprise. These frameworks would typically be used in the context of strategic IT planning concerning the types and timing of IT investments. The models can help managers systematically assess the specifics of planning, control and decision integration, information integration, and business process integration to achieve the goal of seamless integration. Once this is understood, the connectivity required to support such integration (the Reach dimension of the framework) can be determined. At that point, the IT portfolio framework can be used to assess the current state of IT use and capabilities among the relevant set of trading partners, to define and gain concurrence on a target

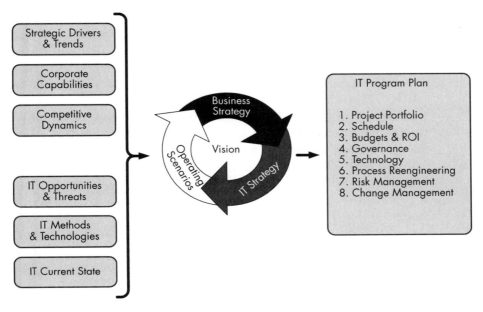

FIGURE 6.6
Possible IT strategic planning process.

end-state, and to define a migration path to the goal. This process would include consideration of alternative IT technologies, IT architecture and tools, and funding, program and project management, and staffing.

Figure 6.6 illustrates a typical IT strategic planning process that might be used in defining and prioritizing IT projects aimed at seamless integration. Although the analysis and planning aspects of this process are relatively straightforward, there are a number of IT-related challenges that must be overcome in order to realize the business value of the extended enterprise.

THE CHALLENGE OF BUILDING CONSENSUS ABOUT IT DIRECTION

One of the principal challenges to achieving seamless integration involves building consensus about IT strategy, which is hard to do in a single firm of any size, let alone across multiple firms. That is why many of the success stories concerning IT use among trading partners feature strong channel leaders who are close to the ultimate customer and who have the buying power to influence the pace and direction of IT investment upstream in the supply chain. The ability to drive IT strategy has the advantage of efficiency because it avoids or minimizes the messiness of trying to achieve consensus on an IT strategy and vision among trading partners, many of whom will have made substantial investments in IT and might have to make new IT investments that could be ill-timed from their specific business perspectives.

With the power of the channel captain comes the ability to execute an IT strategic planning process, then drive the specification of an IT architecture and associated migration path. Absent such power, it is difficult to gain consensus on a technology direction due to the previous IT investments of the respective trading partners and the likelihood that a given company will be operating in more than one extended enterprise, thus facing the need to integrate with more than one IT architecture. Although these problems may eventually be addressed as the IT industry gets better at B2B integration, enterprise application integration, and distributed computing, they will remain a significant hurdle for the next decade or more, due largely to the challenges of IT integration across different firms.

THE CHALLENGE OF IT INTEGRATION

Assuming that a strategic direction and architecture for enabling the extended enterprise can be agreed upon, there still remains the substantial challenge of IT integration, which has been the holy grail of the IT industry for years. Historically, the approach to IT integration has been to develop custom point-to-point integration programs between relevant IT applications. This approach worked fine with a small number of stable applications and business processes, but as rapid IT innovation led to newer versions of existing applications and/or to new applications enabling better business processes, it became clear that point-to-point integration could not be sustained in many large companies due to the difficulty of maintaining the growing number of customized integration programs in the face of change.

The limitations of point-to-point integration led to the need for a more flexible and maintainable approach to integration. The response during the 1990s was ERP systems for internal IT integration, EAI software for companies that wanted to maintain their "best-of-breed" applications in lieu of going to a single ERP platform, and B2Bi software for IT integration across companies with different IT platforms. The 1990s and early 2000s also spawned such integration enablers as XML, integration servers, Web services, and distributed computing. All of these recent innovations are just making their way into the IT mainstream, pushed mainly by the business integration opportunities spawned by the commercialization of the Internet.

The difficulty of IT integration is attested to by the massive costs and the sometimes spectacular failures of ERP deployments, such as at Hershey Chocolate Company in the fall of 2000, at Nike in 2001, and at Agilent Technologies in 2002. ERP systems are intended to replace a collection of functionally oriented business applications with an integrated suite of applications; thus, ERP packages represent a *pre-integrated* IT solution. A core value proposition claimed by ERP vendors is that their ERP packages *reduce the risk associated with custom integration of functional systems*.

In the Hershey case, the initial deployment of SAP's ERP package failed, despite years of planning and multiple millions in consulting fees. The failure cost Hershey millions in profits due to stockouts on store shelves during the weeks leading up to Halloween. Nike's ERP debacle of similar magnitude was widely publicized in the media, as was Nike's publicly putting the blame on its software supplier, i2 technologies. Agilent Technologies blamed trouble in implementing its ERP system—involving a changeover from multiple ERP systems to Oracle software—for a $105 million revenue shortfall and a $70 million shortfall in operating profits, causing the company to lose $228 million in its third fiscal quarter. Agilent's CFO was quoted as saying, "On balance, our implementation experience was about normal."[13] If "pre-integrated" IT solutions can fail in a single-firm environment, as illustrated by the Hershey, Nike, and Agilent examples, there is little reason to believe that custom integration of IT applications across the organizational boundaries of trading partners will be easy.

The difficulty of IT integration is also attested to by the existence of IT integration business units at major systems integration companies. These firms would not have such practices unless they were reasonably certain of significant market opportunities for these services. Whether it is called *enterprise integration, e-technology integration,* or *extended enterprise applications*, these major integrators and their packaged software partners are poised for major IT integration projects aimed at helping trading communities integrate key applications that enable planning, control, decision integration, information integration, and business process integration.

THE CHALLENGE OF MULTIPLE IT INTEGRATIONS

In typical discussions of supply chain integration (or collaborative commerce or virtual integration), a simplified linear view of a supply chain is used to illustrate the physical, informational, and financial flows between companies in the supply chain. Then the discussion turns to how to optimize the subject supply chain, which gets into supply network design, best practices, business process reengineering, collaboration, information sharing, gain sharing, performance metrics, scorecards, and other related topics. In many cases, however, a given company in a given supply chain will also be operating in a number of other supply chains. This raises the challenge of multiple IT integrations.

For example, when Ford, General Motors, and Chrysler each launched e-business initiatives in the late 1990s with a view toward online exchanges (e-marketplaces) to enable collaboration in product development, demand management, production scheduling, order processing, and procurement, tier-1 suppliers balked, citing the difficulty in needing to have IT integration with three separate exchanges. The resistance of key suppliers drove Ford, General Motors, and Chrysler to combine their e-business initiatives into one, which became Covisint.

With the extended enterprise, the challenge of multiple IT integrations will increase and is not easily solved. However, the success of some companies in seamlessly integrating their ERP systems with multiple vendors/customers (such as PolyOne and others described in Chapter 3) shows that multiple IT integrations are being achieved, with huge benefits.

OTHER IT CHALLENGES

Successfully using IT to enable seamless integration in the extended enterprise also requires the ability to manage a range of other challenges, including governance in a multicompany context, navigating IT initiatives through the capital budgeting systems of the trading partners, managing the risk-reward tradeoffs across multiple companies, and reengineering business processes across companies. One metric of the latter challenge is offered by a retired supply chain executive from Procter & Gamble, who notes that major collaboration efforts that entail business process reengineering between just two trading partners can take 12–18 months: 6 months just to figure out what is going on between the two businesses and another 6–12 months to plan and execute changes.

A VIEW OVER THE HORIZON

Business use of IT has come an incredible distance in the past two decades, adding demonstrable value to those companies that successfully harness IT and challenging the competitive positions of laggards. In the last 10 years alone, enterprise applications such as ERP, supply chain management (SCM), and customer relationship management (CRM) have emerged and been adopted by many of the largest companies in the world, as well as a growing number of mid-sized and smaller companies. Individual companies have invested tens of millions of dollars, and the associated business process changes have often been wrenching, as indicated by the examples of Hershey, Nike, and Agilent. The amount of time it has taken to roll out ERP to major companies and the cost of doing so suggests that the journey toward IT-enabled seamless integration may take longer periods of time than one might expect within an extended enterprise context. As with any journey, it helps to have a view of what the final destination will look like, even if it is somewhat hazy. What follows is a view of some key IT-related attributes of the companies that will have successfully used IT to enable seamless supply chain integration.

WINNING COMPANIES WILL EXCEL AT IT INTEGRATION

A key business motivation for the extended enterprise is agility in response to emerging market opportunities. With rapid innovation in many industries comes the need for companies to pool competencies and resources to get to market faster than rivals. A key element of getting to market quickly is IT integration—being able to put quickly in place such key business processes as collaborative product development processes, sales and operations planning processes, and supply chain operational processes via IT. Companies that excel at IT integration will have an advantage in the marketplace.

BUSINESS PERFORMANCE MANAGEMENT SYSTEMS WILL DRIVE CONTINUOUS IMPROVEMENT AND REAL-TIME RESPONSE

A key enabler of planning, control, and decision integration will be multicompany applications of closed-loop business performance management (BPM) systems. The ability to achieve IT integration at the levels of transactional IT and informational IT will set the stage for being able to measure current supply chain operating performance in or near real time, compare actual results with goals, trends, and/or benchmark data, compute variances, notify appropriate people when variances exceed established thresholds, and provide the IT-enabled means to take action. The closed-loop BPM systems of the future work like statistical process control systems do today, except the process being controlled will be supply chain operations. The extended enterprise that becomes proficient at BPM will have the information needed for continuous process improvement and real-time response to performance issues that affect customer service, asset levels, quality, and cost.

DECISION PATHS AND ANALYTICAL ROUTINES WILL ENABLE DECISION INTEGRATION

IT integration and closed-loop BPM systems will deliver the raw information and performance metrics that will enable the extended enterprise to act quickly and in concert in response to performance issues and improvement opportunities. As part of this process, typical categories of supply chain performance problems will be known and catalogued, and standard options for correcting each problem will have been defined. Alerts generated by the BPM system will trigger standard analytical responses and use workflow technology to send the raw information and analytical results to decision makers, who will act according to prescribed decision processes and timetables. The analytical routines will range from simple decision tree analysis to complex optimization routines. The extended enterprise that deploys decision paths and other analytical routines will be more agile than its competitors.

BUSINESS INTELLIGENCE AND ANALYTICAL APPLICATIONS WILL DELIVER PROCESS INTELLIGENCE AND INFORMATION INTEGRATION

Successful extended enterprises will have invested in business intelligence systems and analytical applications to achieve information integration, which will support BPM systems, decision paths, and analytical routines. These systems will draw information from the transactional IT systems of the various trading partners in the extended enterprise and provide secure access to real-time and historical performance information on a self-service basis. The successful extended enterprise will take advantage of supply chain event monitoring, inventory visibility, supply chain analytics, and scorecards to deliver process intelligence at all times and quickly respond to problems and opportunities.

IT EXPERTISE WILL BE MANAGED AS A CORE COMPETENCE AND COMPETITIVE DISCRIMINATOR

Winning companies will recognize the importance of IT to their business strategies and to their ability to participate in extended enterprises. They will understand that they need to make fully considered, careful decisions about which elements of their IT portfolios can be safely outsourced and which have the potential to deliver competitive advantage and should remain in house. They will have invested in the human and technology assets to develop skill in IT integration, business performance management, decision paths, analytical routines, business intelligence, analytical applications, and process intelligence. All of these capabilities affect the company's attractiveness as an extended enterprise partner, and the winning companies will have recognized that not every company will be able to excel at exploiting IT.

SUMMARY

Information technology is a key enabler of the seamless integration that is the goal of the extended enterprise. In conjunction with process reengineering, alliance competence, and change management, IT can be deployed to enable planning, control, decision integration, information integration, and business process integration—which allow key companies in the extended enterprise to operate as though they were a single enterprise. To get there requires strategic IT leadership and the ability to manage an IT portfolio across functional and company boundaries. Managers in supply chains that can achieve the necessary IT integration and deploy the right IT applications faster than their competitors will achieve stronger competitive advantage and deliver higher value to their stockholders, owners, managers, and employees.

7

TRUST, THE GLUE THAT BINDS THE EXTENDED ENTERPRISE

B ecause business issues and personal relationships lie at the core of the extended enterprise, trust must be a condition necessary for firms to work closely. Trust manifests itself in the integrity of information shared, in the belief that partners will do as they say, and in the willingness to share risk and reward equitably in pursuit of common goals and interests. This chapter develops the concept of trust and shows how it is central to developing extended enterprise thinking and to putting these ideas into practice. Trust is truly the cornerstone of any extended enterprise because it is the foundation for social order.

A chapter on trust faces two major challenges, given the state of business in the United States during the early years of the 21st Century. First, there was a pronounced loss of confidence in business in the wake of Enron, Tyco, WorldCom, and a host of other companies where individual greed, financial improprieties, and outright fraud, theft, and management monopolized the daily press for a time. This first point casts a pale over the entire business climate.

The second point is more specifically germane to the supply chain and describes more the nature of how business gets done. The United States is contract-driven to the point that formal contracts are fundamental to how business is conducted, and procurement is no exception. In fact, the reliance on contractual obligations surrounding price, delivery, and other aspects of the purchase order has been the standard by which buyers worked with suppliers. Not having these terms and conditions in writing does not compute for buyers who share a fundamental mistrust of suppliers. Buyers are convinced that suppliers will take advantage of them and will find every loophole and exception. They argue that contracts are the only way to manage when there is no trust.

However, in conversations with alliance managers who orchestrate global collaborative relationships, it would appear that a singular focus on contracts is unhealthy and potentially dangerous. Initially, they ask why a buyer would sign a contract with someone he or she does not trust. Then they state that a contract cannot substitute for trust, and the two should not be confused.

In earlier chapters, you encountered the notion of contract management and considered the number of software tools that enable the contracting process by providing data throughout the different phases of project management or the procurement decision-making process. One objective of these tools is to ensure that suppliers understand the terms and obligations of the contract; another is to communicate to all stakeholders throughout the buying process. Without trust, it is unlikely that firms will achieve or even be willing to entertain the level of collaboration that is essential.

Contracts are important but within the extended enterprise paradigm, buyers and sellers manage relationships and a business. They should not manage the contract so that it takes on a life of its own. This is not to say that contracts are unimportant. To the contrary, contracts ensure among other things that both sides understand what has been agreed to, despite changes in leadership, ownership, etc. Thus, the contract becomes the institutional memory of the formal relationship among trading parties and captures the conditions under which the contract will be enforced.

WHY IS TRUST IMPORTANT?

Why is trust so important? Figure 7.1 shows a typical supply chain. Under the traditional model, separate companies negotiate separate bilateral agreements; each member of the supply chain acts in its own self-interest, and the invisible hand of market tends to rule. You have seen previously that the results of this approach are that the data are often delayed and incorrect and that the system is inherently unstable because members constantly strive for their own gain at the expense of others. The extended enterprise is driven by an alignment in goals and purpose such that exactly what the customer wants is delivered on time and seamlessly among the different levels of the supply chain, without error, with no waste or redundancy in the system, and with each member of the system sharing

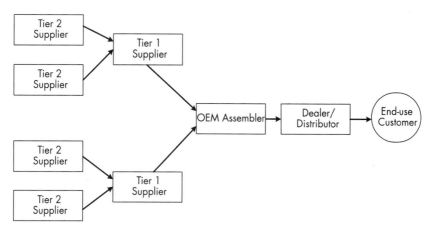

FIGURE 7.1
A prototypical supply chain.

in the benefits. This ideal state hinges on trust among supply chain members—that is why trust is important!

In research on the U.S. automobile makers, Dyer[1] demonstrates that trust lowers transaction costs ranging from the cost to search for potential suppliers to costs associated with negotiating, monitoring, and enforcing contracts. Trust also increases knowledge sharing and encourages partners to dedicate assets on behalf of the others. He argues compellingly that trust creates economic value and is not based primarily on personal relationships. Trust is based on predictable behavior and fair dealing. Dyer credits much of Chrysler's success with its SCORE program to such attributes when working with its suppliers.

In retailing, building relationships remains a key success factor in the light of consolidation and economic pressures that have led to a number of bankruptcies.[2] In the weeks leading to its Chapter 11 filing, Kmart failed to communicate openly with its key constituents (e.g., investors, suppliers, and customers). At a time when close relationships might have helped slow the path to reorganization under Chapter 11, management ignored the signals. As Kmart circled its wagons and stopped communicating externally, suppliers stopped shipping goods, customers went to Wal-Mart and Target, and investors lost confidence. Failure to acknowledge the importance of partnerships with key constituents led to a loss of trust. As a result of this lack of trust, information flows became restricted, key data were not shared, and the perceived need to protect one's self was viewed as opportunistic. The unintended outcome was that any trust that existed was seriously damaged.

Trust manifests itself in other, less dramatic ways. Take, for example, the assembly line running full tilt; the number of Hewlett Packard inkjet printers that roll off the production line is impressive. Upon closer scrutiny, it appears that the factory is not an HP facility and, in fact, is owned by Solectron, a major contract manufacturer with operations and supply networks around the globe. This might seem on the surface to be a typical outsourcing relationship, but what we are observing is an early form of extended enterprise. Here, firms have chosen to focus on what they do best and to partner with others who can provide the needed expertise and capability in non-core activities. HP has chosen to devote its efforts to managing other parts of the value chain and to work with Solectron to manufacture for it. Similarly, Sara Lee has decided that it will be a brand-building and marketing company, and has outsourced many parts of its food preparation operations. Nike made this decision years ago.

Traditional wisdom would have us believe that cost is the major motivation for outsourcing relationships where it is estimated that savings are in excess of 15 percent.[3] The pharmaceutical business, for instance, has also found advantages to contract manufacturing, given that the cost of new drugs often exceeds $500 million, and there are no guarantees that the basic R&D will lead to commercialization of a blockbuster new drug.

A key to managing both the cost of doing business and the effects of certain actions on profitability is visibility across the supply chain that results in accurate demand and supply forecasts. To ensure that collaboration throughout the supply chain is going to work, parties have to agree on one view of the truth. Fact-based decision making is essential but alone is not sufficient. For instance, when asked what items contribute to the success of logistics/transportation operations, the top two responses reported in *Industry Week*[4] are collaboration with suppliers and customers, and real-time information.

A recent McKinsey study reports that the auto industry could almost double its total profits along the value chain through more effective outsourcing.[5] Rather than work in a collaborative trusting manner, the auto manufacturers have kept most of the profit for themselves, have treated suppliers with disdain, and have acted opportunistically. An outcome of excessive price cuts and other concessions has placed some suppliers in the position of sacrificing quality and innovation to stay alive. Although this sounds very dramatic, the auto industry has been so cost-focused that it has neglected to appreciate the true benefits that can accrue from outsourcing to a trusted partner. Additional value can be created through relationships having shared goals that reward suppliers for meeting/beating targets, rely on innovation spawned from cross-company teams, and acknowledge and leverage the skills brought by all members of the supply chain.

Herman Miller developed a new division, SQA (Simply, Quick, and Affordable), to serve small business/home office markets. Through a redesign of its value chain, Herman Miller manages a collaborative network of supply chain partners to meet delivery dates better and more efficiently. Visibility of data from orders to inventory to actual customer demand has taken the order-to-delivery cycle from eight weeks to less than two. Firms that have been successful in building these value networks have a customer-focused attitude that pervades the entire supply chain, reliable and accurate data that are shared openly, and long-term relationships with key suppliers, all of whom do what each does best.

Although it is true that inventory turns and cash-to-cash cycles lie at the heart of many of these business models, trust sets the rules of engagement. Consider Dell and its suppliers. The seamless flow of goods, the accuracy of demand and supply forecasts, and the constant requirement to innovate drive the process. These systems survive and prosper because of a shared vision, a level of trust, and a commitment to shared performance metrics. Although trust lies at the heart of collaboration, there is a school of thought that abides by the Russian proverb—*trust but verify*. For example, if shared metrics are agreed upon, it makes sense to conduct periodic audits to check the accuracy of forecasts, in-stock positions, and average selling price. Accuracy of information is the hallmark of the Dell system.

Dell's integrated value chain provides the flexibility and adaptability that vertical integration lacks. The open and free exchange of information enables the tight coordination that historically has come through vertical integration. Without shared goals and a shared vision, and without planning processes that incorporate the desires of partners, the extended enterprise is likely to crack and break. However, some of these ties have been strained as a result of the 2002 merger between Compaq and HP. With the merger, HP became a very direct competitor of Dell across a number of product lines. Since the merger, Dell has been ranked number two in both the PC and server market. Adding to the tension is the recession in the computer industry that started around the middle of 2000. Several of the close ties have unraveled, and partners are competing to capture more of the value chain. One outcome is that Dell decided to market its own brand of printers, thereby alienating HP. A trusted supplier became a severe competitor, and existing rules and relationships went by the boards.[6] Two points are worth mentioning here: Trust is fragile, and as friends compete, trust may be compromised.

TRUST IS ESSENTIAL

The dilemma surrounding any collaborative supply chain relationship is that with closeness comes the fear of opportunism where one supply chain partner acts in its own self-interest to the detriment of others. Although rationalizing a supply base reduces transaction costs,* it also can increase monitoring costs if the buyer is worried that other members of the supply chain are not likely to be true to their word. With fewer options comes greater dependence. The fear of vulnerability adds cost to the system, encourages redundant activities, and ignores the potential gains that can result by working with companies that offer complementary skills. However, these supply chain partnerships should be more flexible, adaptive to change, and more innovative.

Partners often come to the relationship with history of past supply chain relationships gone bad or of not having lived up to their potential. It appears that the largest barrier to success is organizational, rather than technical or financial. One of the key obstacles is in the "people costs," resulting from old habits that must be changed and cultural legacies that do not support the new mindset and managerial skills required to support these supply chain alliances. The changes required are quite far-reaching and entail developing a climate that fosters trust and open communications, builds commitment, supports a win-win orientation, and sets firmly in everyone's mind the fact that supply chains compete, individual firms do not.

---

*If you consider that the cost to process a purchase order can be in excess of $200, consolidating your supply base and issuing fewer POs can mean a very noticeable impact on the bottom line.

If partners are to share sensitive information, they must be assured that the information will be used as intended. Trust can be seen as your word being your bond—you say you will do something, and your partner knows you will. Another aspect of trust is the security in knowing that each party will act with the interests of all partners in mind. That is, a supply chain member will defer certain decisions to other members of the supply chain, knowing that the final decision will take into account the considerations of all members.

Think back to the earlier examples of vendor-managed inventory or of supply chain partnerships in aerospace, particularly the Joint Strike Fighter project. Lockheed Martin can ill afford to promote its own agenda or interests over those of its partners and maintain the degree of credibility and trust needed to complete its obligations and commitments to the U.S. Department of Defense successfully.

Similarly, Sun Microsystems has reconsidered its relationship with its channel partners and has begun to focus on building their trust by not competing with them and their solutions provider partners. Instead of trying to control the customer relationship, Sun now acknowledges that partnering and sharing the customer can avoid the conflict that permeates many relationships in the enterprise solutions space. Channel partners are looking for consistent messages and behaviors that align with the stated purpose of these relationships.

Firms are dependent on networks to fulfill their mission; these networks, by definition, encourage informal interaction and idea sharing. Hierarchies, on the other hand, create formal reporting relationships, a chain of command that stifles such open flows of information.

Networks such as extended enterprises depend on trust for their lifeblood because formal mechanisms cannot guarantee that rights and obligations will be met. A firm could rely solely on a contract, but these legal documents are limiting, in that they breed compliance and not commitment. Also, a contract does not assure that when conditions change, previously agreed-to outcomes will still be achieved. At a fundamental level, there is a difference in philosophy between alliance-like thinking and contractual thinking. These differences are summarized in Table 7.1. Contracts often are written to

TABLE 7.1 Understanding the Differences in Contractual Thinking and Alliance-like Thinking

FROM CONTRACTUAL THINKING	(TRANSFORMATIONAL THINKING)	TO ALLIANCE-LIKE THINKING
Risk mitigation		Value creation
Overzealous protection and fear	⟶	Facilitation and collaboration
Narrow and rigid interpretation		Expansive, flexible, adaptive
Emphasis on legal correctness		Balance legal logic with common sense

protect against something bad happening to the firm and not to encourage creative thinking when problems arise.* Moreover, contracts cannot easily address the range of contingencies and exigencies that businesses face in today's global competitive arena.

THE ROLE OF CONTRACTS AND TRUST

It has often been said, "Write the contract and put it in the file cabinet; when you have to refer to it, you have big-time problems." However, most procurement organizations rely heavily on contracts to manage their supplier relationships. The challenge is to understand what the interplay is between contracts and the development of trust among members of a supply chain. Lance Dixon, the architect of Bose's JIT2 system,** has stated that Bose will regularly seek outside bids to ensure that its suppliers are cost-competitive. It seems odd that partners would be subject to such scrutiny. Mr. Dixon has stated that verification is just good business practice.

*We are not so naïve as to believe that contracts are not important. We understand the role and the importance that contracts play. We admit further that they force parties to be very clear and precise in how language is crafted so that all parties share the same understanding of what has been agreed upon. At the same time, we believe that absent trust, contracts are essential.

**Under this approach, key suppliers become in-plant personnel who have total responsibility for managing a Bose commodity class or service, such as outbound logistics. These people are often co-located with Bose people and become part (virtually speaking) of the Bose organization.

Ryder Systems is the lead logistics manager for Dell and has a master agreement that specifies that Ryder can use Dell's information only to serve Dell. Ryder's senior person for global markets and e-commerce, Gene Tyndall, warns against placing too much faith in such agreements. He argues that partners don't need contracts to collaborate—trust your partners or get different partners. Therein lies the rub: Absent trust, contracts become important. However, given the importance of protecting intellectual property and such, contracts do play a role. Our point is that you can rely too heavily on a contract and lose sight of other equally important aspects of the relationship.

Think about an extended enterprise as consisting of three major, intertwined considerations: managing the business, managing the relationships, and understanding the underlying spirit of the relationship that guides the development of roles and expectations. If understood at this level, the interplay between contracts and trust becomes more apparent. Managing the business part of the extended enterprise is by far the most easily understood part of the equation. Managers construct a business case for the merits of a virtual supply chain built on arguments made in Chapter 6. The issues are often related to workflow, transparency, allocation of risks and rewards, and other aspects of ensuring the timely delivery of product and services.

Contracts are used to codify the nature of the relationship and become useful in instances where partners have little past experience with one another. The contract reduces uncertainty by formally designating behavior and by adding predictability to the outcome of the exchange.

In cases where evergreen contracts or multiyear commitments might exist, both parties might not view changes to the original agreement in the same light. The U.S. Army's partnering program was initiated to foster better contract administration among the military and its contractors. The term *partnering* is used to define a level of commitment between government and industry to avoid disputes and minimize conflicts during the course of the contract. With a foundation built on common goals and objectives, the partnering process attempts to eliminate the adversarial attitudes that governed past relationships. Interestingly, the process focuses mainly on dispute avoidance and only briefly mentions trust and commitment as key benefits.

The question is not whether formal contracts or informal relationships are better. The important question is how best to leverage the two so that the supply chain accomplishes its objectives with minimal disruption and conflict. One concern among buyers, however, is that a personal relationship might lead to awkwardness and, in the extreme, a conflict of interest. In trusting supply chains, a social contract emerges that begins to frame how the parties will interact and what is acceptable behavior. Part of the process entails sense making[7] where different views are acknowledged and norms are used to reconcile differences and guide partners' interactions. Unlike contracts, these agreements are informal, unwritten, and largely nonverbalized. In practice, the informal and formal rules, emergent roles, and expectations support each other. One result is that supply chain partners are willing to go beyond the letter of the contract.

The spirit of the relationship reflects the psychological contract that guides all interaction in the supply chain and sets the most basic understanding of what it means to partner within the extended enterprise. When buyer and seller do not share the same view of what it means to partner, conflict often results. Partners will, from time to time, test the limits of trust by asking for certain concessions or engaging in actions that will call for a degree of flexibility or adaptation that pushes the boundary of the contract. These tests help calibrate the depth of trust and help set the scope in which trust is operative. Partners who trust will work to adapt to the changing environment while upholding the spirit of the contract.

In one instance, a misunderstanding of a key supplier's perspective caused a serious problem regarding supplier relationship management. At the corporate level, supply chain initiatives were developed to strengthen relationships with key suppliers and to leverage their skills fully. Buyers spoke about shared risk and rewards, long-term commitments, and sharing of confidential information. However, many suppliers believed that the buyers' actions were motivated entirely by cost cutting. In fact, evidence revealed that suppliers were asked to shoulder the risks while the buyer received a disproportionate percentage of the rewards (lower purchase price). Buyer and seller did not agree on what it meant to partner, nor did they share a common vision for their future interaction.

In this industry, a major revenue stream for the OEM has traditionally been the sale of spare parts, and suppliers, according to the tacit agreement, did not compete downstream against OEM manufacturers. Nonetheless, one supplier was thinking seriously about entering the spare parts business. In part, it saw the spare parts aftermarket as a new opportunity to capture more of the value that was going to other members of the supply chain. Digging deeper into recent events leading up to the rift, it is clear that the manufacturer had not lived up to supplier expectations. Promises of increased purchases were made, guarantees that other divisions would work with this supplier on higher value-added goods were offered, and a vision of a closer working relationship between the two firms had been articulated. Excuses were given when none of these promises came to fruition. With the perception of lost revenue resulting from broken promises, it is not surprising that the supplier began to think of its own future.

DECOMPOSING TRUST INTO ITS CORE DIMENSIONS

Given the uncertainty that surrounds any business decision today, it is unlikely that a formal contract can address each possible outcome. When there is trust, partners will meet the implied purpose of the relationship with the knowledge that the additional costs will be acknowledged and future considerations will be made. If following the letter of the contract becomes the focal point, there is little incentive to adapt, conflict arises, and the relationship is jeopardized.

Research devoted to trust in organizations has a 40-year history,[8] and the definition of trust converges on a confidence in others' intentions and motivations. Trust is the belief that one's alliance partner will act in a predictable manner, will keep his or her word, and will act in a way that will not negatively affect the other. This last point is particularly salient under conditions where one partner might feel vulnerable due to a heightened dependence on the other. Trust lessens the concern that this knowledge would be expropriated and used later to compete against the partner. Table 7.2 depicts different dimensions of trust and lends insight into how powerful a concept it is and why it must be a fundamental part of any extended enterprise relationship.

There is some skepticism that supply chain partners would work closely in an atmosphere of trust. Doubt arises from the observation that the relationship between buyer and seller is

TABLE 7.2 Trust and Its Different Dimensions*

TRUST	COMPONENTS	IMPLICATIONS
Character-based	Integrity—honesty and principles Motivations—what intentions are	These elements relate to the qualitative aspects of partners' operating philosophies and cultures.
	Consistency of Behavior— reliable and dependable	Difficult to ascertain and are often known by experience
	Openness—willingness to share information	The glue that bind partners
	Discretion—holds in confidence	If motives are not shared and confidentiality violated, problems arise
Competence-based	Specific—specialized area of expertise	Problem solving was a key element
	Interpersonal—skills in relating and working with others Broad-based—general expertise beyond recognized field Judgment—decision-making ability	Although judgment is important at the level of the relationship, at the firm level there was less confidence

*Based on Judith Whipple and Robert Frankel, "Supply Chain Success Factors," *Journal of Supply Chain Management* 36, no. 3 (Summer 2000): 21–28.

naturally in a state of conflict. Buyers and sellers have traditionally not shared the same objectives, nor have they experienced a balance in power. One partner often has more power than the other, but AMR Research suggests that technology can be used to "equalize" the differences.[9] Having a single platform on which the collaboration is built can enhance these processes. Also, tools should be developed that educate and transfer knowledge across the supply chain.

BUILDING TRUST

It is one thing to understand trust as a concept; it is quite another to develop strategies to build trust. Although trust is the glue that holds the extended enterprise together, it is quite fragile and subject to a number of stresses and strains. One area in which trust is essential is in the area of supplier development, which can be an early step in developing an integrated supply chain. Trust also is relevant to the use of the Internet and the myriad of business-to-business (B2B) exchanges that have formed (and disbanded) over the years. Here, trust takes on a different meaning.

SUPPLIER DEVELOPMENT

Supplier development is a process to improve the performance of a firm's key suppliers so that the buyer's procurement goals are better met.[10] Often, there are two goals sought. One goal is strategic and focuses on improving the supplier's technical capability, product development skills, management skills, and the like. The second goal is performance-oriented and converges on quality, cost, delivery, and service improvements. Often, there is a supplier assessment where formal evaluation, certification, and feedback are used. After the assessment, there is often direct involvement where the buyer will be involved in training, site visits, and other proactive activities to remediate suppliers' weaknesses. At the other extreme, competitive pressure is used to motivate suppliers. Simply, buyers rely on a punitive approach and emphasize that the business can be allocated depending on which supplier performs the best.

Herein lies one of the problems regarding the trust-building process. It is true that supplier development has frequently been used as a code word to wrestle additional cost concessions from key suppliers. Such attempts are initiated without any sense of commitment from the buyer, who often solicits bids to create a competitive situation. Considering the impact that suppliers have on the buyer's costs, quality, and technology, it would make perfect sense to develop an approach that is not singularly cost-driven and offers incentives to the supplier for achieving non-cost performance targets.

Honda of America works with suppliers to meet jointly developed cost targets. The difference is that cost targets are reached through an analysis of inefficiencies and are not taken from supplier profits. To steal savings from profits is to place any level of trust in jeopardy.

Solectron understands the need for developing a cadre of very competent and state-of-the-art suppliers, given the rapid technological changes it faces in the markets it serves. Through a process that strives to achieve strategic alignment with its suppliers, Solectron looks first at capabilities, then at total costs to select its key supplier development opportunities. Supplier performance is tied to profitability, and both can move in the same direction.

Too frequently, buyers switch suppliers on the basis of price. They will keep key suppliers at arm's length while preaching supplier development and will limit the bilateral flow of information among buyer and supplier, insisting on very formal contracts. This will not lead to trust and will damage any long-term relationship. Trust is built on relationship management, and mixed signals from buyers serve to confuse the supplier, raise questions regarding commitment and credibility, and damage the long-term viability/competitiveness of the supply chain.

Sun and Cisco have identified their supply chains and the manner in which they are managed as key differentiators. Each company has a well-articulated roadmap for success and willingly shares this roadmap with its supply base. On one level, the purpose is to show in a logical and consistent manner how all the parts create value for customers. On another level, the roadmaps demonstrate a commitment to the supply base and have given them voice in the planning process. Sun especially has incorporated its suppliers' strategies in its own planning. On a third level, trust is built through the entire strategy-planning and implementation process. There are no surprises, and all parties understand how risks and rewards are shared. Also, because there is a basis of trust, parties work proactively to gain a competitive advantage for all members.

Returning to Honda of America,[11] its supplier development program became formalized in 1990 as the Best Partner (BP)* program. Initially developed to build a U.S. supply base, the program can demonstrate that productivity gains have been around 47 percent, quality has improved 30 percent, and costs have been reduced by 7.25 percent. Note that the emphasis is on continuous improvement and not on cost reduction per se, although all the benefits have bottom-line implications. Moreover, the process is based on communications and senior management commitment to the entire process.

E-COMMERCE, SUPPLY CHAINS, AND TRUST

It is estimated that the growth in global e-commerce will exceed $6.8 billion in 2004.[12] However, the sad fact is that many businesses might not be prepared to deal with the pressures such extraordinary demand will create. There is a huge problem in managing the logistics of such magnitude. At stake here is the credibility of systems where firms can conduct global transactions but cannot fulfill these orders easily. UPS has begun to manage supply chains for its customers through a subsidiary that integrates all the parts of the process.

Neutral exchanges such as FreeMarkets and industry-specific exchanges such as ChemConnect, corporate exchanges, and buying cooperatives (e.g., Covisint) are all

---

*BP also stands for Best Price, Best Performance, Best Position, and Best Productivity.

intended to streamline the front end of the process and gain price reductions along the way. Although each of these exchanges is touted as collaborative, trust takes on a new meaning here. Now trust is defined as *reliability*—it is the guarantee that the transaction will be completed. A number of services have developed in recent years (e.g., SGSonSITE, TradeCard, eCredit.com) that provide independent assurances that the goods ordered will be received. The Internet has re-defined trust, a concept that helped us understand the complexity of interpersonal interaction and behavior, to mean the level of fulfillment assured in an online exchange.

Trust has been trivialized to mean the transactions have been "certified" to be accurate and reliable. The focus on the mechanics of the transaction between supply chain members removes any consideration of developing partnerlike behavior. There is a difference of opinion regarding the Internet and its effect on collaboration. Some contend that, given the range of tools available on the Internet, it will improve the effectiveness of collaboration by augmenting co-located, face-to-face teams.

How is commitment developed if bids are shopped and contracts renegotiated every six months or so? How are suppliers encouraged to innovate if, at the end of the bidding session, the winning bid is based on the lowest price? Trust and reputation have been taken from the realm of experience and repeated interactions that occur as buyer and seller repeatedly work together. Instead, "trust brokers" such as Open Ratings and GeoTrust have emerged. These companies are developing "objective" scales and rating schemes to quantify suppliers' reputations. Do they deliver on their promises?

Open Ratings combines data from other buyers' evalua-tions, performance, demographics about the firm (size, years in existence), financial and credit information, and other business-related data. From this, a rating scheme is developed. One concern has always been that a firm can buy a good reputation through its advertising expenditure. Open Ratings provides a balanced evaluation that is fact-based (mostly). Such a rating scheme begs the question of whether this method will supplant the perceived need of buyers to engage their suppliers and attempt to *know* the company and its people in building a relationship. The insidious, almost perverse nature of relying on these brokers is that, as long as the business is going well, the relationship is less important. As the business suffers, the relationship and the ties formed begin to rise in importance. Unfortunately, because little time is spent cultivating the relationship, there is no safety net to protect the business. Imagine buyers beginning to see shortages and/or materials going on allocation. A close relationship with a dedicated supplier could buffer such a problem. If no time were spent nurturing this relationship because B2B exchanges replaced the perceived need to do so, why would the supplier be inclined to lend a hand?

APPROACHES TO BUILDING TRUST

One element of value creation determines how the different supply chain partners combine resources and skills to create value. The second component is an assessment of how the finances (both dollars and margins) associated with the value created are appropriated among channel partners. It is in the second calculation that trust becomes more important. Are benefits divided equitably or equally? What is the calculus for deciding how a channel partner receives a fair share of the price paid by customers?

KNOW THE COMPONENTS OF TRUST

Trust can be built by understanding the impact of its components. Character-based trust is important because firms have choices. Given a choice, why work with a firm that has a questionable reputation? It is possible to search the Web and find out how past supply chain relationships have proceeded because a great deal of this information is part of the public press. Firms that have not collaborated in the past can learn from others' experiences. Certain companies in the software marketplace have developed reputations for willfully expropriating technology from its partners. Why work with these firms? Market power and the hold these firms have on the marketplace would be one of the few logical explanations. These firms seem to rely on their grip on the marketplace to manage their supply chain relationships; thus, these relationships tend to be both contentious and fragile. These supply chains should be less competitive in the long term, although power dependence might sustain them for longer periods of time than one might predict. Others[13] are more emphatic and state that without a clear and mutual interdependence, it will be very difficult to attain the degree of supply chain integration needed to compete favorably. One question that should be asked is, What would you want your supply chain partner to say after the relationship ends?

If partners can agree on the goals/purpose of the extended enterprise, this lays a foundation of mutual interest and the need to collaborate. In many instances, it would be important for the supplier or buyer (whoever is the protagonist) to set the stage and tell a story that demonstrates the importance of the partnership, the gains to all parties, and the consequences of not collaborating, explicating the path to competitive advantage. Reputation (or goodwill) often serves to get a foot in the door so that the parties can begin this conversation. It is especially critical that mutual gains be stressed, that all partners are given voice, and that their strategic interests become part of the overall plan for the supply chain network. From this starting point, trust can begin to be built among the members of the network who will work closely to implement the plan. To be sure, firms do not trust, people do!

Consider the "seasick syndrome." Seasickness occurs when the inner ear and the eye send inconsistent messages to the brain. In the case of suppliers, these mixed messages occur when they hear the buyer say one thing and do another. They hear *partnership* and *collaboration* but see price pressures and the use of leverage to extract a lower price. Both parties can agree on the importance of collaborative behavior but there can be enough inconsistencies between what the buyer says and does to affect the tone and spirit of the relationship. See Table 7.3 for an illustration of the inconsistencies leading to the seasick syndrome.

TABLE 7.3 Evidence of the Seasick Syndrome and the Inconsistency between Buyer and Seller

BUYER SAYS....	SUPPLIERS SAY....
Suppliers should be developed	Want to be treated as equals
Good suppliers provide low price	Good suppliers provide value through service, solutions, etc.
Communication flows one way	Two-way communication key
Relationship is improving	Relationship is deteriorating
Relationships are important	Contacts constantly changing
Engineering should collaborate more	Collaboration is needed at all levels

Source: Darden Student Project, Darden School, University of Virginia, "Supply Chain Beliefs" (November 2000).

UNDERSTANDING THE RELATIONSHIPS BETWEEN TRUST AND CONTROL

Table 7.4 summarizes the nature of the interaction between trust and control, and suggests that as goals and objectives become less tangible, trust takes on a more important role in managing the nature of the relationship between supplier and buyer. In supply chain relationships where joint learning and technological discovery are goals, formal control mechanisms become less relevant. The discovery process tends to be more random, and partners must trust the process and appreciate the twists and turns that might affect the nature of the relationship. Flexibility and adaptability become essential so that partners have the latitude to vary from the "protocol" as delineated in the contract. Conversely, under conditions of less uncertainty, contracts take on added importance; the rules are the rules, and variance in behavior is less tolerated.

Behavioral control also affects how people interact and sets boundaries for certain behaviors through reporting systems, assignments, and training. Competence trust-building is based on transparency of information and ability to access and analyze data about the skills, capabilities, and expertise of the partners. Both competence-based and character-based trust benefit greatly from social control. Social control also manifests clan-like behavior, due to the strong relationship with shared decision-making processes and common and agreed-upon values, norms, and goals.

TABLE 7.4 A Summary of the Interaction between Trust and Control

TRUST	CONTROL	ENVIRONMENT	INTERACTION BETWEEN TRUST AND CONTROL
CHARACTER-BASED	FORMAL	MORE CERTAIN	
Integrity Motivation Consistent behavior Openness Discretion Goodwill	Output Behavioral	When outputs are more clear and specified the interaction is subject to less interpretation and is mutually understood	Trust (character-based) might help bring the partners together Both formal and output control become more relevant Such a context might be more contractual in nature and a need to build a deep sense of trust can be supplanted by a contract
COMPETENCE-BASED	INFORMAL	MORE UNCERTAIN	
Specific Interpersonal Broad-based Judgment	Social	When outputs are less clear and the nature of the interaction is subject to uncertainty	Trust becomes more critical Formal control mechanics become less useful Social control helps bolster trust

FROM THEORY TO PRACTICE: DEVELOPING AN ATMOSPHERE OF TRUST

There is no easy formula but there are certain key steps that will raise the probability that a more trusting relationship between trading partners can be built.

BEGIN WITH A PLAN

Without a plan, objectives cannot be set, goals cannot be articulated, and outcomes cannot be measured. Understand well why a trusting, collaborative relationship is more beneficial to you, your customers, and your supply chain members than other forms of less collaborative relationships. This plan becomes the basis of the discussion with potential supply chain partners so that a common set of objectives, purpose, and goals can be established among supply chain members. To help understand the process better, the following kinds of questions should be addressed:

- What are the mutual benefits to be realized by the different supply chain partners?
- Are partners treated fairly and equitably? Do risks and rewards balance?
- Do all partners have a voice and are they heard?
- Have we taken the time to mesh strategies from each of our part-ners into the supply chain strategy?
- How does this supply chain meet customers' needs and provide a sustainable competitive advantage?
- What role does each partner play? Are the roles clearly understood and accepted by each supply chain member?
- Why were partners asked to be part of this supply chain? What is each one's unique contribution?
- During the planning process, have we included considerations for managing the relationship and the business?

- Is there senior management support and commitment?

Ensure Open Lines of Communication

The key issues go way beyond technology that allows information to flow openly among the members of the supply chain. The most critical issue is that partners are comfortable exchanging sensitive information and that the flows are encouraged to be less formal and not follow the chain of command. Partners share an understanding of what the scope and depth of information content is that should be exchanged and agree that certain information might be considered out of bounds. Listed below are questions that are intended to help managers understand that communication within the supply chain is less about the technology and more about the level of commitment, degree of comfort, and willingness to exchange sensitive information.

- Do you communicate only when there are problems or is there an ongoing dialogue among supply chain members?
- Do you tend to speak the same language and see issues from each other's perspective?
- Is there a tendency to keep partners aware of new developments and potential problems before they occur?
- Does information flow with equal ease throughout the supply chain?
- Do supply chain members have open discussions that are fact-based?
- Is there agreement among partners regarding oper-ating principles and "rules of engagement?" Does everyone understand the rules?
- Do members work hard to keep others involved in decisions that affect the supply chain?

ESTABLISH AN APPROPRIATE GOVERNANCE STRUCTURE

The governance structure addresses issues related to roles and performance among supply chain partners, assigns responsibility for activities and participation in decision making for supply chain-wide issues, ensures equitable treatment of all partners as it relates to sharing both risks and rewards, and attempts to build a sense of shared commitment to the broader, albeit mutually agreed-upon, supply chain vision. Control is contractually based and limits the level of commitment and trust. Control, as in command and control, is a bankrupt concept within the context of the extended enterprise. You cannot control what you do not own.

Governance structures that are consistent with and supportive of the tenets of the extended enterprise foster a greater sense of trust and emphasize more behavioral control. The keys to a collaborative supply chain are mutual respect, a culture that supports fair dealing and equitable behavior supply chainwide, and a set of values that encourage open discussion and access to the decision-making process for all members of the supply chain. To examine whether such elements are part of the supply chain's governance structure, the following questions are useful.

- Are problems that arise treated as "your" or "our" problems?
- Are there conflict-resolution mechanisms built into the operating principle or do members rush to a legal remedy?
- Do members genuinely work toward common goals and a shared vision?
- Are outcomes viewed as supply chain-wide and linked to the success of the network, rather than to individual members?
- Can partners articulate the norms and values that guide acceptable supply chain behavior?
- To what extent are members comfortable with interdependence and the fact that the success of the supply

chain is linked to partners working for the good of all members?

- Do members value and respect the contribution, input, and differences that each partner brings to the supply chain?
- Are performance outcomes tied to hard objective measures only?

KEEP YOUR EYE ON WHAT MATTERS

The default option for most companies is to act in their own self-interest. Oliver Williamson, who has done path-breaking work in transaction cost economics, states that, left to their own devices, people will act opportunistically with guile. Self-serving behavior renders the supply chain weak because partners will revert to old adversarial habits. Members must constantly be reminded that what is important is that supply chains compete with other supply chains. The extended enterprise is a response to a world where change is unpredictable; costs associated with developing technology, new products, and innovative processes are often too high; and time horizons are too long. Vertical integration affords high degrees of control but lacks the flexibility and adaptability to survive.

The challenge is that managers are comfortable with control and uncomfortable with the notion of trust. Yet effort should align structures, processes, policies, and procedures systemwide. Such alignment sends a consistent message that without trust, our supply chain will fail—plain and simple.

WALK IN YOUR PARTNERS' SHOES

Taking your partners' perspective and understanding what drives their decision processes is important. This is especially true because the formal contracts tend to deemphasize such behavior, instead focusing on "what is good for me." This means also that you must be careful of the signals you send. Balking at a request for information, not fulfilling promises, missing deadlines without prior notification, and showing a

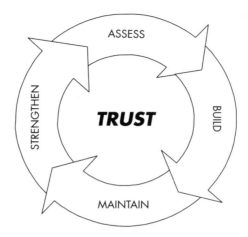

FIGURE 7.2
The virtuous circle of trust. *Source:* Modified from PricewaterhouseCoopers, *Building Trust in Alliances* (October 2000).

lack of concern for the issues of importance to your partners all can call into question the level of trust between partners.

To some degree, managing trust can be seen as a virtuous circle. Partner choice is certainly an important first step but the relationship must be built, sustained, and managed to survive the inevitable difficulties that come with doing business in a turbulent world. PwC (now part of IBM) has developed a fairly simple model for thinking about the trust-building cycle. Figure 7.2 presents the essence of its approach, which provides insight into how to build a trusting atmosphere that is indispensable to maintaining economic ties among extended enterprise members.

PARTNER ASSESSMENT AND DETERMINING TRUSTWORTHINESS

Given the number and range of qualified suppliers, how does the buyer select the right one for membership in an integrated supply chain? A good supplier does not necessarily make a good partner, and the criteria needed to make that assessment go beyond traditional metrics. Certainly, questions of competence, state-of-the-art technology, innovativeness, cost competitiveness, and quality of management still are quite valid. In addition to these concerns, an evaluation should consider mutuality of goals, purpose, and shared vision and values. Moreover, it would be critical to learn about aspects of the firm and its management that reflect the behaviors, attitudes, decision-making style, organizational processes and procedures, and the like that would support or inhibit extended enterprise thinking and actions. The following is a list of illustrative questions that should stimulate thinking regarding the partner assessment process.

1. What is the supplier's level of commitment to us? What has the level of commitment with past supply chain partners been?

2. What do past/current customers say about this supplier? Has it kept its promises to others?

3. Does its management speak of us as a team or do they use "I" and "you," not "we?"

4. What is this supplier's view of the future? How long have past supply chain relationships lasted?

5. Is this supplier willing to share its new ideas and future plans with us?

6. Do its systems and structures permit informal communications across levels, divisions, and functions?

7. Are its people empowered to act? Do all decisions and information flow to the top where action is initiated?

8. Does the supplier use multifunctional teams to solve problems and address issues?

9. Do contractual concerns loom large in the conversations we have held? Are attorneys present at every meeting?

10. Do management personnel seem flexible and appear to be willing to change, or are they rigid in their thinking?

11. Does this supplier seem to know our business and is it willing to contribute to our mutual success?

12. What kinds of assurances does the supplier want from us? Does it appear that this supplier will hold us to the letter of the contract? Does this supplier insist that everything must be spelled out and put in writing?
13. Is everything business or is time taken to initiate a personal relationship?

Answers to these questions provide insight to fundamental questions about the trustworthiness of a potential partner. At the very least, it should raise questions that would not normally be considered simply because managers do not tend to think of these issues, and they are uncomfortable working with these "softer metrics." Sure, it is possible to find a strong supplier that is technically competent and has processes to ensure cost savings now and over time. A trustworthy supplier has those characteristics and will stand by you when the economy falters and will go the extra mile for you because it is the right thing to do.

SUMMARY

This chapter has developed the concept of trust as fundamental to the creation and maintenance of the extended enterprise. This is not intended to be a theoretical discussion; however, the level of trust that currently exists across supply chains tends not to be the level required for the extended enterprise to yield the results it is capable of producing. Trust is far more than the integrity of the data generated and shared among supply chain partners. It is far more than knowing a new supplier can legitimately meet its obligations after it is chosen at auction. Trust exists as a bond among people who are dedicated to a compatible set of goals and objectives. It is the ability to know that your partner will act in the mutual best interest of all extended enterprise members and will execute according to plan, without exception and with no surprises.

8

DEVELOPING THE EXTENDED ENTERPRISE

MANAGERS: PEOPLE, PROCESSES, AND STRUCTURES

Our goal in this chapter is to discuss the changes that are needed to support the extended enterprise. Specifically, we identify the different expectations, roles, and mindset that must become part of management's approach to transforming a firm into a model extended enterprise member. Our premise is that these changes require a different breed of procurement manager/executive. We believe that it is very difficult to effect organizational change without having people who support the processes and have the skills, competencies, and attitudes that are consistent with the principles of the extended enterprise. Purchasing managers who grew up in the era of "three bids and a cloud of dust" lack the foresight, attitude, and skills to maneuver within the demands of the extended enterprise.

Our position is that the extended enterprise symbolizes a new world order. It represents a network of collaborating supply chain partners that, we believe, will more successfully compete on a global scale than other forms of supply chain relationships. The transition from traditional supply chain to the extended enterprise will not happen automatically. Many firms lack the senior management support that is required to drive the change. These firms also do not possess the mindset needed to make the leap to greater collaboration. In fact, many companies seem to be stuck in an adversarial mode where buyer and seller still lack trust, do not share a common vision, and do not easily work for the mutual benefit of the entire set of supply chain members. We have witnessed that buyers are prone to pull the price card to accomplish short-term objectives when the going gets tough.

We begin this chapter with a discussion of the changes affecting organizations in general. We discuss the implications for developing extended enterprise managers and the different skills these new world managers will need. Finally, we talk about the challenges faced by firms that attempt to transform themselves to be more extended enterprise-facile and adept.

GENERAL TRENDS OF FORCES
CHANGING THE WORLD[1]

A discussion of forces changing the world must begin with the Internet, the mother of all discontinuous change. In a supply chain context, the use of the Internet has taken two major paths. One path emphasizes cost reduction and the opportunity to gain greater efficiency in business processes and systems. The Internet has, in some instances, affected pricing by driving products to a commodity status. The worst examples—reverse auctions—come to mind, where prices drop like a rock during the bidding process. The second path accentuates the positive outcomes of extended enterprise thinking that enable communications in real time across the globe and facilitate interaction among partners at all levels, from joint product design and inventory visibility to logistics and transportation.

Related to the Internet is the realization that information rules, and the power asymmetry that might have existed previously between supply chain members now becomes less meaningful and almost irrelevant. Without this power imbalance, the Internet places buyer and seller on a more equal footing. Not only does information move more freely between firms, it also moves up and down the hierarchy within firms. In response, management styles must adapt from command and control to a model of empowerment. Hierarchical structures that promote command and control tend to be risk-adverse systems that crush new ideas.[2]

Instead, senior management should strive for people-centered management, where innovative thinking is valued, a sense of ownership is fostered, and detailed orders will be replaced by performance expectations and regular feedback. On a related note, transparency in information will increase, and firms will come to rely on more specialized firms to complete the value chain. Value creation will be spread across the supply chain, with members contributing their unique skills to the final product/service. This type of specialization requires integration and coordination so that all of the separate firms can act as though they were one. For example, firms such as i2 Technologies have introduced new supplier relationship management software that enables suppliers and buyers to collaborate more easily on sourcing and procurement activities. However, there are cultural changes associated with this new way of doing business, and Harreld suggests that the changes might tax the skills of supply chain members.[3]

SURVIVING IN THE NEW ECONOMY

The challenge, according to Senge and Carstedt,[4] is to develop sustainable businesses that are compatible with the current economic reality. Traditional procurement practices embody the principles of someone attempting to achieve the firm's agenda and goals to the detriment of supply chain partners, who then become adversaries rather than partners. Now both companies and employees are part of larger social networks. Employees seek jobs where there is a match between their goals and values and those of the firm; money and profits alone are not sufficient to engender commitment.

Firms are linked to explore the possibilities of these burgeoning value chain networks that co-design, co-innovate, and together try to keep pace with the expanding knowledge base. In effect, the extended enterprise will benefit from systems thinking where managers begin to appreciate the impact their actions have on a much broader set of companies and decisions. Imagine the complexity and difficulty inherent in coordinating a multi-tier supply chain where partners at each level have outsourced activities to others, and all must be staged and coordinated to deliver products and services. The extended enterprise encompasses far more than integration of workflow; it is based on joint planning and strategy development.

To understand one of the differences between the new and old organizational forms that are needed in the new economy is to contrast American football with rugby.[5] Football has a hierarchy, with the quarterback calling the plays and each player having a predescribed job to execute according to the play. Performance is immediately measurable in distance toward the goal. Rugby is a flow game, with adjustments and problem solving needed at each moment to adjust to the changing movement on the field. Individuals are empowered to act unilaterally in moving the ball down the field, and unlike football, each player is a generalist. In football, the head coach is in total control and often sends in plays from the sidelines. In rugby, the coach has little control once the game begins and often motivates and educates from the sidelines.

BOUNDARY-SPANNING ROLES

We have designed a world where a great deal of activity happens at the boundary of the firm and at the boundary of the functional unit. Specialization and an extended enterprise-wide focus have caused departments/functions/companies to share information and resources in common pursuit of supply chainwide benefits. It is at the nexus of collaborating firms that managerial skills and capabilities need to be developed. There is no question that traditional buyer behavior has been both inadequate and ineffective. A sampling of the differences in skills is highlighted in Table 8.1. An examination of the typical buying organization reveals that most procurement groups are more heavily populated with people who engage in *typical* boundary-spanning activities than with people who possess skills needed to engage in the *emerging* boundary-spanning activities. Think about job postings: Most organizations do not use the list in the right column of Table 8.1 to describe the duties of a senior buyer or even a director of procurement. We wonder whether the correct job title should be Manager of External Supplier Relations; the term *buyer* just does not capture the essence of the emerging role.

TABLE 8.1 Behaviors Required for Boundary-Spanning Roles in the Extended Enterprise

TYPICAL BOUNDARY-SPANNING ACTIVITIES	EMERGING BOUNDARY-SPANNING ACTIVITIES
Transaction accountant	Information exchange broker
Administers interfirm contracts	Guides the formation and implementation of strategic relationships and interfirm supply networks
Primary point of contact with suppliers	
Interfaces with first-tier suppliers/customers	Co-managers of external manufacturing
Minimizes risk to buying (e.g., disruption of supply, incoming defects, etc.)	Responsibilities throughout the supplier value chain
	Manages and leverages the skills of the supply chain

Boundary roles are not a new concept, and the classic boundary-spanning roles[6] include such activities as gatekeeping, transacting, and protecting. *Gatekeeping* is simply the filtering of information and is part of the request for proposal (RFP) and bidding process where the relevant information flows through procurement to the key decision makers in the buying and selling organizations. *Transacting* encompasses all aspects of the workflow from negotiation to the timely receipt of goods. *Protecting* entails activities that watch after the firm's best interests, such as due diligence, forecasting, and monitoring of supplier performance.

We believe that none of these roles track very well with the implicit demands of the emerging boundary-spanning activities. If this observation is true, we envision a very serious skill gap in the near future because these emerging boundary-spanning roles do not fully enable the firm to develop into a successful extended enterprise partner, although they do make some inroads. As firms begin their journeys, the question becomes, what additional skills are needed to support and nurture extended enterprise thinking and behavior? The traditional boundary-spanning roles tend to reflect more tactical kinds of activities related to workflow and completing the transaction.

REQUISITE BOUNDARY-SPANNING ACTIVITES

The new skill sets required extend the boundary-spanning roles listed above and force procurement managers to expand their repertoire and vision in support of the extended enterprise.

GATEKEEPING AND INTERPRETATION

As previously defined, these boundary-spanning activities include responsibility for the unfettered flow of information to key persons both inside and outside the firm. However, the flow is not limited to data. Now the procurement manager must transform these data and interpret the information by utilizing his or her experience, decision support models, and other smart systems. For example, one task might be to help profile, find, and secure world-class supply partners for the extended enterprise. Relying on databases and other sources of information (see Chapters 3 and 6), buyers can make more informed decisions about potential suppliers and understand whether there is a good fit prior to making any commitments. There are systems that allow buyers to explore the future financial stability of potential suppliers, as well as to check other vital signs before they become candidates for supplier development efforts. On a more qualitative level, many of the major oil companies have used, as part of their RFP process, a survey that is intended to discover whether a new supplier thinks like a supply chain partner. Based on past data, the oil firms gain insight into the attitudes and mindset of a potential supplier and will select suppliers accordingly.

TRANSACTION AND INTEGRATION PLANNING

The notion of a traditional purchasing transaction implies that buyers negotiate contracts that are favorable to their companies and take advantage of the relative power position they have over the suppliers. Negotiations and terms and conditions take on a different meaning in the extended enterprise model. More one-sided strategies are replaced by win-win thinking. The buyer now is transformed into a teacher and a planner, a diplomat and a bridge builder. The buyer is well versed in the industry and the nature of competition among other supply chains. He or she also understands the end use market and how value is created in the marketplace. Think of the buyers in your own firm. How many of them possess these skills? Our bet is few, if any.

ENGAGING, MANAGING, AND MONITORING

Recall from the previous section that the third boundary-spanning activity was protecting, which can be interpreted as a policing function to ensure conformance with contractual terms and conditions, schedules, quality, and the like. Policing is associated with antiquated command and control mechanisms and really has no place in the extended enterprise. Now boundary roles activities are more focused on the creation of an environment where parties develop shared norms that serve to bolster and support the notions of the extended enterprise. In Chapter 7, we explained the relationship between trust and contracts, and that discussion is relevant here, as well.

MANAGING ACROSS NETWORKS

There are many challenges facing managers who orchestrate the coordinated efforts of the internal network of cross-functional activities, as well as external linkages. The skills needed are very similar to those possessed by alliance managers, who must also ensure the effective interplay among independent organizations coming together to bring their combined skills to the marketplace. Before we describe the skills and capabilities of the person needed to accomplish these boundary roles, it makes perfect sense first to describe what those roles are likely to be.

Previously, we suggested that the procurement function might undergo a major reorientation. As managers of external partnering, purchasing now engages in activities ranging from manufacturing to distribution to the co-development of new products. These activities are quite consistent with changes occurring across a number of different business sectors.

Consider a new business venture developed by Cardinal Health, Inc. to serve the pharmaceutical business. Positioned as part of Cardinal's collaborative e-commerce platform, the objective of this new business is to develop a number of technologies and services for drug companies that are beginning to rely on outside partners to provide a number of value-added functions. Cardinal's service offerings range from patented drug delivery technologies, contract manufacturing, and packaging to product launch capability. The company has a transparent interchange process with the U.S. Federal Drug Administration to ensure the timely and accurate filing of materials as the new drug works its way through critical trials and the like.

One implication is that the pharmaceutical buyer who works to align his or her firm with a new supplier such as

Cardinal must also take an enterprise-wide view, given the number of touch points Cardinal might have with a drug company. To orchestrate and build these complex relationships would be a challenge for most traditional procurement managers. As virtual integration (where collaboration links firms in the value chain) replaces vertical integration, these new boundary-spanning skills become much more critical. The new role is a far cry from the traditional roles played by buyers. To help gain an appreciation for these different skills, what follows is a description of the kind of manager who can successfully master the challenges of coordinating and integrating across these networks.

Managing across networks creates a complicated set of relationships that require time and talent. Thus, *management requires multi-faceted individuals with the ability to be flexible and adaptive to the development stage of the supply chain network*. That is, supply chains develop over time, as do the relationships among the members. The skills required to navigate these relationships will also change and adapt, depending on the stage of the relationship and the network. The talents required to orchestrate joint action at one stage of the lifecycle might not be the same as what is required at another stage. Early stage networks might need an advocate or champion who can build consensus around the key elements of the network's vision and mission. As the network matures, different skills are needed, such as skills of a facilitator or mediator, and typically entail ensuring the smooth running of the network and attending to those issues that threaten the network or potentially bog down its workflow. The boundary role person (i.e., procurement manager) will have to be an honest broker who is respected by all supply chain members, is viewed as an objective party, and thinks systemwide.

These boundary role managers must attend to a broad range of strategic and operational issues, operating simultaneously on three levels: across two or more separate partner companies, within the partner companies, and within the network and between individuals. Working across different levels with different people having different perspectives and agendas requires the capacity to be in different places at the same time. Individuals must have an ability to take a broad, strategic perspective while also knowing the details. We believe these people are in short supply, and until these skills are developed, many potential extended enterprise relationships will languish.

In some networks, firms work with competitors and begin to realize that they can cooperate and compete without fear of expropriation of their trade secrets and other proprietary information. Members soon become comfortable with the duality of network membership. A reciprocal interdependence exists in which rules emerge regarding what information is shared and when it is acceptable to say, "No, I cannot talk about that." Imagine the patience and clear thinking that must prevail when working with a competitor. At times, this can be quite awkward, especially when it relates to the unintended leakage of information.

Such awkward relationships are commonplace in the aerospace business, where firms cooperate and compete on a daily basis. Pratt Whitney and GE cooperate to build a new engine to compete against Rolls Royce for the new 650+ passenger Airbus while they compete very intensively to be the engine selected for each new Boeing 777 and 767. Pratt and GE have developed sequential work rules where each is responsible for parts of the engine. There is little co-mingling of personnel, and both firms work hard to eliminate any opportunity for information leakage

UNDERSTANDING THE COMPETENCIES
OF AN EXTENDED ENTERPRISE MANAGER

There are unique characteristics that define strong extended enterprise managers. Although not all managers possess these skills, those who do will be valuable assets to their firms and will contribute to their firms' competitive sustainability. The discussion that follows helps to understand what the array of skills are, how to identify these skills, and how to develop them in a purposeful manner. However, for these skills to flourish, there must first exist in the firm a set of building blocks that support and nurture these competencies. Without a supportive environment, it is less likely that these competencies will be deemed important by the firm.

BUILDING BLOCKS FOR EXTENDED ENTERPRISE THINKING

We have spoken about the different mindset and attitudes needed for extended enterprise thinking to grow within the supply chain. There are a number of relationship characteristics that produce less conflict and opportunism, greater cooperation, and heightened performance among supply chain partners.[7,8] These characteristics help explain the nature of close ties among supply chain partners.[9] Trust and commitment are the *sine qua non* of the extended enterprise. Without a basis of trust and a sense of commitment, there can be no long-term relationships. Trust is truly the cornerstone of any collaborative supply chain because it is the foundation for social order.[10] As we discussed in Chapter 7 trust takes time to develop; many companies lack both the patience and the skills that allow trust to emerge.

Commitment is simply one partner's willingness to devote time, energy, and/or resources to the alliance. When one partner demonstrates commitment, there is often a similar response from the other, and on it goes in a virtuous cycle. Monczka and his colleagues[11] found that when trading partners are willing to devote resources to ensure long-term interaction, a higher probability of success ensues. In part, failure in managing supply chains is attributable to management neglect and an inability to understand the set of factors that engender cooperative behavior. A Coopers and Lybrand study[12] reported that executives spend 23 percent of their time developing alliance plans and 19 percent of their time on drafting legal documents, but only 8 percent of their time is devoted to managing relationships. The lack of time devoted to relationship management is seen as a lack of commitment. Our experience is that managers at all levels woefully underestimate the amount of time required to attend to the needs of these collaborative supply chain relationships.

For example, a product recall at Ford highlights the importance of relationship management. Rather than point fingers at each other, Ford and Firestone should have come together and jointly designed new Explorer and Wilderness tires. It is a sad commentary that the current Ford chairman is the great-grandson of both Henry Ford and Harvey Firestone. An alliance of families and businesses that survived a century came to an end when Ford and its tire supplier could not solve the Explorer problem and began their public name calling over who was at fault. The product recall and the associated liability made the relationship almost meaningless, and each worked hard to protect its own assets. Trust in each other was damaged beyond repair, and the trust placed in both manufacturers by the public was called into question. Both firms are worse off for the experience.

Second, *communications* lies at the heart of information exchange among members of the supply chain. Transparency is affected by the frequency, depth, and content of information communicated, and certainly affects what is known supply chain-wide. Partners must have some common basis of past experience from which to benefit from the knowledge. Two points emerge here. The technological linkages must be in place, but the technology is merely an enabler. The true stumbling block is the degree to which partners are willing to share information and establish a common platform or vocabulary.

A third factor that affects the relationship among supply chain partners is the set of *integrative mechanisms* that link the partners on a number of dimensions ranging from procurement-related decisions regarding inventory levels and manufacturing schedules to more strategic issues related to innovative processes and joint business plans. Informal processes and structures enhance learning, and in these relationships, the opportunity to learn tacit knowledge is enhanced. At the same time, when integrative/coordinative mechanisms are limited and/or highly formalized, the full benefits of joint action are truncated.

A fourth factor is *decision-making style*. A firm's decision-making processes determine the way partners interact, affect how information is processed, impact the degree of formal versus informal exchanges and interaction, and influence the readiness with which joint knowledge is created and disseminated. Flexible, adaptive, and open organizations are more conducive to highly interactive exchanges and knowledge transfer.

At the other extreme is a highly bureaucratic organization where all information flows to the top and all decisions are centralized. With little sense of empowerment or little informal flows of information, it is difficult for supply chain partners to engage each other. Such conditions do not breed trust; they stifle commitment and make it virtually impossible for any supply chain-wide initiatives to succeed. In bureaucratic organizations where information is tightly held and protected, there is little appreciation for the importance of value chain optimization.

A fifth factor affecting the partners' ability to achieve supply chain-wide advantages is *company culture*. Culture reflects the central norms that characterize an organization and shape the expectations about what are appropriate behaviors and attitudes. Such a supportive culture is open to continuous learning, encourages questioning behavior, and rewards working hard to improve the quality and transparency of the information, both acquired through partnerships and created internally.

Two companies we have worked with were involved in a joint activity to improve the state of the art in their industry and to bring to the market a truly innovative solution. Although each partner had the requisite set of technical skills and expertise, their joint efforts were almost derailed because of the differences in their corporate cultures. One company viewed information as a public good and was willing to share with its partner so that the project could move along expeditiously. The other partner, although well intended, viewed information as a private good, and it was shared only on a need-to-know basis. These differences in their culture made it virtually impossible for the project team to accomplish its charter without intervention. As a result, the relationship suffered; the damage to the partnership has lingered and has had a debilitating effect on the partners' future efforts.

A final factor is the degree to which partners ascribe to and support a *win-win orientation*. Although somewhat related to the firm's culture, a win-win orientation captures the notion that trading parties will hold in check the tendency to act opportunistically and will work hard for the common good. A win-win orientation can be reflected in the psychological contract that shapes expectations of how trading partners will interact. The extended enterprise is a response to uncertainty that drives partners to cooperate. The same uncertainty that drives firms to ally and share knowledge also creates the circumstances for partners to behave opportunistically. A win-win orientation can mitigate this tension.

These six building blocks establish the degree and depth to which supply chain members engage in partnerlike behavior and maximize the joint benefits that accrue.[13] These building blocks support the development of competencies needed to be a successful extended enterprise manager. In fact, without these building blocks, organizational processes and structures will probably inhibit such competencies from being recognized and nurtured.

PROCESSES AND STRUCTURE NEED TO ADAPT

Developing a supply chain competence flows from recognition that supply chains are really socially constructed networks, and to navigate among the different members, a different set of skills is required. In fact, these relationships are quite unique and almost take on lives of their own.[14] However, there must exist supporting structure, procedures, and policies.

The operational hierarchical management styles of the past will no longer work. Rigid rules and single departmental emphasis to the detriment of the firm and the supply chain can no longer be accepted. These values and actions all support the notions of command and control. With a shift from tasks to process, the structure of the firm—the implicit interaction among parts, both internally and externally—will change. A process focus will raise the level of consideration to the extended enterprise, and supply chain performance will now extend to metrics that reflect the array of collaborating partners.

One effective mechanism for bringing the different partners together is the use team. Teaming crosses boundaries and functions, and focuses people's attention on joint efforts and joint outcomes. A challenge for supply chain members is that, in an extended enterprise context, many of the teams formed are virtual teams. Because work is often done at a distance and not face to face, trust becomes an important precursor to the effectiveness of the working relationship.

To manage the distance and time problems, Dupont relies heavily on teams in the early stages of new business development. The objective is to jump-start the collaborative process and to lay a foundation for completion of the innovative process. These teams consist of internal people as well as partner members who manage the process from concept to commercialization.

To be successful, these teams should possess a number of attributes that enable them to design and execute the workflow of the different projects. Illustrative of the attributes are:

- common focus/vision
- common picture of success
- clearly defined roles and responsibilities for team members
- shared understanding of outcomes and performance measures
- clearly defined performance measures
- valued differences that members bring to the team
- resolution of conflict in a productive fashion
- being good problem solvers
- linking to success of the team and not the individual members

Team leaders should possess unique skills, as well, because they must create and be comfortable with mutual interdependence. They must be strong facilitators and communicators because they cannot dictate action among team members. In light of the pressures for short-term financial performance, these people should also balance long-term commitments.* They must be passionate about the benefits of teaming and dedicated to making it work.

Recall that Honda has dedicated dozens of people to work with suppliers and has a long history of making significant investments in and commitments to its suppliers. Honda works to communicate its vision and ensure that partners are on the same wavelength. At the same time, performance expectations are well known and measurable. Forming an effective team requires the ability of supply chain partners (and team members) to form trusting relationships. It would follow that effective boundary role behavior would also include these capabilities. Without such skills, the business case will be jeopardized, and failure is almost assured.[15]

DEVELOPING EXTENDED ENTERPRISE MANAGER COMPETENCIES

Strong extended enterprise managers are in many ways alliance managers[16]; as a result, they must possess similar skills. Some of these competencies are teachable; others are not. Teachable competencies are those imparted through an "educational" experience. They are the kinds of skill sets and abilities that individuals acquire through more formal education, on-the-job training, or everyday work activities. They are generally competencies that are easily defined and observable. A number of these competencies are strongly associated with effective line management or general management skills. Unteachable competencies (e.g., being clever and creative, embracing other cultures), on the other hand, are more descriptive about how an individual thinks and sees the world. For instance, it is possible to reframe a question or problem so that the tension shifts from the partners to the common threat faced by the extended enterprise. Instead of arguing over how

*In fact, a recent conversation with a senior vice president of manufacturing operations and strategic sourcing worldwide suggested that part of the problem companies have in agreeing to partner and invest in the future is the corporate focus on quarterly reporting to Wall Street.

the pie is to be divided among partners, the more salient issue becomes how to preserve the pie in the face of new competitors and a common enemy. Although these skills may not be "teachable" in a traditional, programmed way, they are learnable. The best and most effective alliance managers have already acquired these skills over time.

TEACHABLE COMPETENCIES

There are three clusters of teachable competencies: functional, earned, and interpersonal. *Functional competencies* relate to actual business experiences and expertise required for general management strength. Strong extended enterprise managers know the business, their markets, their products, the technologies, and general system management. They appreciate better the value of enterprise-wide thinking, although their functional competence may be in manufacturing, logistics, purchasing, or materials planning and scheduling. They have developed a mindset where they understand their business, its core skills, and what role the extended enterprise plays in the firm's strategy.

A second cluster includes competencies that are less acquired and more earned. The word *earned* is chosen to connote that this array of skills stems from acknowledgment of a job well done. Past successes increase the credibility and respect acquired after years of building rapport within and through one's professional performance and interactions. Strong extended enterprise managers have paid attention to building networks throughout their careers, taking advantage of opportunities to serve on task forces and professional societies, and taking assignments that broaden their base of contacts, both internally and externally. They also know how to use their network-building skills quickly to tap into networks of their partners. A "hired gun," for example, may know the context well but will undoubtedly not have the network know-how or connections to get things done quickly and right.

Interpersonal competencies comprise the third cluster of skills and have to do with the ability to interact appropriately in diverse social settings. If relationships are a cornerstone of networks, as they are of strategic alliances, the ability to form relationships often begins with simple social encounters. Because networks are so heavily dependent on relationships between people, a manager's interpersonal skill can show little room for error. Understanding the finesse needed in "meeting and greeting" is not inconsequential or frivolous, and the ability to spend time socializing garners credibility and respect within the company. This social time builds relationships that can serve as a safety net to protect a troubled business relationship by providing the time and confidence to resolve conflicts and other problems.

Interpersonal competencies also include communication skills that encompass speaking and listening well to others in a one-on-one situation. In addition, it is the ability to make another, especially a manager of another culture, comfortable and at ease. Another strong root of interpersonal competencies has to do with cross-cultural tact and sensitivity. Persons with these skills understand how to relate to others who have different values or perspectives without demeaning themselves or their partner. A number of these capabilities track very closely to the team leadership skills presented above.

UNTEACHABLE COMPETENCIES

Unteachable competencies have to do with a way of thinking. Effective managers *think differently and see the world differently*. They tend to enjoy the risk-taking sense of a challenge, act with determination, and engender an entrepreneurial spirit. Often, they are described as adaptive, flexible, and open-minded. Successful managers tend to see multiple points of view *simultaneously* and in multiple dimensions. This is more than simply understanding the perspective of another; they are also guided by the past, learn from it, and are not limited by it. Managers who get locked into their pasts cannot properly diagnose their present problems. Short-term metrics breed short-term thinking. Too often, managers want immediate answers and solutions to their supply chain-related problems. To achieve the quick fix, managers often want to know how the past problem was addressed and exactly what steps were taken. Unfortunately, this "one-size-fits-all" technique is not likely to work because networks are vibrant, ever-changing entities with unique developmental patterns, pitfalls, and possibilities.

Strong extended enterprise managers should have the ability to see patterns in data and order among disorder. They have a talent for dealing with the abstract and are creative and even curious. These are difficult characteristics to train for. These managers are able to improvise and fashion innovative solutions in the present because they see what is possible. They look at supply chain networks as a source of new knowledge and embrace the opportunity to learn.

Do these people exist? We believe they do; these competencies are not so rare. The more relevant question is whether these people populate most buying organizations. Our experience is that herein lies the problem—many traditional buyers do not, in our estimation, possess these competencies. Ignoring the need for finding these people and developing them to fill extended enterprise positions could have serious strategic consequences.

FINDING THE RIGHT PERSON

In all, strong extended enterprise managers require a different kind of individual perspective and world view. This different orientation seems to explain in the most solid form the unteachable competencies we have articulated. A *network perspective* has at its foundation the ability to learn and to implement that learning, using a broad repertoire. Managers with a strong network perspective are able to bring order to chaos, thrive on ambiguity and uncertainty, and engage artfully with others. Those conditions become a catalyst for learning—not a threat to the status quo.

Companies need to acknowledge and appreciate the impact an individual manager can have on network development and success. This may seem obvious, but recognizing the need and importance of who is placed into a network management position can be a key determinant of success. Network manager development is not just a human resources issue; it is a question of developing corporate talent belonging to the entire company. In fact, it is a question of developing talent for the extended enterprise. Given the nature and level of analysis for competitive behavior among supply chains, the choice of network manager can have profound implications. Senior managers must ask questions that seek to identify the depth of teachable competencies and the strength of the unteachable skills. A sampling of the kinds of questions one might ask follows.

NETWORK MANAGER COMPETENCIES: WHAT KINDS OF QUESTIONS TO ASK

Functional Competencies

- Does this person have the necessary or relevant line management skills for this supply chain?
- To what extent does this person understand the company, its products, and its business?
- How might this person's educational background enhance or detract from the position?
- Does this person have a strong understanding of our business and of the supply chain's business?

Earned Competencies

- Has this person developed an extensive network within our company?
- Does this person have an extensive business network in the industry?
- Has this person developed solid relationships within the partner company?
- Does this individual have credibility in our company?
- Does this individual have credibility and respect outside our company, especially with our partners and in the alliance?

Interpersonal Competencies

■ To what degree is this person comfortable in social business situations?

■ How does this person demonstrate sensitivity to differences between cultures?

■ Is this person considered an effective communicator in diverse settings?

■ To what degree does this person easily alter his or her behavior to fit with a new environment or setting?

■ Is the person attuned to nonverbal communication?

■ Can this person easily sense the mood of a group or individual?

Network Mindset

■ Does this person have an affinity for complexity?

■ Can this person think in terms of patterns, connections, and rela-tionships?

■ Does this person thrive on challenges?

■ Does this person continue to learn from his or her experiences?

■ Is this person described by others as "thinks about and sees the world differently?"

■ Can this person simultaneously consider multiple points of view?

Once identified, these same managers can also learn what it means to partner, for the company and for the entire supply chain. Thus, through a series of escalating experiences and exposure to mentors and role models, new management talent can learn from what the others are doing. The more diverse the models, the more broad the learning can be. The emphasis here is on *can learn*. Network managers are an integral part of the firm's larger alliance development and alliance success. However, their development in part depends on their company seeing and valuing extended enterprise activities and the related skills and competencies.

Desiring strong network managers but failing to reward relevant behaviors or to foster a collaborative spirit can undermine a company's efforts. Good network managers grow up in a culture that supports allying behavior in a company where the infrastructure and managerial processes reward and encourage cooperation and collaboration, initiative, risk taking, inquisitiveness, and innovation that alliances demand. Without a supportive environment, good network management is incomplete. Simply, there must be a plan for developing and identifying the critical role played by these managers; the process cannot be left to chance.

EXTENDED ENTERPRISES EVOLVE OVER TIME

Supply chain networks develop over time and, as a consequence, go through phases that tend to solidify the relationship among partners, build trust and commitment, and enable the network to accomplish its objectives. Recall that an extended enterprise/network view represents a transformation. Before firms evolve to appreciate the value of network thinking, there is a stage in which there is *little collaboration* among the potential partners. Here the partners still work in parallel, duplicating effort and not realizing the gains that can be made if they begin to cooperate and work together. They are not acknowledging the skills and expertise each could bring to the network. Often the thought of sharing resources, information, and decision making is an unpleasant thought to many senior managers. It can be seen as a sign of weakness, even failure, to be reliant on another to accomplish a set of goals.

As companies and network managers become more comfortable with the idea that decision making will be shared among partners and as each begins to understand the level of resources each is willing to dedicate to the network, there develops a degree of *at-stakeness*. At-stakeness suggests that partners share similar levels of commitment and are comfortable with the notion of sharing power. There is recognition that skills and resources across the firm must be integrated if the network is to provide value to the marketplace.

At the next stage in the transformation there exists a *transparency*. There is an open exchange of information within the network. Partners understand each other's motivations and as a consequence, belief systems begin to align, and common values and norms start to emerge. You can easily imagine that such transparency also serves to lower the boundaries that might still separate network members; clearly, with added insight, barriers are likely to fall.

As companies begin to integrate their relevant operations more closely, commitment grows, social norms guiding network behavior become widely accepted, and systemwide thinking supplants any opportunistic behavior. This level of mindfulness serves to unite the network in meeting the goals that first brought the network together. At the final stage of the transformation, network members achieve the full *synergy* that permits unexpected gains. Such closeness breeds gains that arise by chance because risk-taking behavior is considered safe and leads to experimentation. Through experimentation, managers learn to trust, commit additional resources, and accomplish goals beyond their initial expectations.

The challenge is how to create the environment that encourages, supports, and nurtures such thinking. Silo thinking, centralized decision making, and the like run counter to the network view. There is a major transformational experience that must occur. Traditional models and templates no longer apply. Senior management must lead the charge and provide both the opportunity and the facilitating structure and processes. You do not change the organization overnight; rather, it evolves. Yet the evolution must be planned, and the change required for this "new world" must begin today.

Managers must have an ability to look to the future while focusing on the present. This duality provides a link between the two worlds in which the firm operates and sets a clear path to be followed. Although urgency can be established and a new vision can be articulated, change requires that the organization clearly see the path forward and understand the positive impact it will make. Simply, there must be a plan, and there must be mechanisms (e.g., structures and processes) in place to support the plan.

It should be apparent that a network fostered by an absence of boundaries is not the goal or an end point. The need for network managers is a response to an uncertain and complex world in which one firm has neither the resources nor the expertise to navigate these uncharted and often rough waters. Thus, leaders must be comfortable setting a path and knowing that the outcome is not fully known at this juncture. Managers need the strength of conviction to know that the direction is right and that midcourse corrections are allowed. Moreover, systems and measures must be adaptive enough to reflect this reality; cultures must be receptive to the idea that with learning comes mistakes, and there are hard lessons to learn.

SUMMARY

The new world order that is symbolized by the extended enterprise requires a different kind of manager. We believe that the changes that are required to become a successful member of an extended enterprise network cannot be achieved with traditional thinking about the roles and responsibilities of a procurement manager. We believe that the title of this new person should reflect the different demands and capabilities needed to manage effectively across boundaries. To the reader who cannot imagine this new world, this chapter reads more like science fiction. The ability to think about this new breed of manager requires both some imagination and courage. Imagination is needed to envision this new world in which work happens across boundaries at the nexus of firms and not always within the comforts of "my" department or company. Courage is needed to act on this realization and to work to change the status quo. The extended enterprise is not the default option for companies. It will take work, organizational changes, and managers who can lead through uncertain times with conviction and with the ability to compel others to do the same.

CHAPTER 9

METRICS FOR EXTENDED ENTERPRISE PERFORMANCE MEASUREMENT

As noted in Chapter 1, the overarching objectives of the extended enterprise are to maximize the value generated for the ultimate end customer and to minimize total costs along the entire value chain. In this context, metrics for performance are of key importance because they influence the ability to conceptualize the extended enterprise. More importantly, they affect managerial behaviors that impact the capabilities required to implement the tenets of the extended enterprise. To repeat an old adage, "What gets measured gets rewarded; what gets rewarded gets done."

This chapter reviews briefly some of the traditional performance measures used in purchasing and supply chain management (SCM) before discussing the kinds of measures needed for the extended enterprise. It was noted in Chapter 4 that performance measures should be aligned with strategic objectives. Supply chain strategies may differ from company to company, depending on the firm's business strategy, its position in the supply chain, its competencies, and top management desires. Some companies may be at a point where they need to develop expertise and competencies *within specific functions*, such as purchasing, customer service, or manufacturing. Their performance measures should focus on functions and departments. Other companies may have a greater need for *cross-functional capabilities* within their own firms and need cross-functional metrics, and still other companies have a need for *interenterprise capabilities* and need metrics that focus on supply chain activities. All three categories of metrics are discussed in this chapter.

TRADITIONAL PERFORMANCE MEASURES: FOCUS ON FUNCTIONS

The traditional approach to performance measurement has been with metrics that focus on individual functional departments, such as purchasing, manufacturing, logistics, and customer service. Table 9.1 shows some examples of these functional unit-focused types of metrics for three different functional areas. Note that all emphasize measures of efficiency, and all have as major objectives how to reduce costs or raise productivity.

With respect to supply management, the approach is often purchasing-centric, with major emphasis on *efficiency of transactions*. Metrics such as number of purchase orders per buyer, dollars managed per buyer, line items managed per buyer, and time required to process orders are usually favored over "softer" measures, such as degree of supplier cooperation, supplier commitment, and quality of supplier support services. The measures are often department-centered, with few, if any, linkages to company goals.

Traditionally, purchasing performance goals have been set on the basis of historical data, and there have been few

TABLE 9.1 Performance Metrics across Three Functional Areas

PURCHASING-RELATED METRICS	MANUFACTURING-RELATED METRICS		LOGISTICS-RELATED METRICS	
Material inventories	Product quality	Line breakdowns	Finished goods inventory turns	Warehouse space utilization
Supplier delivery performance	Work-in-process inventories	Plant utilization	Finished goods inventory days of supply	End-of-life inventory
Material quality	Adherence to schedule	Warranty costs	On-time delivery	Obsolete inventory
Material inventories	Cost per unit produced	Source-to-make cycle time	Lines picked/hour	Inventory shrinkage
Unit purchase costs	Setups/changeovers	Percent scrap	Damaged shipments	Cost of carrying inventory
Material acquisition costs:	Setup/changeover costs	Material usage variants	Inventory accuracy	Documentation accuracy
■ Cost per purchase order	Unplanned stockroom issues	Overtime usage	Pick accuracy	Transportation costs
■ Dollars managed per buyer	Bill of materials accuracy	Production cycle time	Logistics costs	Warehousing costs
■ Expediting costs	Routing accuracy	Manufacturing productivity	Shipment accuracy	Container utilization
Line items per buyer	Plant space utilization	Master schedule stability	On-time shipment	Truck cube utilization
Time per purchase order	Process yields		Delivery times	Premium freight charges
No. of purchase orders per buyer				Warehouse receipts
Invoice errors				

industry-wide standards. There have been attempts by numerous consultancies to establish best-in-class performance, and some of these efforts have resulted in improvements in efficiency of their clients' procurement logistics and materials management activity. However, in general, traditional measures tend to be narrowly focused, are often tied to measures of efficiency and not effectiveness, and are less likely to reflect the more behavioral aspects of the relationship among departments (and companies). If the adage "what gets measured, gets done" is true, the traditional focus will lead to suboptimal performance and outcomes.

SUPPLY CHAIN PERFORMANCE MEASURES: THE ENTERPRISE VIEW

As purchasing and logistics morphed into SCM, new and different approaches to performance measurement were called for. Over the past decade, there has been growing recognition that the role and goals of supply management needed to be linked more closely with company goals and top management expectations. Monzcka, for example, has noted that the traditional measures focusing on supply management *efficiency and transactional processing* are insufficient. Managers should also develop *measures of effectiveness* to help drive continuous improvement and change in people's behavior.[1] Rather than ask whether procurement is doing things right, the question now is, Are they doing the right things? Measures of effectiveness that truly capture both the goals of the firm and the intent of the extended enterprise become important. Also, as noted in Chapters 1 and 2, the new competitive realities demand much higher levels of cross-functional integration and cooperation.

With the advent of SCM concepts, firms began to look more at enterprise-wide integration and to focus on cross-functional processes, as well as individual departmental functions, such as purchasing and manufacturing. The perspective is still on "our company," and "us" versus "them" (i.e., other members of the chain), but the view is across several functions/departments instead of just one. In an attempt to break down the traditional functional "silos," many companies created cross-functional teams with responsibility for specific processes, such as order fulfillment and new product development. Some companies institutionalized this focus by emphasizing the "horizontal organization." Organizing around major cross-functional processes, these firms created new process-focused management titles, such as Vice President of New Product Development and Director of Order Fulfillment.[2] To support such organizational changes and in pursuit of enterprise-wide integration, new process-based metrics began to appear. Table 9.2 lists a few of these for illustration.

TABLE 9.2   Enterprise-Oriented Cross-Functional Metrics

PROCESS CROSS-FUNCTIONAL METRICS	
Forecast accuracy	New product time-to-market
Percent perfect orders	Planning process cycle time
Cash-to-cash cycle time	Schedule changes

An example of process-based performance measurement shown in Table 9.2 is the "perfect order concept," which measures the percentage of customer orders that are flawlessly fulfilled.[3] Like the process it reflects, the metrics cross the boundaries of traditional functional departments to measure the effectiveness of order fulfillment. A failure in any step of the process, such as an inventory shortage on a packaging line or an incorrect invoice in the accounting department, results in a failure to meet the goal of perfectly fulfilling an order. To measure performance against this goal, a number of individual metrics are involved, such as order availability, order entry accuracy, warehouse picking accuracy, production accuracy, on-time product shipment, on-time product delivery, product quality, paperwork accuracy, customer inquiry service, and invoice accuracy.

Another cross-functional, process-based metric shown in Table 9.2 is cash-to-cash cycle time. This measures the average time it takes to convert dollars expended on raw materials into dollars collected for finished product. It cuts across purchasing, manufacturing, logistics, customer service, and other functions to provide a combined measure of overall efficiency of particular importance to top management.

Many companies have utilized cross-functional metrics such as these in creating their own systems for measuring supply chain performance, as noted in the next section. Probably the best-known supply chain model today—the Supply Chain Council's SCOR (Supply Chain Operations Reference) Model[4]—incorporates cross-functional, enterprise-wide measurements of supply chain performance. The approach followed in this widely adopted industry standard model involves a set of supply chain performance measures comprised of a combination of the following:

- Cycle time metrics (e.g., production cycle time and cash-to-cash cycle)
- Cost metrics (e.g., cost per shipment and cost per warehouse pick)
- Service/quality metrics (order fulfillment, on-time shipments, and defective products)
- Asset metrics (e.g., inventory turns, return on controllable assets)

Many different sets of metrics can be used with the SCOR Model, depending on the particular strategic objectives and competencies of the individual firm, as noted earlier. Figure 9.1 shows one representative set of metrics arranged according to the SCOR Model's four standard supply chain processes (plan, make, source, and deliver). The measures shown here include both function-specific (e.g., production costs) and cross-functional (e.g., order fulfillment) measures.

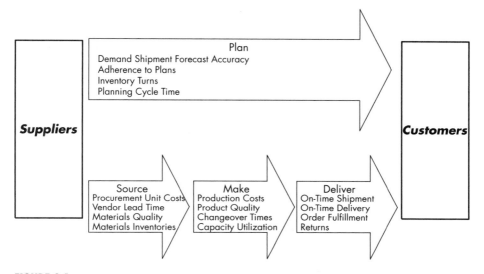

FIGURE 9.1

Illustrative performance measures based on the Supply Chain Council's SCOR Model. *Source:* Supply Chain Council, SCOR Overview, 2001.

SUPPLY CHAIN PERFORMANCE MEASURES—THE SUPPLY CHAIN-WIDE VIEW

The examples of PolyOne and other companies in Chapter 3 showed that the cross-functional process approach to measuring supply chain performance can be extended across firm borders to create cross-enterprise processes. Alternatively, enterprise-wide metrics such as cash-to-cash cycle time can be applied consistently to the succession of individual firms along the value chain. The challenge faced with either approach is that the chain is typically composed of independent business units and legal entities with separate stockholders and managers, and differing business goals and objectives. Rarely does one firm control an entire supply chain's performance. However, as Chapter 3 showed, considerable evidence attests to the significant benefits that can occur when cross-enterprise processes are integrated and synchronized, and separate firms cooperate to optimize the supply chain. Because of this recognition, considerable effort has been expended in recent years to develop metrics for cross-enterprise and supply chain-wide performance measurement. Three of the more prominent such proposals for coordinated chain-wide performance measurement are:

1. A different set of SCOR Model metrics
2. The Supply Chain Performance Scorecard developed by the Performance Measurement Group (PMG)
3. The Balanced Scorecard (BSC) for SCM

SCOR MODEL

Table 9.3 shows another set of metrics proposed for use with a recent version of the SCOR Model, intended to be applied to all enterprises along a particular supply chain, from beginning to end. Five broad supply chain performance attributes (reliability, responsiveness, flexibility, cost, and assets) are intended to be measured by 13 metrics, some of which are precisely specified (e.g., cash-to-cash cycle time) and some that require further specification for measurement in a particular application (e.g., value-added productivity). Both customer-facing (e.g., delivery performance) and internally facing measures (e.g., asset turns) are included in this set.

PMG SUPPLY CHAIN PERFORMANCE SCORECARD

In 1994, a consortium from academia and industry led by the consulting firm of PRTM looked at the challenge of measuring performance across a total, or "integrated," supply chain in pursuit of ensuring end-customer satisfaction. The consortium proposed a comprehensive group of integrated supply chain performance measures.[5] Four broad areas of performance measurement were addressed:

TABLE 9.3 SCOR Metrics for Supply Chain-wide Performance Measurement

PERFORMANCE ATTRIBUTE	PERFORMANCE ATTRIBUTE DEFINITION	METRIC
Supply chain delivery reliability	The performance of the supply chain in delivering the correct product to the correct place, at the correct time, in the correct condition and packaging, in the correct quantity, and with the correct documentation to the correct customer.	Delivery performance Fill rates Perfect order fulfillment
Supply chain responsiveness	The velocity at which a supply chain provides products to the customer.	Order fulfillment lead times
Supply chain flexibility	The agility of a supply chain in responding to marketplace changes to gain or maintain competitive advantage.	Supply chain response time Production flexibility
Supply chain costs	The costs associated with operating the supply chain.	Cost of goods sold Total supply chain management costs Value-added productivity Warranty/returns processing costs
Supply chain asset management efficiency	The effectiveness of an organization in managing assets to support demand satisfaction. This includes the management of all assets, fixed and working capital	Cash-to-cash cycle time Inventory days of supply Asset turns

Source: Supply Chain Council, *SCOR Overview* V5, Pittsburgh, PA (August 2001).

1. Customer satisfaction/quality
2. Cost
3. Time
4. Assets

A total of eight primary metrics and ten secondary metrics were proposed by the consortium to measure performance across these four areas. The eight primary measures suggested by the 1994 consortium, with slight revision, were subsequently used as the basis for a Supply Chain Performance Scorecard developed by the PMG, a subsidiary of PRTM. Table 9.4 shows an early version of the PMG scorecard.[6]

TABLE 9.4 PMG Supply Chain Scorecard Metrics

PERFORMANCE METRIC	CUSTOMER-FACING		INTERNALLY FACING	
	Delivery	Responsiveness	Cost	Assets
Delivery performance to request*	✔			
Delivery performance to commit	✔			
Order fulfillment lead time		✔		
Upside production flexibility*		✔		
Total SCM cost			✔	
Cash-to-cash cycle time*				✔
Total inventory day's supply				✔
Net asset turns*				✔

*Metric used in later versions of Scorecard.

PMG reports that this scorecard or some subset of it has been used by hundreds of companies, including a large number of the more than 700 technology-based enterprises that are part of the Supply Chain Council. Originally containing the eight metrics shown in Table 9.4, the scorecard has evolved into a balanced set of the four metrics highlighted in the table. These include two customer-facing (delivery performance to request and upside production flexibility) and two internally facing metrics (cash-to-cash cycle time and net asset turns).

Annual surveys conducted in the years 1995–1998 produced evidence that companies that ranked among the best in class according to these four measures were market leaders, commanding up to 75 percent higher profits than average performers. The 1998 survey reported that a company with strong SCM performance was likely to have 60–100 percent better asset utilization, freeing up cash to use on investment opportunities or reduction of debt.[7]

Despite the positive benefits associated with use of these performance measures, PMG's 2001 survey found that they were still in the early stages of adoption by industry. Only about 36 percent of the respondent companies were using scorecard metrics to steadily increase the capability of their supply chains.[8] And despite the adoption by many companies of the BSC concept for their general business practices, less than one-third of the companies surveyed (which included blue-chip companies such as Johnson & Johnson, IBM, Dow Chemical, Mobil, AT&T Wireless, Colgate-Palmolive, Honeywell, and Raytheon) were measuring supply chain performance from all four perspectives of the supply chain scorecard (delivery performance, flexibility and responsiveness, cost, and assets). An overwhelming majority of these companies implemented their measurement programs in the two years prior to the survey, showing again the emerging nature of these applications.

BALANCED SCORECARD FOR SCM

The BSC, created by Kaplan and Norton,[9] was originally developed for general application to business organizations as an alternative to traditional profit-oriented performance measurement systems. It is designed primarily to help firms that have historically overemphasized short-term financial performance. The BSC provides a structured mechanism for influencing managers to achieve a balance between nonfinancial and financial results across short- and long-term planning horizons. As indicated in Figure 9.2, Kaplan and Norton

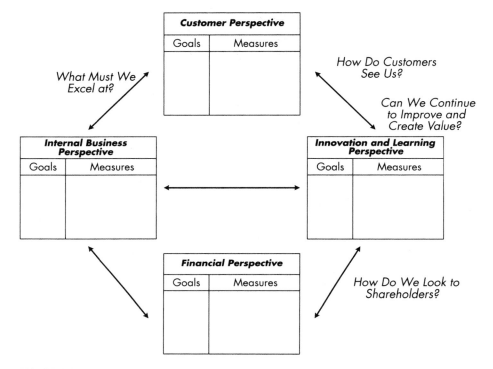

FIGURE 9.2
The BSC framework. *Source*: Peter C. Brewer and Thomas W. Speh, "Using the Balanced Scorecard to Measure Supply Chain Performance," *Journal of Business Logistics* 21, no. 1 (2000).

suggest that balance is obtained by adopting performance measures of the firm that represent, respectively:

- customer perspective
- internal business process perspective
- innovation and learning perspective
- financial perspective

Kaplan and Norton's BSC concept was subsequently adapted for application to SCM by Peter Brewer and Thomas Speh.[10] Their adaptation, shown schematically in Figures 9.3 and 9.4, substitutes a total supply chain view for the individual firm view of Kaplan and Norton's BSC.

The supply chain cost of ownership measure (for example)

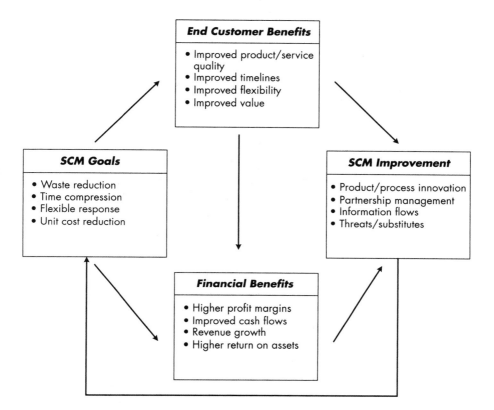

FIGURE 9.3

An SCM framework. *Source:* Peter C. Brewer and Thomas W. Speh, "Using the Balanced Scorecard to Measure Supply Chain Performance," *Journal of Business Logistics* 21, no. 1 (2000).

is intended to capture the costs across the supply chain associated with purchasing, holding of inventory, poor quality, and delivery failures. Similarly, in the financial perspective category, the cash-to-cash cycle measure is intended to show how long it takes, on average, to convert a dollar spent for raw materials into a dollar collected for finished product along the chain. The premise is that supply chains that have successfully increased product and information flow and have effectively integrated operations among partners will have faster cash-to-cash cycles than ones that have not done so.

Like the SCOR chain-wide metrics and the PMG Scorecard, the SCM BSC extends management's perspective to

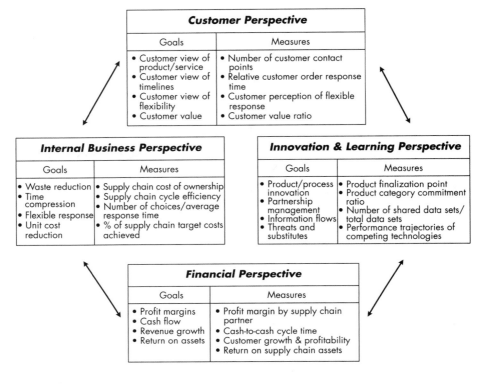

FIGURE 9.4

The supply chain BSC framework. *Source:* Peter C. Brewer and Thomas W. Speh, "Using the Balanced Scorecard to Measure Supply Chain Performance," *Journal of Business Logistics* 21, no. 1 (2000).

upstream and downstream supply chain partners. However, what distinguishes some of the measures shown in Figure 9.4 from traditional metrics and the other chain-wide approaches described here is that they begin to focus on behaviors and situations other than the arm's-length business practices associated with traditional adversarial open-market negotiations. For example, the financial perspective measures shown in Figure 9.4 include profit margin by supply chain partner and customer growth and profitability.

Although the SCM BSC was proposed as recently as 2000, some of the supply chain-wide metrics shown in Figure 9.4 (e.g., cash-to-cash cycle time, net asset turns) have been used and tracked for several years, as reported in the PMG studies noted above. It is significant to the thesis of this book that the most recent PMG survey suggests that use of these measures is at least to some degree associated with better-than-average financial performance, as noted earlier. On a related note, a study sponsored by the Conference Board found that companies whose stock outperforms their rivals are more likely to have a formal strategic performance measurement system such as Kaplan and Norton's BSC.[11] For example, under the category of internal business perspective, Figure 9.4 shows four business process measures that are intended to track performance across the entire supply chain.

The shift in philosophy that takes place when a supply chain point of view is embedded within the BSC framework is that the scorecard's internal perspective is expanded to include both the "interfunctional" and "partnership" perspectives. In essence, the SCM BSC begins to force the incorporation of integrative measures, in addition to the traditional nonintegrated measures that motivate employees to view their firm's success as also being dependent on the success of others in the supply chain. As noted earlier, the cash-to-cash cycle time and total cost of ownership metrics are examples of integrated measures that embrace several functions (accounting, manufacturing, logistics, and sales) across more than one business firm. This type of integrated measure spans functional and firm boundaries to show all members how the chain is performing and fosters incentives to work with other members of the chain.

EXTENDED ENTERPRISE MEASURES*

The BSC perspective affords a number of benefits from which an appropriate set of extended enterprise metrics can be proposed:

1. The metrics used flow from the supply chain members' shared vision and strategy.

---

*This section benefited greatly from discussions with Jeffrey Trimmer, currently a Batten Fellow at the Darden School and a former executive with DaimlerChrysler.

2. The approach can be used to evaluate and refine supply chain-wide implementation of measures in support of the strategy.
3. The BSC helps managers understand the future by focusing selectively on the drivers of present performance.
4. The BSC application process itself educates supply chain members about their contribution to the total picture and demonstrates how each fits into the picture.

As noted previously, the assumptions around which the BSC was created fit logically within the extended enterprise framework. For example, the focus on both financial and non-financial measures is very appropriate because extended enterprise members become involved in ensuring equitable financial returns for all partners, based on inputs and value-added capabilities. At the same time, the ability to build and sustain a trusting and committed relationship is fundamental to achieving the goals of the extended enterprise. Also, the focus on the end customer lies at the core of the extended enterprise because its objective is to bring superior value to the marketplace. Finally, the emphasis on process-related measures and learning highlight two of the key attributes of the extended enterprise. Process-related measures tend to capture indirectly how well an activity is being accomplished and to serve as an early warning signal of possible problems.

Ideally, performance measures for the extended enterprise should push every firm in the supply chain and all employees in every firm to focus their efforts on increasing the total profits for all chain members as this supply chain competes with other supply chains for the hearts and minds of end-use customers. Such rewards can come only through an integration of all chain members' logistics, procurement, operations, and marketing processes with other upstream and downstream members so that materials, information, component parts, and finished product flow seamlessly from point of origin to the final consumer at low cost and with high levels of service.

A 2000 survey in *Industry Week* reported that although there is much talk about value chain management and collaborating with partners across the entire supply chain, less than 2 percent of executives report that their firms function as full extended enterprises.[12] The survey suggests that much of the inertia can be traced to cultural and corporate barriers. Leading the list was a lack of senior management commitment and an inability to tie supply chainwide efforts to strategy. Also on the list was the need to develop common processes for partner selection that span the supply chain to ensure consistency.

However, despite the inertia, managers in the survey did acknowledge that there are many benefits gained from information sharing with partners, as summarized in Table 9.5.

TABLE 9.5 Summary of Major Benefits Gained from Information Sharing with Supply Chain Partners

MAJOR BENEFITS GAINED	% OF COMPANIES IN SUPERIOR SUPPLY CHAINS	% OF COMPANIES IN POOR SUPPLY CHAINS
Increased sales	41	14
Cost savings	62	22
Increased market share	32	12
Inventory reduction	51	18
Improved quality	60	28
Accelerated delivery times	54	27
Improved logistics management	43	15
Improved customer service	66	22

The *Industry Week* article also noted a prediction that firms that fail to create external supply chain-wide metrics will become less preferred as partners. Without such metrics, it is more likely that management will act in a self-serving manner. Even more supportive of an extended enterprise perspective is the forecast by industry experts that price pressures, a historic barrier to value chain optimizing, will fade in importance, and collaborative benefits of time saving, reliability, and market share will become more important.

For example, one of the key predictions in a 1998 study conducted jointly by the Center for Advanced Purchasing Studies, A. T. Kearney, Arizona State University, and Michigan

State University was: "In order for organizations to gain a competitive advantage in the future . . . more focus will be placed
on trust-building, communications, and joint planning and
developments. . . . The emphasis [will be] placed on selecting
supply partners that are considered to be solid relationship
candidates, as opposed to selecting them on traditional metrics
such as price." As one manager put it, speaking about supplier
selection, "I foresee a day when the source evaluation process
will be entirely focused on the relationship potential. A cross-
functional team will evaluate suppliers based on a variety of
relationship factors, but not price."[13]

The challenge is to extend current thinking to capture
issues such as the ones presented above and to acknowledge
that for many managers it is a stretch to consider performance
measures that affect the entire supply chain versus only what
impacts them directly. The most critical pieces of the puzzle
are the people and their ability to embrace change. Each of
these issues must be reflected in the extended enterprise's
BSC. To begin the process of creating an extended enterprise
scorecard, partners must agree on a more comprehensive set
of metrics to reflect a value chain-wide perspective.

For example, two dimensions of the model presented by
Brewer and Speh that would benefit from additional measures
aligned with the goals of the extended enterprise would be the
financial and customer perspectives. The objective here is to
reflect more fully the set of performance measures that
support and encourage extended enterprise thinking and
action. These proposed metrics are summarized in Table 9.6.

A second way to extend current thinking is to fill any
apparent voids in the current BSC model. For example, two
key missing components in the model are measures for:

1. *Determining the degree to which key business
   processes are synchronized and complemented
   across all supply chain partners.* This would include
   processes for managing inventory, workflow, and the
   like, as well as processes for improving quality, time to
   market, all aspects of the new product development
   and innovation, and processes for information gather-
   ing and knowledge management across all firms. Other

TABLE 9. 6 Transforming the Supply Chain BSC to an Extended Enterprise Focus

DIMENSION OF SUPPLY CHAIN BSC	EXISTING METRICS	PROPOSED METRICS
Financial	1. Profit margin by supply chain partner 2. Cash-to-cash cycle time 3. Customer growth and profitability 4. Return on supply chain assets	1. Equitable division of profits across the supply chain 2. Cash-to-cash cycle time across the chain 3. Total return on assets across the supply chain 4. Systemwide cost savings
Customer	1. No. of customer contact points 2. Relative customer order response time 3. Customer perception of flexible response 4. Customer value ratio	1. Market share of priority segments 2. Share of wallet 3. Conversion rate of customers to loyal customers 4. Speed of market/segment entry 5. Level of cross-selling

process-related metrics might relate to mechanisms for resolving conflict and serious disagreements.

2. *Assessing the relationship-specific measures that must lie at the heart of the extended enterprise.* For example, it is essential that measures exist for estimating the degree of collaboration, trust, and commitment, as well as the level of perceived conflict. These qualitative metrics would reflect much of the behavior in the extended enterprise and help ensure the full and dedicated involvement of trading partners.

These two components complement the current BSC approach. The consideration of external processes in effect raises the level of analysis from the firm and its internal functions to the level of the supply chain. The objective is to supplement the traditional internal processes with other processes that are unique to managing the workflow, cash flows, and information flows across the entire supply chain. An illustration of these measures is summarized in Table 9.7.

TABLE 9.7 Possible Additional External Process Measures for the Extended Enterprise

POSSIBLE PROCESSES TO MEASURE

1. Compatibility of software systems that span the supply chain
2. Time taken to implement supply chain-wide IT changes
3. Processes to ensure shared strategic plans at all levels
4. Percentage of new product successes over X period of time
5. Average time to develop and implement new product/services
6. Processes to ensure that relevant technology and knowledge is shared supply chain-wide
7. System-wide partner selection processes

Another implication of the external processes component is the highlighting of the processes that affect each member of the supply chain and that have a profound impact on how well the extended enterprise performs, relative to other competing networks. Demand and supply forecasting processes, technology sharing, and cross-supply chain learning and knowledge transfer all improve the accuracy of the information shared, ensure a common view of the world, and lead to firm-level improvements that are a function of systemwide effects. Moreover, these processes are more likely to lead to a common vision and gain alignment of the goals and objectives across the extended enterprise.

In his highly revealing study of the automotive industry, for example, Jeffrey Dyer showed that specific types of behavior between buyers and suppliers led to higher levels of mutual trust, which in turn resulted in lower transaction costs, higher return on investment, higher levels of knowledge sharing, and higher levels of investment in dedicated assets.[14] Dyer distinguishes between interpersonal trust (between two individuals) and interfirm trust (between groups of individuals); he found that U.S. suppliers trust Toyota more than they trust U.S. automakers, not because of greater levels of interpersonal trust but because they find Toyota's *business processes* for working with suppliers to be fairer and more consistent. Dyer refers to this *process-based trust* as critical for creating a trust orientation between individuals in large organizations.

Dyer notes that a firm is viewed as trustworthy when it has institutionalized a set of practices and routines (i.e., business processes) for dealing with a partner organization that transcend the influence of particular individuals. He found that key processes that can either foster or destroy supplier trust include the automaker's supplier selection process and the processes by which automakers transfer knowledge to suppliers to help them improve productivity and quality. Thus, measures and metrics that indicate the effectiveness of such critical processes are vital to the success of the extended enterprise.

From the above it is clear that performance metrics that help measure the degree of collaboration, trust, commitment, and related behavior are necessary in the BSC approach for the extended enterprise. The objective of this BSC dimension is to understand the extent to which the different supply chain members engage in appropriate behaviors that reinforce and bolster the principles and ideals of the extended enterprise. Table 9.8 illustrates the types of behaviors related to collaboration that might be the basis for specific measures.

The challenge is to ensure that senior management understands the strategic importance of this type of metric and is willing to accept more behavioral measures to help determine supply chain success. Equally important, management must be willing to invest in training and education to develop supply chain managers who have the requisite skills implied by these metrics. As stated in preceding chapters, this is a nontrivial challenge. These metrics carry very significant changes for the traditional OEM or supplier. For example, managerial mindsets will have to change across a number of dimensions:

- From functional to process integration
- From information hoarding to information sharing
- From adversarial to collaborative behavior
- From customer service to relationship management

TABLE 9.8 Collaboration and Related Behaviors

ELEMENTS OF THE BSC	EXAMPLE STATEMENTS OF BEHAVIOR RELATING TO HOW THE ELEMENT MIGHT BE MEASURED
Collaboration	The extent to which partners: ■ share business plans ■ take into account the needs of all supply chain members ■ work on behalf of all members of the supply chain ■ are willing to adapt to changing conditions without renegotiating the contract ■ share similar long-term objectives and goals ■ share a consistent view of how to do business ■ have a strong chemistry among supply chain members
Trust	Trading partners have a reputation for fairness. Trading partners do not take advantage of each other. Trading partners are confident that sensitive information will be used as intended. Trading partners do what they say they will do. Trading partners consistently monitor the benefits and costs that accrue. Trading partners share in gains proportional to their risk. Trading partners compare costs and benefits to those of other partners to ensure that the partnership is equitable. Contracts with partners tend to be as complete as possible. Members of the supply chain show a great deal of integrity.
Conflict resolution	When faced with problems or disagreements, supply chain members generally: ■ Enter into a direct discussion of the problem ■ Attempt to get all concerns on the table ■ Seek win-win solutions ■ Try to seek a middle ground ■ Use give and take to reach a compromise ■ Try to find a solution between the two extremes ■ Use power to push through their own position

TABLE 9.8 Collaboration and Related Behaviors (Continued)

ELEMENTS OF THE BSC	EXAMPLE STATEMENTS OF BEHAVIOR RELATING TO HOW THE ELEMENT MIGHT BE MEASURED
	■ Refer to the written contract ■ Use the contract as a tool for others to agree with their position ■ Evade discussion of diverse opinions ■ Avoid open discussion of opposite views ■ Cover up opposing views and opinions
Commitment	Supply chain members are dependent on their trading partners. Suppliers have dedicated significant investments in the relationship with the OEM. Supply chain members have tailored their operating processes to meet the requirements for working together. Training and qualifying companies to serve as supply chain members has involved substantial commitment of time and money.
Communication	All partners tend to communicate formally and follow the chain of command. Information is shared frequently and informally, not only at prespecified times. Partners share information with their suppliers to assist in improving supplier operations.

Note that most incentive and reward systems resemble organizational silos and do not reward people for cross-functional or supply chain-wide efforts. In contrast, the BSC focuses on processes that cross boundaries and disciplines. BSC measures have been chosen that affect both behavior and performance; the two must be linked. Beyond this linkage, alignment must exist with these measures and the strategic objectives of the members of the extended enterprise.

SUMMARY

Although many different measures have been discussed here, the metrics chosen for a particular application should be relatively few in number, easy to measure, fairly high level, and discernable in real time. Metrics that are hard to measure, totally retrospective, and obtuse (i.e., the impact on supply chain-wide performance is difficult to appreciate) are of little use and ultimately can affect the usefulness of the scorecard.

The BSC helps to foster commitment among managers along the supply chain because those managers participate in the process that creates the measures. In addition, the BSC helps promote the sharing of best practices and stimulates communications up and down the value chain. Think of a series of cascading scorecards, beginning with extended enterprise-level metrics and ending with individual managers' scorecards in support of the extended enterprise. Now the entire process is linked, and individual behavior is aligned with the goals of the extended enterprise. Because there is a common knowledge base across the supply chain, it is easier to fix problems and to implement change consistent with mutually agreed-upon goals.

10 CONCLUDING REMARKS

C hapter 9 began with the comment, "What gets measured gets rewarded; what gets rewarded gets done," and it seems appropriate to end the book with the same comment. It is appropriate because the observation is true and emphasizes one of the major challenges facing companies that attempt to embrace the notions of the extended enterprise. Although a number of the benefits of extended enterprise thinking can be easily measured, other gains cannot be as easily quantified. Both the business and the relationship outcomes have been shown to be important, and both are worthy of attention, although the relationship metrics are less easily quantifiable.

Another challenge focuses on the deployment of technology and its role in the development of the integrated supply chain. We have emphasized that technology alone does not ensure competitive advantage. Technology and trust must run hand in hand.

Still another challenge is the emphasis given to cost reduction, with little attention given to revenue growth. We have been very emphatic that cost should not be the sole focus; managers should look also for market opportunities. If metrics emphasize technological enhancements and cost reduction but diminish the importance of relationship building, customer satisfaction, and revenue growth, extended enterprise thinking will not flourish.

The extended enterprise is a new approach to managing buyer-supplier relationships. It cannot be emphasized enough that this process represents a change in culture that must not be overlooked or underestimated. Expect resistance, prepare for it, and know that the changes advocated here often run counter to years of accepted business practice.

To equate the extended enterprise to the use of software and technology that enable the flow of products, the information about them and the money that exchanges hands among the supply chain members tells only part of the story. Even more problematic, such a focus masks the true opportunities and obstacles that drive successful extended enterprise behaviors. To highlight some of these concerns, a 2003 article published by *Forrester Brief*[1] reported that, despite the advancements provided by a number of extended enterprise-wide software solutions, these much-touted tools are slow to move beyond early adopters. In part, an inability to reach full enterprise-level acceptance is due to an absence of internal collaboration bolstered by a lack of integration across the full supply chain. As has been discussed throughout the book, herein lies part of the reason why there is a slow adoption of extended enterprise behavior by supply chain partners: *The technology overpromises, and people underdeliver*.

McKinsey suggests that, by itself, software cannot fix short-comings in supply chain management; in fact, it can make them worse.[2] It is important to remember that many of the enterprise software solutions require massive business process redesigns. If the processes are not fixed and attempts to manage these massive changes are not implemented, it is quite likely that the hoped-for gains will not come to fruition. Again, people issues are key to managing the requisite changes.

The evidence has been presented that well-performing supply chains are built on, among other things, lean supply, the transparency of data across boundaries, *and* the quality of the relationship. These attributes are bolstered by structures and systems that support the flows and linkages across the levels of the supply chain. Quality is often described by the degree of closeness among partners, the level of trust and commitment, and other characteristics mentioned throughout this book. The point is that the quality of the data and the quality of the relationship are essential to the success of the extended enterprise.

A recent article published by *The Economist*[3] presents a number of suggestions for developing successful extended enterprises that align very well with the principles developed throughout the book. Among the suggestions are:

- Before integration of the supply chain is possible, the firm must mirror the same behaviors. Integration and cooperation must exist internally before you can do the same outside. This means that there can be no silos; information must flow openly, and functions/disciplines must cooperate and trust each other.
- Know what the role of each member of the supply chain is and have members agree to their roles. When roles are not clear or when they overlap, it is inevitable that duplication will increase costs, that conflict will surface, and that trust will be damaged.
- Each member of the supply chain should know why an integrated supply chain is important. Firms must share a common destiny and agree on the reasons why it makes sense to collaborate. As importantly, each member of the extended enterprise must jointly own the strategy. It is critical that the entire process be driven from strategy and alignment across members.
- Know what your strengths are. Focus on what you do best, and stop doing what others can do better. Firms partner because by working together they can all better

meet the needs of the marketplace. Comparative advantage must exist if a new partner is asked to join the network. Cost savings is important but is not sufficient for achieving the full benefits of the extended enterprise.

■ Commitment is key, the work is hard, and performance metrics help articulate the objectives. Senior management must be committed to the concept of the extended enterprise and must drive the ideals and principles throughout the organization and across its boundaries.

It is ironic that on one level, extended enterprises are built on the use of technology to communicate among supply chain partners with little need for human interaction. Simply, what makes such interactions possible is a very human condition. Relationships must be established, and these relationships must be built on trust. With trust and the need for close working relationships comes heightened dependence (really interdependence), and managers become very uncomfortable. Whether discomfort is a function of perceived risk, a loss of control, or both is not the point. The point is that building these relationships takes time, takes effort, and ultimately takes a different type of manager than previously has been assigned to procurement, materials management, or strategic sourcing. Technology might enable supply chain integration, but trust ensures that it will survive. Trust serves as the glue that binds the members of the extended enterprise.

Borrowing from our knowledge of alliances, the new extended enterprise manager is facile at managing external manufacturing, building coalitions, resolving conflict, and behaving as an honest broker. This person must understand how to manage across companies, cultures, and contexts. The extended enterprise works when seamlessness is a virtue and an absence of boundaries is encouraged instead of an attitude of protecting "my information" from "you." It is a "we" and not an "I" mentality that lies at the heart of the extended enterprise.

Ultimately, the extended enterprise model will work smoothly when there are metrics that capture the performance of the partnership. Some of these measures are defined by hard financial and/or quantifiable results. Other measures will be softer and will reflect the dynamics of the relationship-building/-managing process. Managers must develop faith in the process and appreciate that although there are notable risks, the rewards are far greater and result in greater customer satisfaction, improved market share and market penetration, higher profits, and a sustainable competitive advantage. Faith in the process and public support for the ideals of the extended enterprise must begin at the top and must permeate the very soul of the firm.

The book began with a reference to Thomas Jefferson and the Lewis and Clark expedition, and we will end the book with another reference to Thomas Jefferson. Long-held cultural biases can very easily sub-optimize the performance of the supply chain. One of the fears that runs through any supply chain is the fear that unintended information leakage might compromise the competitive position of one supply chain member. To avoid such a problem, firms often consider not sharing any information so as to minimize the potential problem.

Thomas Jefferson once said, "He who lights his taper from mine does not diminish my light at all." Mr. Jefferson speaks to the essence of the extended enterprise. Partners who espouse extended enterprise thinking acknowledge that information sharing enhances the quality of the relationship among supply chain members and improves the competitive aptitude of the entire supply chain. Rather than worry that individual advantages might be compromised, managers now reframe the discussion and see that the entire supply chain benefits.

Win-win thinking results in a winning supply chain that can successfully compete on a global scale. This is the goal of the extended enterprise. We have shown a path to adopting the tenets and principles of the extended enterprise, and we hope the trail is well marked and that the cautions have been adequately highlighted along the way. Good luck!

CHAPTER 1

1. Edward Teach, "Working on the Chain," CFO (September 2002): 83–88.

2. Doug Smock, "Buyers Shift Strategies as Cost Reduction Goals Grow," *Purchasing* 131 (September 5, 2002): 13–14.

3. Ed Leddy, "Consortia Procurement: A Look Inside," *Inside Supply Management* (July 8, 2002).

4. See Robert Spekman, Joe Spear, and John Kamauff, "Supply Chain Competence: Learning as a Key Component," *Supply Chain Management: 7* 41–55 (2002).

5. *CEO Agenda 2002, The Extended Enterprise*, The Economist White Paper Series, November 2002.

6. Cyrus Freidheim, *The Trillion-Dollar Enterprise* (Reading, MA: Perseus Books, 1998).

7. For a further discussion of agility, see Steven Goldman, Roger Nagel, and Kenneth Preiss, *Agile Competitors and Virtual Organizations* (New York: Van Nostrand Reinhold, 1995).

8. John McClenahen, "Calibrated for Flexibility," *Industry Week* 250 (October 2001): 47–48.

9. David Bovet and Joseph Martha, *Value Nets* (New York: John Wiley & Sons, 2000).

10. Anthony Velocci, "Strategic Sourcing Mostly a Neglected Opportunity," *Aviation Week & Space Technology* 155 (October 15, 2001): 70–71.

11. George Taninecz, "Forging the Chain," *Industry Week* (May 15, 2000): 40–46.

12. Robert Spekman, John Kamauff, and Niklas Myhr, "An Empirical Investigation into Supply Chain Management: A Perspective on Partnerships," *Supply Chain Management* 3, no. 2 (1998): 53–67.

13. William Copacino, *Supply Chain Management* (Boca Raton, FL: St. Lucie Press/APICS Series on Resource Management, 1997).

14. Charles Stabell and Oystein Fjeldstad, "Configuring Value for Competitive Advantage," *Strategic Management Journal* 19, no. 5 (May 1998): 413–437.

15. Modified from Philip Andrews and Jerome Hahn, "Transforming Supply Chains into Value Webs," *Strategy and Leadership* 26, no. 3 (July–August 1998): 6–11.

16. Keach Choon Tan, Vijay Kannan, and Robert Handfield, "Supply Chain Management: Supplier Performance and Firm Performance," *International Journal of Purchasing and Materials Management* 34, no. 3 (Summer 1998): 2–9.

17. Charles Corbett, Joseph Blackburn, and Luk Van Wassenhove, "Partnerships to Improve Supply Chains," *Sloan Management Review* 40, no. 4 (Summer 1999): 71–82.

18. Gene Tyndall, Christopher Gopal, Wolfgang Partsch, and John Kamauff, "Ten Strategies to Enhance Supplier Management," *National Productivity Review* 17, no. 3 (Summer 1998): 31–44.

CHAPTER 2

1. Adam Fein, *Facing the Forces of Change* (New York: DREF, 2000).

2. Michael Tracey and Chong Leng Tan, "Empirical Analysis of Supplier Selection and Involvement, Customer Satisfaction, and Firm Performance," *Supply Chain Management* 6, no. 3/4 (2001): 174–188.

3. Michael Maloni and W. C. Benton, "Power Influences in the Supply Chain," *Journal of Business Logistics* 21 (2000): 49–73.

4. David Arminas, "The Mother of e-Marketplaces: Will It Pass the Test?" *Supply Management* 7, no. 10 (May 9, 2002): 22–26.

5. David Burt, Donald Dobler, and Stephen Starling, *World Class Supply Management* (New York: McGraw Hill/Irwin, 2002).

6. James L. Patterson and Kim M. Amann, *Strategic Sourcing: A Systematic Approach to Supplier Evaluation, Selection, and Development* (Tempe, AZ: Center for Advanced Purchasing Studies, 2000).

7. Deloitte Consulting Report, "Energizing the Supply Chain" (1999).

8. Gregory Owens, Olivier Vidal, Rick Toole, and Donovan Favre, "Strategic Sourcing: Aligning Procurement Needs with Your Business Goals," in John Gottorna, et al. (eds.), *Strategic Supply Chain Alignment* (Burlington, VT: Gower Publishing Limited, 1998): 285–301.

9. Michael Leenders and David Blenkhorn, *Reverse Marketing* (New York: Free Press, 1988).

10. David Nelson, Patricia Moody, and J. Stegner, *The Purchasing Machine* (New York: Free Press, 2001).

11. Michael Leenders, Jean Nollet, and Lisa Ellram, "Adopting Purchasing to Supply Chain Management," *International Journal of Physical Distribution and Logistics*, vol. 24, # 1, (1994): 40–51.

12. Jeffrey H. Dyer, *Collaborative Advantage* (New York: Oxford University Press, 2000).

13. See for instance K C Tan, "A Framework of Supply Chain Management Literature," *European Journal of Purchasing and Supply Management* 7 (2002): 39–48.

14. Michael Milgate, "Supply Chain Complexity and Delivery Performance: An International Exploratory Study," *Supply Chain Management* 6, no. 3/4 (2001): 106–118.

15. AT Kearney, *The Extended Enterprise* (May 2002).

16. Adapted from David Ross, *Competing Through Supply Chain Management* (Boston: Kluwer Academic Publishers, 1998).

17. William Copacino, "Masters of the Supply Chain," *Logistics Management Distribution Report* 37, no. 12 (December 31, 1998): 23.

CHAPTER 3

1. Oliver Wight, *Production and Inventory Control in the Computer Age* (Boston: CBI, 1974).

2. Wallace J. Hopp and Mark L. Spearman, *Factory Physics*, 2nd edition (New York: Irwin McGraw-Hill, 2001).

3. Norman Gaither and Greg Frazier, *Production and Operations Management*, 8th edition (Cincinnati, OH: South-Western College Publishing, 1999).

4. Andre Martin, *Distribution Resource Planning*, revised edition (Essex Junction, VT: Oliver Wight Publications, 1993).

5. Jennifer Baljko, "Sun Clears Out Inventory Costs Through New Supplier Program," http://www.cmpnet.com (March 22, 2002); accessed 8/14/02.

6. Tom Vollman, William Berry, and Clay Whybark, *Manufacturing Planning and Control Systems*, 3rd edition (Homewood, IL: Irwin Business One, 1992).

7. Jay Hizer and Barry Render, *Operations Management*, 6th edition (Upper Saddle River, NJ: Prentice Hall, 2001).

8. Eliyahu Goldratt, *The Goal*, 2nd revised edition (Croton-on-Hudson, NY: North River Press, 1992).

9. Eliyahu Goldratt and Robert Fox, *The Race* (Croton-on-Hudson, NY: North River Press, 1986).

10. Joseph Manetti, "How Technology Is Transforming Manufacturing," *Production and Inventory Management Journal* (First Quarter, 2001) 54–64.

11. Hopp and Spearman, *Factory Physics*.

12. Sunil Chopra and Peter Meindl, *Supply Chain Management* (Upper Saddle River, NJ: Prentice Hall, 2001) 345.

13. Hopp and Spearman, *Factory Physics*.

14. Peter Senge, *The Fifth Discipline—The Art and Practice of the Learning Organization*, (New York: Doubleday, 1990) 3.

15. Chopra and Meindl, *Supply Chain*, 344.

16. Jim Kilpatrick, "Advanced Planning Systems Spark the Supply Chain," *APICS—The Performance Advantage* (Falls Church, VA: American Production and Inventory Control Society, August, 1999): 25–28.

17. Steve Banker, "The Make-to-Order Fulfillment Supply Chain: HON Company Case Study," *Arcweb Newsmagazine*, arcweb.com; accessed 7/27/02.

18. Susan Scheck, "APS Helps Balance Supply/Demand," *Electronic Business News Online* (January 29, 1999); accessed 8/14/02.

19. Javed Sikander, "Extended Tools Needed for Supply Chain Management," *Electronic Business News* (March 14, 2002); accessed 8/15/02.

20. Jennifer Baljko, "Software Vendors Honing Supply Chain Offerings," *Electronic Business News Online* (February 28, 2002); accessed 8/14/02.

21. Chopra and Meindl, *Supply Chain*.

22. Doug Bartholomew, "Turbocharging the Supply Chain," *Industry Week* (September 2001).

23. Norman Mayersohn, "Dell's Killer App: Keeping Close to the Customer," *Consumer Goods Technology* (June 2001).

24. Presentation by Dell Managers, The Darden School, University of Virginia, (February 2002).

25. Gene Bylinsky, "The E-Factory Catches On," *Fortune Magazine* (July 23, 2001).

26. Bylinsky, "The E-Factory Catches On."

27. "Brave New Factory," *Business Week* (July 23, 2001).

28. Steve Konicki, "Let's Keep This Private," *Information Week* (July 30, 2001); accessed 8/20/02.

29. "Brave New Factory," *Business Week*.

30. Michael Hammer, "The Superefficient Company," *Harvard Business Review* (September 2001): 82–91.

31. Conversation with PolyOne management (August 20, 2002).

32. Konicki, "Let's Keep This Private."

33. Kurt Hoffman, "Fulfilling B2B Sellside Promises," Supply Chain Brain.com (April 2001); accessed 9/6/02.

34. Jean Murphy, "Customer-Driven Supply Chains Begin with Real-Time Visibility," Supply Chain Brain.com (March 2001); accessed 9/6/02.

35. Deven Sharma and Chuck Lucier, "From Solutions to Symbiosis: Blending with Your Customers," *Strategy + Business* 27 (2002): 39–48.

CHAPTER 4

1. Mike Verespej, "Supply Chain Collaboration," *Frontline Solutions* 3, no. 9 (2002): 20–24.

2. Tim Gouldson, "Supply Chain Glitches and Shareholder Value Destruction," Ivey School Report, "The Life of Business Is Its Supply Chain," *Computing Canada* 27, no. 22 (October 19, 2001): 19.

3. Lisa Ellram, George Zsidisin, Sue Siferd, and Michael Stanley, "The Impact of Purchasing and Supply Management. Activities on Corporate Success," *Journal of Supply Chain Management* 38 (2002): 4–17.

4. The term *strategic intent* is taken from Gary Hamel and C. K. Prahalad's *Competing for the Future* (Boston: Harvard Business School Press, 1994).

5. John Hagedoorn, "Inter-Firm R&D Partnerships: An Overview of Major Trends and Patterns Since 1960," *Research Policy* 31, no. 4. (May 2002): 477–492.

6. Ciaran Brady and Kim-Sun Chan, "Implementing a Worldwide Cash Management Solution in an ERP Environment," *AFP Exchange* 21, no. 5 (October/September 2001): 98–102.

7. August-Wilhelm Scheer and Frank Habermann, "Making ERP a Success," *Association for Computing Machinery, Communications of the ACM 43*, no.4 (April 2000): 57–61.

8. Shira Levine, "The ABC's of ERP," *America's Network* 103, no.13 (September 1, 2001): 54–58.

9. Heather Harreld, "Supply Chain Collaboration," *InfoWorld* 23, no. 52/53 (2001): 22–25.

10. Roberto Michel, "Content before Commerce," *MSI* 20, no. 2 (February 2002): 50.

11. Daewoo Park and Hema Krishnan, "Supplier Selection Practices among Small Firms in the United States: Testing Three Models," *Journal of Small Business Management* 39, no. 3 (July 2001): 259–271.

12. "Carrier and GE Industrial Systems: A Supply Chain Partnership," UVA-OM-0933 (Charlottesville, VA: Darden Graduate School of Business Administration, University of Virginia, 1999).

13. "Tier-1 Suppliers Raise the E-Business Bar," *Industrial Distribution* 90, no. 10 (October 2001): 31.

14. Anitesh Barua, Prabhudev Konana, Andrew Whinston, and Fang Yin, "Driving E-Business Excellence," *MIT Sloan Management Review* 43 (Fall 2001): 36–44.

CHAPTER 5

1. "Outsourcing's Inexorable Growth," *Investors Business Daily* (October 24, 1996).

2. "Companies Increasingly Look to Outsourcing for Competitive Advantage," KPMG Peat Marwick LLP (1997).

3. James Brian Quinn and Frederick G. Hilmer, "Make vs. Buy: Strategic Outsourcing," *The McKinsey Quarterly*, no. 1 (1995): 48–70.

4. Charles Handy, *The Age of Unreason* (Boston: Harvard Business School Press, 1991).

5. Fourth Annual Manufacturing Outsourcing Survey, Bear Stearns, Inc. (May 2001).

6. Stephen J. Doig, R. Ritter, Kurt Speckhals, and D. Woolson, "Has Outsourcing Gone Too Far?" *The McKinsey Quarterly*, no. 4 (2001): 25–32.

7. Cited in "Outsourcing's Next Wave," Michael F. Corbett & Associates, Firm-builder.com; accessed 7/15/02.

8. Christine Spivey, "U.S. Outsourcing Decelerates," *Forrester Research Techstrategy Reports* (February 2002).

9. Robin Cooper and Regine Slagmulder, *Supply Chain Development for the Lean Enterprise* (Portland, OR: Productivity Press, 1999).

10. "Few Companies Capitalize on Strategic Outsourcing," *Industrial Distribution* (September 2002).

11. Christopher Lonsdale and Andrew Cox, *Outsourcing: A Business Guide to Risk Management Tools and Techniques* (London: Earlsgate Press, 1998).

12. *The Fifth Annual Outsourcing Index*, Outsourcing Institute, Outsourcing.com; accessed 8/14/02.

13. "Few Companies Capitalize," 16.

14. Jane Linder, et al., "Business Transformation Outsourcing: Partnering for Radical Change," *Accenture Inc.* (July 2001).

15. James Carbone, "Reinventing Purchasing Wins the Medal for BIG BLUE," *Purchasing Magazine* (September 16, 1999): 38–41

16. Carbone, "Reinventing Purchasing," 39.

17. James Brian Quinn, "Strategic Outsourcing: Leveraging Knowledge Capabilities," *Sloan Management Review* (Summer 1999): 9–21.

18. Quinn, "Strategic Outsourcing."

19. Geoffrey A. Moore, *Living on the Fault Line* (New York: HarperCollins, 2000).

20. Dun and Bradstreet, Inc., *Barometer of Global Outsourcing* (February 24, 2000).

21. Steven J Kafka, "The Collaboration Imperative," *Forrester Techstrategy Report* (May 2001).

22. Alex Anderson, "Cisco Gets to the Point (of Sale)," *Manufacturing Systems* (February 24, 2003).

23. "New OneChannel Software Enables Companies to Predict Demand," OneChannel Web site (2003.

24. Paul Kaihla, "Inside Cisco's $2 Billion Blunder," *Business 2.0* (March 2002).

25. Bill Lakeman, et al., "Why Cisco Failed: Outsourcing and Its Perils," *Strategy & Business*, no. 24 (2001).

26. Doig, et al., "Has Outsourcing Gone Too Far?"

27. Lakeman, et al., "Why Cisco Failed."

28. Cooper and Slagmulder, *Supply Chain Development*.

29. See, for example, Linder, et al., "Culture and Control," *Strategic Finance*, vol. 84, no. 6 (2002): 5–16.

30. Les Blumberg, "How to Engage in Strategic Outsourcing Relationships," *Pharmaceutical Technology North America* 26, no. 7 (2002): 74–80.

31. This section is adapted from an Accenture Report, *Business Process Outsourcing Big Bang* (2002).

CHAPTER 6

1. Donald J. Bowersox, David Closs, and M. Bixby Cooper, *Supply Chain Logistics Management* (New York: McGraw Hill, 2002).

2. Donald Bowersox, D. Closs, and T. Stank, *21st Century Logistics: Making Supply Chain Integration a Reality* (Oak Brook, IL: Council of Logistics Management, 1999).

3. Hai Lee and S. Whang, "E-Business and Supply Chain Integration," *Stanford Global Supply Chain Forum* (November 2001).

4. Lee and Whang, "E-Business."

5. Adaptec, Inc. Web site.

6. Thomas Davenport and J. Short, "The New Industrial Engineering: Information Technology and Business Process Redesign" (Cambridge, MA: MIT Sloan Center for Information Systems Research, 1990).

7. Information compiled from Cisco Systems 10K for 2002; from A. Hartman, J. Sifonis, and J. Kador, *Net Ready: Strategies for Success in the E-conomy* (New York: McGraw-Hill, 2000); and from Harvard Business School case 9-398-127, "Cisco Systems, Inc."

8. Lee Sherman, "A Matter of Connections," *Knowledge Management* (July 2000).

9. Franklin Grosvenor and Terrence Austin, "Cisco's e-Hub Initiative," *Supply Chain Management Review* (July–August 2001).

10. Peter Weill and M. Broadbent, *Leveraging the New Infrastructure* (Boston: Harvard Business School Press, 1998).

11. Weill and Broadbent, *Leveraging*.

12. Peter Keen, *Shaping the Future: Business Design Through Information Technology* (Boston: Harvard Business School Press, 1991), 180.

13. Tom Smith, "Price Tag of Latest Software Failure Well Over $100 Million," *Internet Week* (August 20, 2002).

CHAPTER 7

1. Jeffrey Dyer, *Collaborative Advantage* (New York: Oxford Press, 2000).

2. Mike Duff, "12 Hot Issues Facing Mass Retailing," *DSN Retailing Today* 41, no. 10 (May 20, 2002): 10.

3. Pete Engardio, "Souping up the Supply Chain," *Business Week* (August 31, 1998): 110.

4. David Drickhamer, "Rough Road Ahead," *Industry Week* 251, no. 3 (April 2002): 59–60.

5. Stephen Doig, Ronald Ritter, Kurt Speckhals, and Daniel Woolson, "Has Outsourcing Gone Too Far," *McKinsey Quarterly* 4 (2001): 24–37.

6. Pui-Wing Tam, Gary Mc Williams, Scott Thurm, "As Alliances Fade, Computer Firms Toss Out Playbooks," *Wall Street Journal* (October 15, 2002): A1.

7. See Peter Ring and Andrew Van de Ven, "Development Processes of Cooperative Interorganizational Relationships," *Academy of Management Review* 19 (January 1994): 90–118.

8. See Roy Lewicki, Daniel McAllister, and Robert Bies, "Trust and Distrust: New Relationships and Realities," *Academy of Management Review* 23, no. 3 (July 1998): 438–458.

9. Nicole Lewis, "Collaboration Is Not Easy to Achieve," *EBN* (March 12, 2001): 72.

10. See Robert Handfield, Daniel Krause, Thomas Scannell, and Robert Monczka, "Avoid the Pitfalls in Supplier Development," *Sloan Management Review* (Winter 2000): 37–49. Portions of this section are adapted from this article.

11. See Dave Nelson, Rick Mayo, and Patricia Moody, "BP: Developing Excellence in a Global Enterprise," *Hospital Materiel Management Quarterly* 22 (August 2000): 68–70.

12. Chris Mahoney, "Global Supply Chains," *Executive Excellence* 18, no. 8 (August 2001): 8–9.

13. Andrew Cox, Joe Sanderson, and Glyn Watson, "Supply Chains and Power Regimes," *Journal of Supply Chain Management* 37, no. 2 (Spring 2001): 28–35.

CHAPTER 8

1. Portions of this section are adapted from Marvin Cetron and Owen Davies, *The Futurist* 35, no. 2 (March/April 2001): 27–42.

2. John Mullins, Margaret Lineham, and James Walsh, "People-Centered Management Policies: A New Approach for the 21st Century," *Irish Journal of Management* 22 (2001): 127–139.

3. Heather Harreld, *InfoWorld* 23, no. 52/3 (2001): 22–25.

4. Peter Senge and George Carstedt, "Innovating Our Way to the Next Industrial Revolution," *MIT Sloan Management Review* 42, no. 2 (Winter 2001): 24–38.

5. Ray Suutari, "Organizing for the New Economy," *CMA Management* 75, no. 2 (2001): 12–13.

6. George Hallenbeck, Jacob Hautaluoma, and Scott Bates, "The Benefits of Multiple Boundary Spanning Roles in Purchasing," *Journal of Supply Chain Management* 35 (Spring 1999): 38–43.

7. See James Brown and Chris Hendry, "Industrial Districts and Supply Chains as Vehicles for Organizational Learning," *International Studies of Management & Operations* 27, no. 4 (Winter 1997/1998): 127–157.

8. Keith Goffin, Marek Szejczewski, and Colin New, "Managing Suppliers: When Fewer Can Mean More," *International Journal of Physical Distribution & Logistics Management* 27, no. 7 (1997): 422–436.

9. See Dave Wilson, "An Integrated Model of Buyer Seller Relationships," *Journal of the Academy of Marketing Sciences* 23, no. 4 (1995): 335–345.

10. See Roy Lewicki, Daniel McAllister, and Robert Bies, "Trust and Distrust: New Relationships and Realities," *Academy of Management Review* 23, no. 3 (July 1998): 438–458.

11. See Robert Monczka, Kenneth Petersen, Robert Handfield, and Gary Ragatz, "Success Factors in Strategic Alliances: The Buying Company Perspective," *Decision Sciences* 29, no. 3 (Summer 1998): 553–577.

12. Reported in Ranjay Gulati, Tarun Khanna, and Nitin Nohira, "Unilateral Commitments and the Importance of Process in Alliances," *Sloan Management Review* 35, no. 3 (Spring 1994): 61–69.

13. Robert Spekman, Joe Spear, and John Kamauff, "Supply Chain Competence: Learning as a Key Component," *Supply Chain Management* 7 (2002): 41–55.

14. Simon Croom, "The Dyadic Capabilities Concept: Examining the Process of Key Supplier Involvement in Collaborative Product Design," *European Journal of Purchasing and Supply Management* 7 (2001): 29–27.

15. Stephen Dent, "Partnering Intelligence: How to Profit from Smart Alliances," *The Journal of Quality and Participation* 23, no. 3 (May/June 2000): 23–26.

16. This material is used with the permission of John Wiley & Sons, Inc. Parts of this discussion are taken from Robert Spekman and Lynn Isabella (with Thomas MacAvoy), *Alliance Competence: Maximizing the Value of Your Partnerships* (New York: John Wiley & Sons, 2000).

CHAPTER 9

1. Robert M. Monczka and James P. Morgan, "Today's Measurements Just Don't Make It!" *Purchasing* (April 21, 1994): 46–50.

2. Thomas Stewart, "The Search for the Organization of Tomorrow," *Fortune Magazine* (May 18, 1992): 92–98.

3. Larry Lapide, "What about Measuring Supply Chain Performance?" *The Supply Chain Yearbook*, 2001 Edition (New York: McGraw-Hill, 2001).

4. Supply Chain Council, *SCOR Overview*, version 5a, Pittsburgh, PA (2001).

5. PRTM Consulting, *Integrated Supply Chain Performance Measurement: A Multi-Industry Consortium Recommendation*, Waltham, MA (1994).

6. The Performance Measurement Group, LLC, (PMG) *Scorecard User's Guide*, Waltham, MA (2001).

7. Stephen Geary, "Leading Companies Show Less Than 5% Total Supply-Chain Costs," PRTM's *Insight* magazine 2, no. 3, Waltham, MA (Winter 1999).

8. PMG, *Scorecard User's Guide*.

9. Robert S. Kaplan and David P. Norton, "The Balanced Scorecard—Measures that Drive Performance," *Harvard Business Review* (January–February 1992): 71–79.

10. Peter C. Brewer and Thomas W. Speh, "Using the Balanced Scorecard to Measure Supply Chain Performance," *Journal of Business Logistics* 21, no. 1 (2000): 75–93.

11. Ark Frigo, "Nonfinancial Performance Measures and Strategy Execution," *Strategic Finance* 84, no. 2 (2002): 6–9.

12. George Taninecz, "Forging the Supply Chain," *Industry Week* (May 15, 2000).

13. Roberta Duffy, "The Future of Purchasing and Supply: Elevating Relationships," *Purchasing Today* (February, 2000): 31.

14. Jeffrey H. Dyer, *Collaborative Advantage* (New York: Oxford University Press, 2000).

CHAPTER 10

1. Noha Tohamy, Laurie Orlov, and Ryan Hudson, "CPFR Arrested Development: Moving Beyond Pilots," *Forrester Brief* (January 29, 2003).

2. K. Kanakamedala, G. Ramsdell, and V. Srivatsan, "Getting Supply Chain Software Right," *McKinsey Quarterly*, no. 1 (Winter 2003): 1–5.

3. "Extending the Enterprise," *Economist Intelligence Unit* (December 2002).

The *Financial Times* delivers a world of business news.

Use the Risk-Free Trial Voucher below!

To stay ahead in today's business world you need to be well-informed on a daily basis. And not just on the national level. You need a news source that closely monitors the entire world of business, and then delivers it in a concise, quick-read format.

With the *Financial Times* you get the major stories from every region of the world. Reports found nowhere else. You get business, management, politics, economics, technology and more.

Now you can try the *Financial Times* for 4 weeks, absolutely risk free. And better yet, if you wish to continue receiving the *Financial Times* you'll get great savings off the regular subscription rate. Just use the voucher below.

Where to find tomorrow's best business and technology ideas. TODAY.

- Ideas for defining tomorrow's competitive strategies — and executing them.

- Ideas that reflect a profound understanding of today's global business realities.

- Ideas that will help you achieve unprecedented customer and enterprise value.

- Ideas that illuminate the powerful new connections between business and technology.

ONE PUBLISHER.
Financial Times Prentice Hall.

WORLD BUSINESS PUBLISHER

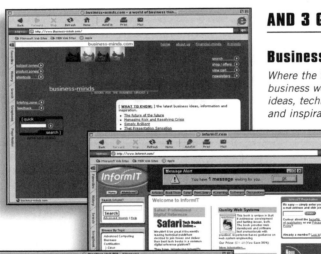

AND 3 GREAT WEB SITES:

Business-minds.com

Where the thought leaders of the business world gather to share key ideas, techniques, resources — and inspiration.

InformIt.com

Your link to today's top business and technology experts: new content, practical solutions, and the world's best online training.

ft-ph.com

Fast access to all Financial Times Prentice Hall business books currently available.